AND THE WORLD
CLOSED ITS DOORS

AND THE WORLD CLOSED ITS DOORS

*The Story of One Family
Abandoned to the Holocaust*

David Clay Large

BASIC BOOKS

A Member of the Perseus Books Group

Published by Basic Books,
A Member of the Perseus Books Group

Designed by Lisa Kreinbrink
Set in 10-point Meridien

Library of Congress Cataloging-in-Publication Data

Large, David Clay.
And the world closed its doors : the story of one family
abandoned to the Holocaust / by David Clay Large.
p.   cm.
Includes bibliographical references and index.
ISBN 0-465-03808-5
1. Schohl, Max, 1884-1943.   2. Jews—Germany—Flörsheim—
Biography.   3. Holocaust, Jewish (1939-1945)—Germany—
Flörsheim.   4. Schohl family.   5. Schohl, Max, 1884-1943—
Correspondence.   6. Flörsheim (Germany)—Biography.   I. Title.

DS135.G5S35755   2003
940.53'18'0922—dc21

2002153720

03 04 05 / 10 9 8 7 6 5 4 3 2 1

To
Käthe Schohl Wells
and in memory of
Dr. Max Schohl

Shall we refuse the unhappy fugitives from distress that hospitality which the savages of the wilderness extended to our forefathers arriving in this land? Shall oppressed humanity find no asylum on this globe?

THOMAS JEFFERSON, 1801

Hitler was quicker than the consuls on whose moods depended the visas that could save us.

ALFRED POLGAR

And you still thought, after the Nuremberg Laws and other horrors, that you were Germans? But we *were* Germans; the gangsters who had taken control of the country were not Germany—*we* were.

PETER GAY

Contents

Acknowledgments

THE BOILERPLATE FORMULA in which an author swears that he could not have written his book without the help of many others is actually true in this case; this book could not even have been conceived, much less written, without the inspiration, guidance, and support of a host of individuals and institutions. Jody Hotchkiss, of Hotchkiss and Associates, New York, convinced me that a magazine piece published by Michael Winerip in the *New York Times* in 1987 constituted the raw material for a full-length historical study; my thanks to Jody for his prodding, and to Mr. Winerip for his original spadework. To translate the initial conception into a viable enterprise I needed the assistance of Dr. P. J. Wells, Max Schohl's grandson, who gave me access to the trove of family letters and documents that his mother, Käthe Schohl Wells, entrusted to him. P. J.'s wife, Fran, organized and catalogued the documents in a way that made them much easier to use. My agent, Agnes Krup, pushed the book along with her usual blend of patience and tenacity. I've had editorial help at Basic Books from Don Fehr and, after he moved on, from Sarah McNally, who made useful suggestions for the final draft.

For contacts, leads, and the literal opening of archive doors during my research in Flörsheim I am indebted to Bernd Blisch, formerly the head of that town's cultural office. Two other local experts on Flörsheim, Werner Schiele and Peter Becker, shared with me their immense knowledge of their town's history and traditions; moreover, their published works constitute an invaluable source for this project. For her memories of life in Flörsheim in the 1920s and 1930s I thank Frau Irmgard Radczuk, who was a neighbor of the Schohls in that era. Thanks also to Jan Radczuk for his own stories, as well as for the several bottles of vodka that fueled our conversations (and on whose influence any errors in my recollection of those stories can be blamed). Mr. Janun Wloral, who works as a guide at the Auschwitz concentration camp, kindly sent me documentation from the camp archive on the death of Max Schohl.

Work in many archives and libraries in America and Europe was indispensable for this book. I wish to acknowledge the staffs at the American Jewish Archives, Cincinnati, Ohio; the Hessisches Staatsarchiv, Wiesbaden; the Library of Congress Manuscripts Division, Washington, D.C.; the National Archives, Washington, D.C.; the Public Records Office, London; the Stadtarchiv, Flörsheim; the Wiener Library, London; the Yivo Institute for Jewish Research, New York; the archive of *The Charleston Newspapers*, Charleston, West Virginia (especially Mr. Bob Schwarz); the Landesbibliothek, Wiesbaden; the Leo Baeck Institute, New York; the University of California Library, Berkeley; the Green Library, Stanford University; the Hoover Institution, Stanford; the New York Public Library; and the Renne Library, Montana State University, Bozeman.

Professor Robert Rydell of Montana State University vetted the manuscript from his vantage point as an expert on modern American social and cultural history; my wife, Dr. Margaret Wheeler, vetted the manuscript from her vantage point as an expert on just about everything. My thanks to them both.

Another convention in acknowledgment writing is to save the greatest debt for last, and in this case the convention again has genuine meaning. Käthe Schohl Wells has been my partner in this project from beginning to end, sharing with me sometimes painful memories of her family's experiences during the early phases of the Holocaust in Flörsheim, of exile in Yugoslavia, and of slave labor in the war-torn Reich. She also painted vivid verbal portraits of the American relatives who tried to help her family escape to the United States during the Hitler era, and with whom she became personally close following her emigration to America after the war. To the degree that I have been able to bring the Schohl family and their would-be American rescuers to life, and thereby to endow this story with a vital human dimension, I have done so only with the constant assistance of my partner. This is her book as much as mine.

Introduction

"THE LAST TIME I saw my father," recalls Käthe Schohl Wells, "we were sitting on my bed in our flat in Ruma [Yugoslavia]. He said he would be back in a few days, and not to worry. We, my mother and sister and I, believed him, because he had been arrested several times before and always come back. We had no idea when they took him away that summer in 1942 that this time it was for good." A year later the Schohl women learned that the head of their family, Dr. Max Schohl, had been deported to Auschwitz, where he died in December 1943.

Käthe Schohl Wells is now a handsome and vital seventy-nine-year-old widow who uses her cane less as a walking aid than as a pointer with which to give directions. Although she has resided in the United States since emigrating from Germany in 1946 and is a proud American citizen, she comes across as a quintessential German-Jewish grandmother, which in fact she is. A visitor to her home is invariably treated to generous helpings of matzoth-ball soup followed by cake and coffee "mit Schlag." If Käthe takes a shine to her visitor, he'll likely come away with provisions for a week and a month's supply of Nürnberger Lebkuchen. Similarly, Käthe's comfortable apartment overlooking the Kanawha River in Charleston, West Virginia, is in many ways a little outpost of the country she left behind over a half-century ago. The china cabinet is filled with Meissen porcelain, and the walls are covered with pictures of her German family and the village near Frankfurt where she grew up, Flörsheim-am-Main. The most arresting photo in her picture gallery features a handsome young man in a German army officer's uniform from World War I; it is Käthe's father, Max, of whom she still has trouble speaking without her voice cracking. She says today that it is the ever-vivid memory of her father that inspires her to travel up and down the eastern seaboard giving talks to Jewish groups about her experiences in the Holocaust.

At the time of Max Schohl's final arrest the Schohl family had been living in exile in Yugoslavia for a little more than two years. They had fled there in March 1940 because as a Jew Max was no longer permitted to live and work in his own country, which he had served loyally and with distinction in World War I. Five years earlier he had lost his chemical factory due to the racist economic policies of the Nazis. In spring 1940 the Gestapo had given him a deadline to leave Germany immediately or face incarceration in a concentration camp. (In Nazi Germany, a policy of forced emigration preceded the program of mass murder in the evolution of the Holocaust.)

Although Yugoslavia provided a temporary haven for the Schohls, it was by no means their first choice as a refuge. Like many German Jews, Max and his family had hoped above all to emigrate to America, where Max believed that he could find work as a chemist, a field in which he had already distinguished himself in Germany. Moreover, Max had some relatives in America, including a cousin named Julius Hess, a clothing store clerk and part-time insurance salesman based in Charleston, West Virginia. Julius promised to help the Schohls obtain immigration visas to America. Max penned his first SOS appeal to "Cousin Julius" in September 1938, when the Nazi persecution of the Jews was already well in progress, and when prospects for finding refuge in America were becoming slimmer because more and more German Jews were applying for visas under a national quota system that remained highly restrictive. Nonetheless, both Max and Julius were confident that the Schohls' visa applications would be successful. After all, Max was a talented chemist and proven entrepreneur; his wife Liesel and his two daughters, eighteen-year-old Helene and fifteen-year-old Käthe, were all willing and anxious to work hard in their prospective new home. Were not Max and his family just the kind of new citizens that America needed?

After roughly two years of effort—of increasingly desperate attempts to find a way through or over the "paper walls" of American immigration policy—Max had to accept the grim reality that America did not, in fact, really need or want the Schohls. In 1939 the American consulate at Stuttgart allotted Max and his family a number within the annual German immigration quota (part of a racially based national quota system for all immigrants to the United States) that would not have allowed them to leave Germany for America until 1944, a delay that Max understandably believed would be fatal.

Despairing of reaching America, Max next sought to emigrate to England, where he had business contacts who promised to help him gain admission to that nation. But here too he ran into government-mandated impediments, which became insurmountable with the outbreak of war in September 1939. Facing the Gestapo-imposed deadline to leave Germany or face arrest, the Schohl family chose Yugoslavia as a temporary refuge in hopes of using that Balkan state as a springboard to emigration to Brazil. But before they could secure entry permits, Brazil too closed its doors. With the Nazi conquest of the Balkans in spring 1941, the Schohls' Yugoslavian refuge turned into a trap. A year after Max's deportation his wife and daughters were ordered back to Germany to work as slave laborers. They survived this ordeal, and by emigrating to America shortly after the war Käthe Schohl was finally able to make the passage that was denied to her father.

As the foregoing outline makes evident, the Schohl story constitutes a small part of a much larger story, or collection of stories. One of the bigger pictures here clearly involves the reaction of deeply assimilated German Jews to the gradually escalating Nazi racial persecution in their country. In putting off his bid to abandon Germany to such a late date, Max was allowing his love of country to obscure his survival instincts, a miscalculation that he shared with thousands of his co-religionists. Like all too many of them, he believed that the German people were too sophisticated, too cultured, to tolerate for long the barbarous brownshirted gangsters who had taken over his country in 1933. The chemist was sure that the Germans would soon wake up and throw the bastards out.

Of course, another of the larger issues at play here—indeed, the central one in this book—is the West's, especially America's, response to the human tragedy unfolding in Nazi Germany and in Nazi-occupied Europe. The Hitler regime's racist policies caused occasional criticism from Western leaders and in the Western press, but there were no concerted efforts by the democratic governments to pressure the Nazis to alter their policies. In essence, the Jewish persecution was regarded as an "internal matter," off-limits to outside "interference."

Initially, the majority of German Jews who elected to escape the Nazi persecution through emigration sought sanctuary in other European countries or in Palestine, but as the oppression intensified a growing number chose to emigrate to the United States—or, more accurately put, they attempted to emigrate to the United States. In the end, the number of Jewish refugees who found safety in America was far less than the number of those who sought sanctuary there. Only about one-quarter of the Jews seeking to emigrate to America from the German Reich between 1933 and 1941 obtained visas under the quota system for Germany, which allocated 27,370 places annually. From Hitler's seizure of power until the closure of U.S. consulates in Germany and Austria in 1941, American consuls granted roughly 60,000 visas directly from the Nazi Reich. Over the thirteen-year period between 1933 and 1945 only about 35.8 percent of the German-Austrian quota was actually used, the quota being filled for the first time in 1939. Peak immigration occurred in the crucial eighteen-month period between March 1938 and September 1939, when some 45,210 ethnic German aliens, most of them Jews, entered the United States under the newly combined German-Austrian quota. Anti-immigration activists complained that the alien newcomers threatened to "flood" America, but the number was more like a trickle in a nation of some 130 million people. The far more significant number was the tens of thousands of Jews—from Germany and elsewhere in Nazi-occupied Europe—who were unable to join even the small stream of refugees flowing through the narrow sluice-gates of American immigration law during this time of crisis.

Severe limitation of immigration was a new phenomenon in the history of Jewish migration to the United States. Despite periodic upsurges of anti-Semitic sentiment in America during the late nineteenth and early twentieth centuries, German Jews, along with Eastern European Jews fleeing political oppression and economic misery in their homelands, flocked to the United States in large numbers. More than 2.5 million Jews found refuge in America during this period. Restrictive new immigration laws passed in the early 1920s, which established the national quota system, significantly slowed the tide of Jewish immigration, especially from Eastern Europe, but even in the 1920s roughly twice as many Jews gained entrance to the United States as in the decade between 1933 and 1943, when the average (from all sources) was only 15,284 a year. In the decade immediately preceding World War I, *eight times* as many Jews entered the United States as in the Nazi era. In other words, the prospects for gaining entrance to America were the slimmest at precisely the moment when that sanctuary was most desperately needed.

Much has been written about the Western democracies' policies toward Jewish immigration in the 1930s and during the Holocaust. Although most commentators have been critical of the West's unwillingness to give sanctuary to a larger percentage of Germany's—and later Europe's—Jews, there is no consensus in the scholarly literature regarding the number of Jews who might have been saved, the timeframe in which any rescue might have been possible, the degree to which Jewish organizations in the West might have been able to push political leaders toward a more pro-refugee position, and the motivation behind the restrictions on Jewish immigration. That being said, there has been a tendency among professional historians in recent years to move away from popular indictments of policy makers whose alleged "abandonment of the Jews" made them "complicit" in the crimes of the Nazis, in favor of an emphasis on the various constraints under which the policy makers had to work.

Focusing as it does on one specific case, this book cannot provide definitive answers to all the big questions regarding the overall shape of Western immigration policy during the Holocaust. As will become evident in the following discussion, however, my view is that one cannot understand what happened to Max Schohl without being aware *both* of a narrow-visioned (and sometimes anti-Semitic) policy-making apparatus in the Western democracies *and* a broader political-economic environment that militated against a substantially more liberal stance. One must always bear in mind that in a time of severe depression and chronic unemployment there was very little popular support in any of the Western nations for throwing open the doors to masses of newcomers, however desperate they might have been. Yet in the end, my central concern here is not so much to "expose" the shortcomings of American and British policy toward Jewish refugees during the Hitler era as to examine the consequences of high-level public policy at the "low" level of individual personal experience. What I try to do in this narrative is to attach a specific human face and voice to the otherwise bloodless record of political calculations and bureaucratic regulations. The ordeal of the Schohls, and to a lesser extent that of their would-be American rescuer, Julius Hess, can serve to remind us that abstract policies regarding national quotas, financial guarantees, and "ethnic balance" were anything but abstract to people whose own lives, and those of their loved ones, were in peril.

While the broader parameters for this study include Nazi racial persecution, the dilemmas of assimilated German Jews, and the West's woefully inadequate response to the challenges of the Holocaust, most of the action takes place on the tiny stage of a smallish German town—Flörsheim-am-Main—during the crisis decades of the 1920s and 1930s. It was in this modest town on the Main River near Frankfurt that Max Schohl settled upon his return from World War I, and it was here that he started his family and launched his career as a chemical entrepreneur. Dr. Schohl quickly became a pillar of the community, someone his fellow

Flörsheimer could lean on in hard times. During the horrific inflation of the early 1920s he paid his workers in solid American dollars, and in the depression of the early 1930s he established a soup kitchen for the hungry. When Hitler took power in Berlin—and local Nazis accordingly seized control in Flörsheim—Max assumed that his past contributions to the community, along with his heroic war record, might afford him a certain protection. The reality was that he and the other Jewish businessmen in town were quickly reduced to pariah status: economically ruined, politically disenfranchised, socially marginalized, and subjected to constant harassment from officials and even ordinary townsfolk. During the infamous "Night of the Crystals" of November 1938, Max's house was thoroughly ransacked by Nazi thugs, some of whom had once been on the receiving end of his largesse. The Schohls' experience in Flörsheim, which essentially mirrored that of the other Jewish families in town, has much to tell us about the workings of Nazi politics at the grassroots level, about the evolution of the Holocaust from the bottom up.

A family history like this one is possible only if the author has access to a substantial body of firsthand information. The most important written record for this book is a unique collection of letters between members of the Schohl family (especially Max) and his American relatives (especially Julius Hess). The existence of correspondence from both sides of the Atlantic is a tremendous advantage. Whereas the letters from Max obviously give us a picture of what was happening in Germany, the letters from Julius Hess open up a window on the mental world of an "ordinary Joe" from the American provinces who was suddenly faced with a set of challenges unlike any he had ever known. Julius's sponsorship of Max's fruitless immigration suit brought home for him not only the horrors of Nazi racism but also the iniquities and capricious cruelties of America's policy toward Jewish refugees. Hess remained a patriotic American citizen throughout this ordeal (just as Max, more amazingly, remained a patriotic German to the bitter end), but he seems to have lost some of his unqualified faith in America's leaders and political institutions. Of course, in experiencing a negative epiphany as a result of prolonged contact with American officialdom Julius was taking part in yet another larger story, and one that is ongoing.

I would like to say that I "discovered" the cache of letters reproduced (generally in their entirety and always without grammatical corrections) throughout this book, but that is not the case. Some of the letters were excerpted in a *New York Times Magazine* piece by Michael Winerip entitled "Dear Cousin Max" (April 27, 1997). Winerip's article contained little commentary, and it occurred to me upon reading his piece that the letters he quoted could pack an even more powerful punch if placed within the framework of their various backstories, large and small. As I conducted research for this project I found other primary documents, including records relating to the Nazi era in Flörsheim, that give the Schohl family letters added meaning. To gain perspective on the American and British immigration policies that kept Max and thousands of other Jewish refugees at bay, I consulted, in addition to the wealth of secondary literature, various public and private document collections in U.S. and U.K. archives. For additional background information, and for many of the more intimate and personal details that help bring this story to life, I turned to witnesses of the Nazi era still living in Flörsheim, to local authorities on the history of that city, and above all to Käthe Schohl Wells, now the sole survivor among Max Schohl's immediate family.

Among the items that Käthe Schohl brought with her to America when she emigrated in 1946 was a framed inscription by Friedrich Schiller that now hangs in her kitchen in Charleston. It reads: "*Es gibt kein Übel so gross, wie die Angst davor*" ("No evil is as great as the fear of it") There is tremendous irony here, for it was, among other misjudgments, precisely an *inadequate* fear of the evil of Nazism that prompted Max Schohl to delay his efforts to get his family out of Germany. Yet at the same time one can understand why Käthe would prize this adage. Although Max was unable to deliver his wife and daughters from harm's way during the Nazi terror, his hope that they would be spared was ultimately realized, and that salvation was achieved in large part because neither he nor they became so overcome with fear that they gave up the fight to live. The fact that Max's family survived an evil that killed so many, and that his daughters were ultimately able to lead prosperous and fulfilled lives, lends the Schohl family story an element of redemption, even of transcendence.

There is an element of hope, too, in the postwar effort (albeit belated) on the part of the German people to come to grips with the great evil committed in their name, and to offer recompense (however begrudging and inadequate) to the victims of that evil. Here too the Schohl story figures in a larger picture: namely, in the tangled process of what the Germans call *Vergangenheitsbewältigung*—"reckoning with the past."

It took the postwar Germans some time even to think about dealing with the legacy of the Nazi past; they were too busy dealing with the challenges of the present, which included digging out from under the ruins left behind by Hitler's "Thousand Year Reich." Under pressure from the Allies, however, regional governments in western Germany began in the late 1940s to bring mid- and lower-level Nazis to justice (admittedly, an often all-too-lenient justice) and to offer limited financial compensation to German Jews who presented claims for their losses to the courts. Shortly after the war, the surviving Schohl women all filed claims for material losses and injuries suffered under the Nazis. The requirement to "prove" their victimization, and the modest fruits of their legal quest, certainly rankled, but the Schohls found satisfaction in regaining their home and in furnishing it with items that the American occupiers had confiscated from local Nazis.

The Schohls' hometown of Flörsheim was, like the nation as a whole, hardly anxious to face up to its own small part in the Holocaust. In the 1980s, however, some local citizens began looking into the town's persecution of its Jewish population. Max Schohl, as the most prominent Flörsheimer to be murdered by the Nazis, came to symbolize the fate of the town's Jews. In 1984 the city named a small street in his honor; it runs next to the site where his factory once stood. Walking down this lane today, or indeed strolling anywhere in the tidy and pleasant little town of Flörsheim, whose major communal preoccupation these days is the noise pollution generated by nearby Frankfurt Airport, a visitor would be hard pressed to imagine what transpired here some sixty to seventy years ago, when folks like Max Schohl were seen as dangerous "aliens" to be driven away rather than as valued citizens whose legacy is to be cherished and kept alive for posterity.

CHAPTER ONE

Max

GERMAN FIRST, JEW SECOND

Max Schohl was born on November 15, 1884, in Pirmasens, a small town in the Bavarian Palatinate famous for its leather goods industry; people called it "the German shoe-city." Max's father, Julius Schohl, owned a wholesale leather business and was among the town's wealthier citizens. He was also a registered member of the local Jewish community organization. Max and his two brothers, Oskar and Arthur, grew up in solid upper-bourgeois comfort and attended the best schools, where they were steeped in the enlightened ethos of German *Bildung*, which taught self-cultivation as well as deep reverence for Germany's cultural heritage. This kind of education had long been crucial in the assimilation of middle-class Jews into mainstream German society, and many German Jews viewed high culture as a kind of religion, making a "cult of *Kultur*." The Schohls certainly did so: leatherbound sets of Goethe and Schiller figured prominently in the family book collection, and Max and his brothers dutifully learned to play musical instruments. Max's instrument was the violin, and he would later insist that his children learn to play the piano. Like many German Jews, he became a great admirer of Richard Wagner, not letting that composer's notorious anti-Semitism get in the way of his enjoyment of *Die Meistersinger* and *Lohengrin*.

The Schohls' Judaism posed no substantial threat to their legal or economic status in the young German nation, which had become unified by the force of arms and Bismarckian diplomacy in 1871, just thirteen years before Max's birth. The constitution of the German Empire, following the lead of the short-lived North German Confederation (1867–1871), granted equal political and civil rights to all citizens regardless of religious confession. Legal equality did not end social discrimination, however, and Jews still found themselves largely shut out of the active officer corps, the upper civil service, and high court society. Moreover, the financial downturn of the mid-1870s that followed the economic boom of the immediate post-unification years generated a backlash against the newly emancipated Jews, who, as so often in the past, were blamed for the Germans' travails. *"Die Juden sind unser Unglück"* ("The Jews are our misfortune"), pronounced the nationalist historian Heinrich von Treitschke, in a fatal slogan that would later be adopted by the Nazis. Otto von Bismarck himself resorted to racist rhetoric to channel resentment away from his government toward Jewish members of the parliamentary opposition. And yet, although the persistence of anti-Semitic sentiment was deeply troubling to Germany's Jews, the more significant reality, in the eyes of most of them, was their new civil equality and the right to advance themselves professionally and economically without undue restrictions from the authorities. Although many gentiles still did not consider Jewish citizens fully "German," the German Jews themselves identified strongly with their nation, refusing to make a choice between being Jewish and German. Even religious Jews took this stance. As *Der Israelit*, the organ of Orthodox Judaism, declared in 1870: "We German Jews are German and nothing else." As a beneficiary of legal emancipation and economic freedom, Julius Schohl, although Orthodox in his faith, taught his children to think of themselves as Germans first and Jews second.

Julius Schohl's direct influence on his sons was cut short by his sudden death in a horseback riding accident in 1896, when Max was only twelve years old. Max's mother Johanna, a physically tiny but emotionally strong woman, took over the upbringing of the three boys. More devout than her husband, she saw to it that Max and his brothers took religious instruction and completed their bar mitzvah. For young Max, however, his secular studies, along with sports and girls, took precedence over piety. In school he proved adept in the natural sciences, especially chemistry. Deciding early on that he wanted to be a scientist, he worked hard in his classes and crammed to pass the *Arbitur* examination that allowed entrance to university-level studies. Here he was acting in accordance with an old tradition; as Alfred Einstein once quipped, the Israelites had spent the past two millennia of the Exile preparing for their entrance examinations. Max performed well enough to qualify for admission to the prestigious Technical University of Munich; after two years there, he transferred to the Technical University of Karlsruhe in Baden. His field was physical chemistry, with an emphasis on applied technical procedures.

Karlsruhe turned out to be an exciting place to study chemistry during the years Max was there. Among its faculty was the great chemist Fritz Haber, who had come to the institution in 1894 and had already attained a full professorship in 1906 at the relatively young age of thirty-seven. While in Karlsruhe, Haber made the discovery that would make him famous and win him the Nobel Prize in 1918: the process of synthesizing nitrogen, a breakthrough that proved crucial in the development of artificial fertilizers and explosives. (During World War I, after moving to the newly founded Kaiser-Wilhelm-Gesellschaft in Berlin, Haber also worked on the development of poison gas, which Germany deployed against its military adversaries in the First World War, and, albeit in a different form, against its civilian "enemies," especially the Jews of Europe, during the Holocaust. Haber himself did not witness this later atrocity; he died in exile in 1934.) We do not know how many courses Max Schohl took from Haber, but the illustrious chemist served as the second reader of his dissertation, titled "*Über Fulvenperoxyde. Ein Beitrag zur Kenntnis der Autoxydation*" ("On Fulvene Peroxide: A Contribution to the Understanding of Auto-Oxidation"). Accepted in 1907, the dissertation entitled Max to append the title "Doktor" to his name, which he did with understandable pride. Here too he was in good and numerous company; so many Central

European Jews were getting Ph.D.'s in this era that, as another quip had it, *"Doktor ist ein jüdischer Vorname"* ("Doctor is a Jewish first name").

At the university Max associated primarily with gentiles, not other Jews. His best friend was a young nobleman named Herman Matterstock, who lived on a large estate in West Prussia. Once the young noble took Max home during a university holiday to meet his parents. Max was invited to kiss the hand of the lady of the house. This, of course, was standard practice, but Max demurred on the grounds that the only female hand he would ever kiss was his mother's. In later years Max did not see much of Matterstock, who went on to become an official in the Nazi Party. In November 1938, when the Nazis interned Max in Buchenwald, Matterstock was unreceptive to pleas for help from his old friend's wife. He could not really remember Max, he said. After the war, however, his memory suddenly improved; during his de-Nazification trial he asked Max's widow for a character reference stating that he had been "a friend of the Jews." Frau Schohl did not comply.

Upon completing his studies Max served a one-year hitch as a volunteer in the Bavarian army, the customary commitment for graduates of Germany's preparatory high schools and universities. He seems to have felt thoroughly at home in the military world, although Jews in general were hardly welcomed in the armies of the various German states, even after 1871. In 1906, the year before Max completed his active service, the Bavarian army had only 281 Jews out of a total strength of 61,432. Following his active duty Max transferred into the reserves, which was the typical procedure. He must have been a very good soldier, for in 1912 he was promoted to second lieutenant in the Bavarian Reserve Officer Corps, which definitely was not typical. The officer ranks in the German army, even at the reserve level, were on the whole notoriously anti-Semitic. The old-line aristocrats who made up the bulk of the Officer Corps regarded Jews as "the paradigm of the new industrial and financial forces which challenged their privileged class position," to quote one authority. Germany's war ministers justified keeping Jews out, or nearly out, of the officer ranks by arguing that people of this "race" were not fit physically or emotionally to occupy leadership positions in the military. According to a pseudoscientific theory widely popular among German officers, Jews were descended from a different species of apes than were gentiles, which accounted for their weak bodies, sloping shoulders, flat feet, poor teeth, and bad eyes. On the basis of such reasoning, Prussia excluded Jews entirely from its Reserve Officer Corps, not to mention its active-duty equivalent. Luckily for the patriotic Max, Bavaria did not go this far, deigning to accept a few highly qualified Jews each year to its reserve officer ranks (though not to the active corps). While allowing that some Jews could make good officers, Bavaria's chief military official went on record in 1907 with the caveat that one had to be extra careful in admitting Jews even to the reserve officer ranks, since "the entire Jewish character and way of thinking and acting differ fundamentally from [those of] the German Officer Corps," rendering "a significant penetration of Jewish elements into the officer ranks not only harmful but downright ruinous." In 1907, the year Max was promoted to Bavaria's Reserve Officer Corps, that institution had only eighty-five Jews, or 2.1 percent of the total, throughout its various specialty branches, and virtually all of them were in the least prestigious divisions like transportation and engineering.

During his years in the reserves Max continued to hone his skills as a research chemist, hoping to follow his idol Fritz Haber into academia. Accordingly, in 1908 he took a teaching assistantship post under Professor Heinrich Schultz at the Technical University of Munich, where he had begun his studies. Although not as hostile to Jews as the military, German universities were hardly bastions of tolerance. It is not known whether Max suffered any anti-Semitic slights in this environment, but he certainly had to contend with miserable pay and the probability of very slow advancement in the rigidly hierarchical German academic system. In 1911 he decided to retreat from academia into industry, taking a job as an analytical chemist at the Tellus A.G. in Frankfurt. He acquitted himself so well in this position that in the following year he was offered the job of *Betriebsleiter*, or unit supervisor, at the Nassovia chemical factory in nearby Flörsheim, the town in which he would eventually settle. He had been in his new post for two years when World War I broke out.

Max Schohl was among the tens of thousands of young Germans who rushed to the colors in August 1914 following the opening of hostilities.

Just two days after the war began he enlisted in the 17th Bavarian Infantry Regiment, whose motto was *"Mit Hurra in den Tod!"* ("With a Hurrah We Go to Our Deaths!") His unit joined the German invasion of Belgium and France. Max's Jewish background was no deterrent to his enthusiasm for the war effort; on the contrary, like many of his co-religionists he saw the war as an opportunity for Germany's Jews to prove once and for all that they were just as "German" as everyone else. He would certainly have concurred with the Jewish Reichstag delegate, Ludwig Frank, who wrote home just before being killed in battle: "I go as all others—full of joy and certain of victory . . . glad to let my blood flow for the fatherland." It is worth noting, however, that not all Jews were certain that their willingness to serve the fatherland would put an end to age-old racist stereotypes. As Fritz Mayer, a member of Max's regiment, wrote on November 21, 1914 (two years before falling on the Western Front): "I am happy in a time of blood-soaked trial to be allowed to prove my loyalty to the sacred truth of our cause, as the love for fatherland burns hotter in us now than ever. We [Jewish soldiers] are not discouraged by the fact that the disgraceful voices of slander against us back home have not entirely died out, but these slurs do make us sad, very sad. What more can they want than our blood? Let them carry out their 'racial studies' on the blood shed by our fallen brothers. At least the enemy bullets make no such distinctions [in the blood they spill]. Thank God for that!"

In fact, the German Jews' support for the war effort did lead to a momentary lull in the chorus of anti-Semitic calumny. In the first months of the war there were actually more professions of admiration for the Jewish national commitment than aspersions on Jewish patriotism. The Jewish industrialist Walther Rathenau, who headed the Reich's industrial mobilization for the war, was able in that heady moment to view the war as a kind of giant smithy in which a firm and lasting German-Jewish partnership might be forged.

Alas, it was not to be. The early wartime expressions of ethnic harmony, like the so-called Spirit of August—that more general feeling of national togetherness that marked the beginning of the war—did not survive the transformation of the conflict from an anticipated joyous crusade crowned by quick victory into a protracted nightmare of meat-grinder attrition in the trenches and unimagined deprivation at home. One of the "explanations" for the German army's failure to bring the war to a quick and successful conclusion was alleged "un-German" behavior on the part of the nation's Jews, who were accused of dodging the killing at the front to stay home and make killings in war-related business. Press reports of Jewish contributions to the war effort, which included thousands of casualties and hundreds of decorations for valor (Jews won 710 Iron Crosses in 1914 alone), were derided as exaggerations or inventions designed to mask the "real" Jewish practice of war profiteering. Shamefully caving in to popular demands to "expose" supposed Jewish underrepresentation at the front, the Prussian War Ministry in 1916 conducted a *Judenzählung*, or census, of Jews serving in the military. Understandably, this move appalled the patriotic Jews fighting at the front. It seemed that no matter how much they sacrificed, their own government continued to treat them as pariahs. This wartime revival of old prejudices made some Jews wonder if they would ever find lasting acceptance. As the Jewish philosopher Hermann Cohen lamented in 1916: "We younger people had hoped that slowly we would be successfully integrated by the 'nation of Kant' . . . , that we could in time let the love of fatherland speak through us without restraint, and that we could be allowed to cooperate with fully conscious pride in the tasks of the nation and with a sense of equality. This trust has been broken; the old oppressive anxiety has awakened again."

When the "Jewish census" did not prove what its framers had intended, the results of the count were hushed up. Statistics compiled after the end of the war revealed that some 100,000 Jews, or about 18 percent of the total Jewish population, had served the German colors, about four-fifths of them on the front lines. Thirty-five thousand Jews had won battlefield decorations, and some 12,000 had died for their country. For the first time, Jews had been awarded commissions in the active officer corps of the German army.

Max Schohl was one of those German-Jewish soldiers who, by throwing himself fully and selflessly into the fray, won promotion to the active officer corps. In 1916 he became a first lieutenant, and at the end of the war he made captain, one of the few Jews in the German army to reach this rank. If, like some of his fellow Jewish fighters, he suffered from the persistence of anti-Semitic sentiment back home, he gave no indication of it in a diary he kept at the front. Here the talk was all of bold (though often costly) engagements with the enemy and gratification over a job well done. Max never held himself back in battle, and he was injured seriously twice, getting shot in the chest (which cost him a lung) and through the leg (which left him permanently crippled). In recognition of his leadership and self-sacrifice he won the Iron Cross, First and Second Class, the Bavarian Service Medal, and the Bavarian Honor Cross for Front Service. His war medals and the certificate attesting to his status as a wounded veteran joined his academic diploma as his most treasured possessions, ones he would later use in attempting to bargain for his life and the safety of his family.

Max's enthusiasm for the German war effort was diminished neither by his own crippling injuries nor by the death of his beloved younger brother, Arthur, a doctor, on the Romanian front. His older brother, Oskar, also became a war casualty, dying at home shortly after the war from wounds incurred in the fighting. Later, Max wrote a moving story about a chance encounter with Arthur during the war, describing him as "so young, so full of life, so much to live for . . . a dedicated, faithful doctor, a brave soldier killed on enemy soil." In short, Max was one of those passionate "bitter-enders" who remained committed to the cause long after many others had begun to waver. For him Germany's humiliating military defeat, not the blood sacrifice on the front or the material deprivation at home, was the true horror of this disastrous conflict.

Germany's military defeat, of course, stemmed largely from the Reich's inability to match the superior firepower of its opponents, but many embittered Germans saw their national humiliation as the product of a "stab in the back" by alleged enemies at home, most notably the Jews. The fact that some Jewish political figures played important roles in the revolutionary events that brought down Germany's royal and imperial rulers at the moment of the nation's military defeat was additional "proof," insisted anti-Semitic agitators, that the Jews were by nature disloyal and subversive. In fact, the majority of Germany's assimilated Jews, particularly those belonging to the middle and upper-middle classes, opposed the revolution and lamented the fall of the monarchy. Many continued to see the old regime as "their world" despite the fact that this world, throughout most of its existence and certainly in its death throes, had been loath to match the enthusiasm of the Jewish embrace.

When it came to lingering loyalty toward the old regime, Max Schohl took an extreme position even among the patriotic German-Jewish veterans' community. He elected not to join the main Jewish ex-servicemen's organization, the Reichsbund jüdischer Frontsoldaten, but chose instead the predominantly gentile and extremely conservative Kyffhäuserbund. Founded as an umbrella association of existing veterans' organizations in 1898–1900, the group took its name from the Kyffhäuser Mountain, where according to patriotic mythology the medieval Germanic warrior-emperor Frederick Barbarossa was "sleeping," awaiting a call to resume his heroic struggle against the Slavs. (Hence Hitler's decision to codename Germany's attack against the Soviet Union in 1941 "Operation Barbarossa.") In 1898 the association erected an enormous and suitably pompous monument to Kaiser Wilhelm I, modern Germany's first emperor, on the Kyffhäuser Mountain. A few years later the group's president, Professor Alfred Westphal, described the organization's "highest and most sacred mission as that of cultivating monarchical and patriotic values, thereby countering the revolutionary and anti-fatherland forces of Social Democracy with a nationalistic people's movement of former soldiers." The Kyffhäuserbund stayed true to its monarchist, antisocialist values even after the collapse of the monarchy and the creation of a democratic republic. Moreover, as in previous years, the group remained unreceptive to Jewish membership. Max Schohl was admitted only because of his brilliant war record and overt monarchist-nationalist convictions. Throughout the 1920s he made a point of regularly attending Kyffhäuser meetings in Frankfurt. He invariably listed membership in the group among his key social affiliations. It would therefore come as a terrible blow to Max when, following Hitler's seizure of power in 1933, the Kyffhäuserbund summarily expelled him from its ranks.

Upon his demobilization from the army in 1918 Max was anxious to return to work as a practicing chemist in Germany, but like many returning veterans he found it difficult to find suitable employment in his battered homeland. For want of other opportunities, he signed on as a chemistry instructor at a private secondary school in St. Gallen, Switzerland. The job was not very demanding, and he was able in his spare time to go hunting and to learn to ski, a sport he pursued vigorously despite the leg injury he had sustained in the war. Little did Max know that, like his war record, his experience as a teacher in Switzerland would later figure importantly in his effort to save his family during the Holocaust.

The pleasures of hunting and skiing in Switzerland notwithstanding, Max was relieved when, after a little more than a year, he was offered a position back home with a chemical firm in Wiesbaden-Biebrich. The company in question, Electro, had recently taken possession of the Nassovia chemical factory in Flörsheim, where Max had worked before the war. The Flörsheim firm had fallen on hard times during the war under its then owner, Dr. Ludwig Stamm, who had been forced to operate under bankruptcy protection for three years before selling out to the Wiesbaden company, which then changed the firm's name to Electro, like its parent. Still under Stamm's inept management in the immediate postwar period, the Flörsheim factory continued to flounder. Max Schohl proved to be one of the beneficiaries of Stamm's incompetence, when, along with two other Jewish partners from Wiesbaden, he was able in mid-1919 to buy the ailing plant from his bosses at Electro for a mere 190,000 marks. On October 8, 1919, he moved back to Flörsheim, now as principal owner (with 40 percent control) of his own company. Among his first acts was to get rid of Dr. Stamm, the former owner and present director. Max could not have known that this apparently routine business decision would have serious consequences later on. The embittered Dr. Stamm would go on to head the Nazi Party in Flörsheim and become the town's mayor during the Third Reich, a position that enabled him to make and break local businesses, including Max's.

In 1919, however, the future looked bright for Max Schohl. In addition to being a newly minted factory owner, he had recently married a beautiful young woman, Frieda Luise (Liesel) Gims, who had been his nurse at the military hospital in Wiesbaden where he was treated for his wounds in 1918. Falling instantly in love with her, Max penned a love poem ending with the strophe, "Oh, rest on my heart/Only kiss my lips/Take all the pain from me/Kiss me back to health!" To marry this angel of mercy he had to overcome staunch resistance from his mother, because Liesel Gims was a shiksa, a Catholic from the nearby village of Amüneburg. Liesel's blue-collar family—her father was a factory foreman at the local Kaliwerke, where three of her four brothers also worked—heartily approved of the marriage, but Max's mother believed that Jewish boys had no business pairing with Christian girls, least of all blue-collar Catholic girls. "Get yourself a nice Jewish Fräulein!" she admonished her son. But Max insisted that he would marry only Liesel, who for her part helped to pacify Johanna Schohl by converting to Judaism. Eventually Liesel became much more serious about religious matters than her husband, displaying the fabled ultra-devotion of the convert. She never had much luck, however, in turning Max into a strictly observant practitioner of their mutual faith. Fortunately, she had somewhat more success in winning over Johanna, who after a few years allowed Liesel to enter her kitchen and do a little cooking. She even allowed Max to inform his wife that her kosher cakes were "not bad."

Upon settling in Flörsheim the Schohls took possession of a handsome three-story house that belonged to the domain of the Electro firm and was situated at Albanusstrasse 2, directly across the Hauptstrasse from the factory. As for the factory itself, it began quickly to prosper as a result of Max's vigorous management and introduction of new technical processes, which included converting celluloid derived from discarded camera film into chemical dyes for leather. To promote the marketing of its products outside Germany, Flörsheim Electro, in tandem with its former parent company in Wiesbaden-Biebrich, opened sales offices in Milan, Paris, and São Paulo. By the mid-1920s the firm had 150 workers on its payroll, making it one of Flörsheim's larger employers. (By far the largest employer in the region was the huge Opel factory across the Main River in Rüsselsheim, which had a workforce of several thousand.) Thus, within a few years of taking the helm of the ailing Electro plant, Max had turned it into a model industrial operation and a force to be reckoned with on the local and regional economic scene.

The "Golden Twenties"

Max achieved his early business successes at a time when Germany in general and Flörsheim in particular were suffering from extreme political, social, and economic dislocation. The Weimar Republic, so called because the constitution for the new state was drawn up in the city of Weimar, which was associated in the German tradition with the humanistic ideals of Goethe and Schiller, barely survived the chaos of its birth and early years, and these traumas of infancy crippled the fragile child for the duration of its short life. In the first two years of its existence the newborn republic was rocked by coup attempts from both the far left and the far right. In January 1919 left-wing Spartacists, hoping to turn Germany into a communist state on the Soviet model, staged an insurrection against the provisional government in Berlin. After two weeks of bloody fighting, remnants of the old army, assisted by rightist "Free Corps" volunteers, managed to crush the rebellion. A little more than a year later, during the so-called Kapp Putsch, a band of disgruntled army officers and rightist political figures briefly took control of Berlin with the aim of establishing an authoritarian regime. The rebels threw in the towel after a few days when the workers of Berlin shut down the city in a general strike.

The Weimar state was weakened also by its association with the armistice and the postwar treaty arrangements that governed Germany's relations with its conquerors. The Imperial German Army may have lost the war, but civilian authorities of the new republic bore the primary onus for the defeat because it was they who signed the 1918 armistice and accepted the subsequent Treaty of Versailles, which among other sanctions deprived Germany of all its colonies, reduced its army to an all-volunteer force of 100,000 men, and held Berlin solely responsible for the war, thus establishing the legal basis for reparations. Not surprisingly, most Germans considered the treaty a travesty of victor's justice. Civilian politicians also shouldered the thankless tasks of finding a modus vivendi with Germany's aggrieved neighbors and making the steep reparations payments demanded by the victors. Believing that such "treachery" merited death, right-wing fanatics launched a campaign of terror and assassination against prominent figures of the new order. Matthias Erzberger, Germany's new finance minister and one of the armistice signers, was gunned down while walking in the Black Forest; Philipp Scheidemann, the first republican chancellor, was nearly blinded by an assailant who threw prussic acid in his face; Hugo Haase, the leader of the Independent Socialist Party, was shot to death on the steps of the Reichstag; and, most notoriously, Walther Rathenau, Germany's foreign minister, who worked as hard to strengthen Germany's diplomatic posture after the war as he had to strengthen its industry during the conflict, was murdered in June 1922 while driving to work.

Rathenau, of course, was a Jew, and in the eyes of those who killed him his "race" made him doubly deserving of this fate, for he was seen as part of a larger Jewish conspiracy to keep Germany permanently weak and open to the predations of international finance. Rathenau was hardly the only victim of anti-Semitic assaults in the early years of the Weimar Republic. In November 1923 *Ostjuden* (Jewish immigrants from Poland and Russia) were attacked in the streets of Berlin following rumors that they were buying up unemployment funds with the intention of lending out the money at usurious rates later on. These pogrom-like attacks in Berlin coincided with the Nazis' Beer Hall Putsch in Munich, Hitler's abortive first attempt to seize power and "save" Germany from its putative internal enemies, including the Jews.

The coup attempts, assassinations, and racist assaults that plagued the early Weimar Republic must be seen against the backdrop not only of national humiliation but also of severe economic crisis. In the period between 1919 and late 1923 the German mark lost virtually all its value, first gradually, then with dizzying speed. Deficit spending by the wartime and immediate postwar governments had put pressure on the mark, which was further weakened by the political instability of the era. Who could have confidence in the currency of a state under siege? But unsettling as the mark's slide was during the first postwar years, things got much worse in 1923 following the decision by France to punish

Germany for defaulting on its reparations payments, by sending troops into the industrial Ruhr Valley. The German government countered this move by instituting "passive resistance," encouraging coal companies and railways to suspend their operations and then compensating owners and striking workers with freshly printed currency from the national treasury. The mark went into free fall. In early February 1923 it hit 42,000 to the dollar, in July 160,000, and in August 3 million. To meet the demand for paper currency more than 2,000 presses worked around the clock, churning out bills in ever-higher denominations: a 50 million mark note in September 1923, 5 and 10 billion bills in October, and a 100 trillion note in November. Even the biggest bills were like chaff in the wind at the height of the hyperinflation in late November, when one American dollar was worth a mind-boggling 4,210,500,000,000 marks. As the mark sprouted zeros, so did prices, with a glass of beer finally fetching 150 billion marks, a loaf of bread 80 billion, and a tumble with a prostitute 300 billion—or a cigarette. Of course people tried to get rid of their cash as quickly as possible, before it lost further value. They rushed from pay counter to store or bar, often transporting their load of bills in backpacks or even wheelbarrows. Commenting on this surreal scene, when the old virtues like thrift and saving had become suicidal, a national newspaper wrote: "People throw themselves on the stores, buy what is there to buy. They hoard necessary and superfluous things. . . . Illogic, blind emotion, and panic rule the hour." When the insanity had finally run its course in late 1923, millions of people were left destitute. For many Germans, the Great Inflation proved to be a catastrophe they could never overcome or forget.

One of the by-products of early Weimar Germany's political and economic tribulations was an upsurge of separatist sentiment in certain parts of the country. In Bavaria, which had been unhappy with the domination of Germany by Prussia since the nation's unification in 1871, there were loud cries for a decoupling from the republic and the creation of a separate alpine state including western Austria. The *Loss von Berlin* ("Away from Berlin") movement was fueled also by religious differences between Catholic Bavaria and Protestant northern Germany, and by the conservative Bavarians' distrust of the more liberal or leftist policies emanating from the national capital. The central government's apparent inability to maintain law and order or protect the economy naturally made the idea of bolting from the republic all the more attractive. Such was the case also in the Rhineland, which like Bavaria had a long tradition of anti-Prussian resentment, especially since Prussia had annexed large sections of the territory in 1815. After World War I France stationed troops in the Rhine-Main region to prevent it from becoming a launching pad for revanchist German attacks. Not surprisingly, the French believed that they would be even safer from attack if the Rhineland were completely decoupled from Germany and allied to France. Accordingly, Paris did what it could to foster separatist sentiments among the Rhinelanders, whose receptivity to such notions was enhanced by their own national government's obvious failings. Partly because of France's high-handed tactics, however, the separatist forces in the Rhineland ran into plenty of opposition from unionist patriots. Moreover, as in Bavaria, the pressures to secede dropped off at the end of 1923, when a viable new currency was introduced that helped the young republic finally find its economic and political footing. Nonetheless, like the Great Inflation, separatism left an enduring legacy of distrust and ill will among the citizens who had been most deeply affected by it.

Max Schohl's adopted hometown of Flörsheim, small though it was (about 6,000 residents in the Weimar era), could not and did not escape the turbulence of these times; on the contrary, it became a kind of ministage on which all the passions of the era were acted out.

Like distant Berlin, Flörsheim was polarized politically between radicalized left-wing elements emboldened by the collapse of the monarchy and conservative forces that greeted the new order with trepidation, if not outright hostility. In the first postwar national and municipal elections, the largest vote-getters in town were the moderate leftist Social Democrats and the Catholic Center Party, which in Flörsheim had a particularly conservative cast. When campaigning for the Reichstag in January 1919, the Center Party declared that the Social Democratic Party (SPD) bore "blood-guilt" for the loss of the war. The SPD, for its part, had increasing difficulty holding its preeminence on the left against the more radical Independent Social Democratic Party (USPD), which berated the mainstream socialists for backing away from Marxism's revolutionary ideals. Picking up support among the town's growing ranks of unemployed workers, the USPD surpassed the SPD as the largest party on the left in the Reichstag elections of June 1920. In subsequent elections the USPD in turn was superseded by the KPD, or Communists, as the dominant force on the extreme left. Meanwhile, on the right, the Center found itself competing for the conservative vote with the extreme nationalist German National Peoples Party (DNVP), which took an openly antirepublican and anti-Semitic line. Here as elsewhere in the Rhine-Main region, the DNVP capitalized on widespread patriotic opposition to the French military occupation, which in Flörsheim had begun on December 13, 1918. Local anti-French agitators made much of the fact that France used black colonial troops to keep the locals in check, a tactic that indignant Germans denounced as *"Die Schwarze Schmach am Rhein"* ("The Black Shame on the Rhine").

The presence of black occupation troops in their town was actually the least of the Flörsheimers' problems at this time. The end of the war brought no end to the food shortages that had weakened the wartime home front's resolve, for the Allied blockade of agricultural imports remained in place for more than a year, while local farmers resisted delivering their crops to market at the low prices set by government officials. A Flörsheim Workers and Peasants Council, which shared power with the elected municipal government in the immediate aftermath of the war, appealed to local farmers to continue supplying the town with food products or face armed attacks by hungry citizens. In fact, because many farmers indeed chose to hold back deliveries of crops, armed strife is precisely what happened. Bands of gun-toting townsfolk mounted foraging raids in the countryside, only to be met by farmer-militias with guns of their own. The recently concluded war of nation against nation in the trenches of Flanders and eastern France had segued into a battle between town dwellers and farmers in the fields and orchards of the German homeland. Hoping to curtail this internecine warfare, in August 1919 the Flörsheim municipal government voted to station guards in the fields and to make bulk purchases of food and coal to distribute to the destitute.

Like agricultural and energy resources, adequate housing was in terribly short supply in postwar Flörsheim due to an influx of refugees from larger cities and to the predatory policies of the French occupiers, who commandeered the best houses and official buildings for their own use. Inadequate shelter drove city folks to the countryside, where they bedded down in chicken coops and pigsties, much to the alarm of the farmers—not to mention the chickens and pigs. In an effort to alleviate the housing crisis, the municipality passed ordinances against demolishing habitable structures or converting such places to nondwelling uses, tactics that landlords were employing to exacerbate the living space shortage and drive up rents.

At the root of Flörsheim's social misery was a blossoming economic and financial crisis mirroring that in Germany as a whole. By mid-1919 the number of unemployed in town had climbed to 200, about one-quarter of the workforce. Unemployment relief provided only 5 marks per day to married men, 1.50 per day to their wives, and 1 mark to each child under age 14. Single unemployed men received 4.50 marks per day. These tiny allotments would have been hard to live on in the best of times, but with the galloping inflation of the postwar period they were more of an insult than an asset. It was not only the unemployed, however, who could not keep their heads above the rising tide of prices; anyone whose income was not adjusted on an almost daily basis to meet the mark's collapsing purchasing power was bound to suffer. On September 14, 1920, the workers at the Opel factory in Rüsselsheim went on strike to protest their inability to feed their families on their current wages; they demanded wage increases as well as a reduction in the price of potatoes from 20 to 15 marks per *Zentner* (metric hundredweight). Later that month demonstrators marched through Flörsheim to the property of a nearby farmer who had announced that he would let his potatoes rot in the fields before selling them at less than 30 marks per *Zentner*. Only the threat of renewed violence persuaded the local peasantry to agree to sell 3,500 *Zentner* of potatoes to the municipality for 20 marks per unit. Soon, of course, 20 marks would not buy a single potato, much less a *Zentner*. By July 1923, a loaf of "mixed bread" (wheat mixed with "substitute" ingredients like turnips) fetched 27,000 marks. The farmers in the region preferred to feed their crops to their pigs rather than sell them in town for useless currency. Farmers also bartered their food products for valuable home accessories or services. It was said that one local peasant had an oriental carpet in his pigsty, a village beauty in his hayloft, and the first decent haircut of his life. The townspeople had plenty of time to service the farmers because, as of September 1923, 1,500 of them were unemployed, almost one-third of the total population.

As in the rest of the Rhine-Main region, in Flörsheim the socioeconomic misery of the times generated a separatist movement, a campaign for an independent Rhineland, whose proponents battled fiercely with German nationalist patriots for control of the political environment. Initially, the separatist cause in Flörsheim was led by elements from the Center Party, who believed that their values would be better protected in a rump Rhine-state tied to Catholic France than in an impoverished Germany dominated by Protestants, socialists, and liberal secularists. However, with the increasing meltdown of the local economy, along with a more conservative trend in national politics after 1920, various leftist and working-class folks jumped on the separatist bandwagon, highjacking it from the Center's control. A local USPD politician named Heinrich Theis, whom the SPD organ in Wiesbaden mocked as "the little Lenin from Flörsheim," assumed leadership of the movement and gave it a pronounced radical coloration. On October 22, 1923, Theis mounted the steps of the St. Gallus Church and, backed by some forty followers, announced Flörsheim's allegiance to a new "Rhine Republic" that had just been proclaimed in nearby Mainz and Wiesbaden. Theis demanded that the St. Gallus bells be rung to celebrate this momentous occasion, but the resident priest, anticipating just such a sacrilege, had removed the main bell cord, forcing the putschists to make do with the clanging of two tiny bells. While the flag of the new republic was being hoisted over the Rathaus, French troops secured the town center. A few days later, on October 27, the head of the French occupation forces in the region, Colonel Wimpfen, named Theis acting mayor in place of the existing office holder, Jakob Lauck, who had refused to countenance the coup.

Lauck, it soon turned out, had made a wise decision. In response to the separatist action in Flörsheim and vicinity, the central authorities in

Berlin and Frankfurt suspended all material and monetary relief to the region. Suddenly bereft of any financial resources to pay its bills or salaries, the new separatist administration of Flörsheim began printing an "emergency currency" of its own, as did other towns of the region. The municipality's 50 billion and 500 billion mark bills featured in the lower right-hand corner a homely piece of wisdom, "Most of Our Worries Consist of Ungrounded Fears," as well as a notice saying that the bills were legal tender in "the entire district of Wiesbaden." The notes' optimistic homily notwithstanding, these colorful bits of paper were rejected by merchants and farmers throughout the region despite threats of draconian punishment from the municipality for not accepting them. Even the hopelessly inflated national currency looked substantial compared to this *"Flörsheimer Notgeld."* With local farmers again refusing to make food deliveries, merchants sitting on their inventories, and unemployed workers threatening to riot for want of their relief payments, the French wisely decided to wash their hands of the Rhine-region separatists. In Flörsheim Colonel Wimpfen hastily dumped the would-be local Lenin, Heinrich Theis, and asked ex-Mayor Lauck to resume his duties. Lauck consented to do so on condition that the separatists be thrown out of the Rathaus. (In acknowledgment of his defense of Flörsheim's German virtue, the town later named a street in his honor.) As of December 1, 1923, Flörsheim's brief moment in the separatist spotlight was over.

Many Flörsheimer did not come off very well in the turbulent years between the revolution of 1918 and the separatist putsch of 1923. Farmers took advantage of townsfolk, and townsfolk raided farmers' fields. Landlords gouged renters and did their best to force housing costs up. Conscientious political leaders, such as the local SPD chief Jakob Altmaier, who had called for an end to the ruinous policy of passive resistance against France's occupation of the Ruhr, were accused of being in the pay of Paris. Some citizens abandoned what they believed was a sinking national ship in favor of a separate Rhineland raft that proved incapable of floating at all. Animosities generated in those tension-filled times continued to fester for years beneath the apparently placid surface of village life.

One Flörsheim citizen who managed to acquit himself quite ad-
mirably in this less-than-admirable time was the newcomer to town,
Max Schohl. As a major employer, Max could have done what virtually
all of his factory-owner colleagues did to turn the Great Inflation to their
advantage—namely, pay his employees in near-worthless national currency, thereby eliminating a large part of his overhead. Rather than advance his own fortunes on the backs of his workers, Max elected to pay
his people in dollars, to which he had access through the foreign
branches of his company. Not surprisingly, this heretical approach incurred the wrath of the other business barons in the area. Branding Max
a *Nestbeschmutzer* (nest-befouler), they took him to court for his breach of
prevailing business ethics, which they denounced as a clever ploy to steal
workers from his competition. Agreeing with this assessment, the district
court (made up largely of magistrates from the imperial era) found Max
guilty and imposed a heavy fine for his "divisive" action. His employees,
on the other hand, saw his behavior in a different light; if he had be-
fouled his nest, they were very happy to roost in it. While some factories
in the region lost workers and suffered strikes, Max's Electro did not.

Paying his employees in viable currency was not the end of Max's
benevolence. In 1920, as more and more Flörsheimer began to suffer
from genuine hunger, Max established an institution that dispensed hot
meals on weekends. He also financed a program to distribute food to
schoolchildren on school days. At Christmas time he presented his
neighbors in Albanusstrasse with Christmas trees and bountiful food
baskets. During the winter neighborhood kids could stop by his home
for hot chocolate, while in summer cold drinks and ice cream were on
hand for the asking. Some eighty years later, a Flörsheim native who as
a little girl had lived next door to the Schohls could still remember Max
as a kind of year-round Santa Claus, a man whose generosity, especially
to children, seemed to know no bounds.

Having managed to get through tough economic times with his company intact and his reputation as a good neighbor firmly established,
Max settled in during the more tranquil years of the mid-1920s as a ver-
itable pillar of the community. In his case, the community of which he
was a pillar was both Jewish and gentile.

The Flörsheim Jewish community in the 1920s was small and had been getting smaller for years. In 1866 it had numbered sixty-nine souls, but it dropped to thirty-five in 1895 largely because of emigration. During this time the percentage of Jews relative to the total population fell from 3.17 to 1.09. Although the number of Jews in town climbed to fifty-seven in 1904, their percentage of the total slipped further because the Christian population grew more substantially. After World War I the Jewish population fell again to fifty, holding more or less constant at that number throughout the Weimar era.

On the whole, Flörsheim's Jewish community was not wealthy, and it had become even poorer since the mid-nineteenth century because many of the more prosperous Jews had chosen to move to larger cities. At the beginning of the twentieth century most of the town's Jews were classed in the lowest tax bracket and therefore found it difficult to pay the "cultural tax" that supported local religious institutions. Without a regular subsidy from the regional government in Wiesbaden, Flörsheim's Jewish Gemeinde would not have been able to provide religious instruction or to maintain a rabbi. As for the kinds of employment that prevailed among the Jews of Flörsheim and neighboring towns, these had not changed much over the years. The most common occupations were cattle broker, fruit and vegetable dealer, retailer, baker, kosher butcher, and tailor. In the years before Max Schohl's arrival, one prominent exception to this picture of modest circumstances and traditional occupations was Dr. Hugo Noerdlinger, a chemical factory owner. At the turn of the century Noerdlinger was by far the richest man in town. In 1900 he also became the first Jew in Flörsheim's history to be elected to the municipal council.

That a Jew like Noerdlinger—albeit one who played no role whatsoever in the religious life of his community—could be elected to the village council in an overwhelmingly Catholic town said something quite positive about the relations between Flörsheim's Jews and gentiles at the turn of the century. True, there had been, and would continue to be, signs of a willingness on the part of some local gentiles to buy into the prevailing anti-Semitic prejudices. In the late nineteenth century the main regional newspaper, the *Kreisblatt für den Landkreis Wiesbaden*, devoted considerable space to racist agitators at the national level, including the imperial court preacher Adolf Stoecker, who championed a defense of the "German-Christian spirit." In 1887 the paper reprinted a series of scurrilous anti-Semitic articles under the title "The Usurers." Six years later Jewish stores in Flörsheim and neighboring towns were burglarized and vandalized. In 1913 a local cultural evening devoted to the works of the nineteenth-century German-Jewish poet Heinrich Heine generated a flurry of angry letters to the Catholic-owned *Flörsheimer Anzeiger*. One letter called the event "a betrayal of German poetry" and denounced Heine as a "poison plant in the garden of poetry." Revealingly, however, these letters were anonymous, as if their authors were not fully confident of their support within the community. And in fact, until the early 1930s, Jews and gentiles in town worked and lived together relatively harmoniously. Communal organizations like the Singing Club, Gymnastics Association, Rowing Club, and Volunteer Fire Department included both Jewish and non-Jewish members. In July 1918, when the town's synagogue celebrated the 200th anniversary of its consecration, Christian homeowners in the neighborhood decorated their houses with bunting, and the Rathaus and Catholic parish-house hoisted flags in the temple's honor. Mayor Lauck and Father Reinhold Klein of St. Gallus Church attended the anniversary service at the synagogue, which was presided over by the district rabbi, who reminded his audience that "flowers shrivel, grass rots, but the word of God lasts forever." The Jewish congregation took this opportunity to reaffirm its loyalty to the fatherland by praying for the Kaiser, the German generals, and the troops in the field.

As a soldier in the field himself at this point, Max Schohl was not present at this joint Jewish-Christian celebration of Flörsheim's primary Jewish institution, but he would certainly have applauded its patriotic sentiments and ecumenical nature. Max, after all, was a great believer in the German-Jewish partnership, and upon settling in Flörsheim he quickly joined predominantly gentile organizations like the Singing Club. He also became a registered member of the Jewish community organization, although he made no big thing of religious observances. He attended synagogue services only on high holidays, not, like his wife, on every Sabbath. He not only gave away Christmas trees to his neighbors but also displayed a huge candle-festooned tree in his own house every holiday season. Politically Max remained a nationalist-conservative, giving his vote to the center-right Deutsche Volks Partei (German People's Party—DVP), which distinguished itself from the farther right DNVP by not mixing its nationalism and antisocialism with anti-Semitism.

In following this political course Max was in the company of many highly assimilated German-Jewish business leaders in the Weimar Republic, but he was somewhat out of step with most of the politically active Jews of Flörsheim, who tended to back the left-liberal Deutsche Demokratische Partei (German Democratic Party—DDP) or the moderate socialist SPD. Where Max *was* fully in step with his fellow Flörsheim Jews was in his rejection of Zionism, which since its foundation in the late nineteenth century had never found a following in town. Even after 1933, when some of the local Jews began to flee Germany, they generally did not make Palestine their goal. Max's rejection of Zionism was part of his broader German patriotism, which was also reflected in his staunch stand against the brief separatist campaign in Flörsheim in late 1923. In his eyes, the separatists were little better than traitors, and for the rest of his days in Germany he could never forgive them for their "betrayal" of the fatherland.

Max Schohl had good reason in the mid-1920s to feel comfortable in his German fatherland, in his adopted hometown of Flörsheim, and in his own skin. He was one of the wealthiest men in town. He could afford to go skiing every year in Switzerland, to regularly attend the theater and opera in Frankfurt, and even to travel over to Paris to see Josephine Baker dance in her banana skirt at the Folies Bergères. His chemical factory was flourishing, not least because of his good relations with his workers. Max was the proud father of two little daughters, Hela, born in 1920, and Käthe, born in 1923. As of 1926, he had a live-in servant named Maria Caballo who helped keep up the house and do some of the cooking. To assist in the care of his girls, Max employed a Swiss-Catholic nurse who, when Max and Liesel were out of town, took her young charges with her to church on Sundays. (The church visits, by the way, made a strong impression on little Hela, who loved all the pomp and circumstance; after the war, she would convert to Catholicism and marry a Catholic.) In his comfortable and well-appointed home Max had a book-lined study, where in the evening he enjoyed smoking a fat Havana cigar while reading his beloved German classics. In the basement he had a well-stocked wine cellar and a special little room where he shined his many pairs of shoes. Befitting his stature as a man of parts, he always wore natty bowties and immaculate suits with a sharp military crease in the pants. As he surveyed his domain in that relatively peaceful and prosperous time, he must have felt not only proud of his accomplishments but also confident that the good times would continue for himself and his fellow German Jews, who seemed finally to have found a secure and rewarding place in the nation they loved.

CHAPTER TWO

"No Entry for Jews"

Depression and Political Polarization

Germany's economic recovery in the 1920s, such as it was, depended in part on an influx of foreign capital, much of it in the form of short-term loans. The foreign power upon which Germany was most dependent was the United States, which provided the lion's share of the credits. Thus when America's financial faucet suddenly ran dry in the wake of the stock market crash of October 1929, Germany began almost immediately to choke with thirst. Trade, both foreign and domestic, fell off dramatically; banks failed; businesses and factories closed; and unemployment figures soared. Germany had about 3 million unemployed before the American crash, which was bad enough, but that figure rose steadily over the next two years, reaching 4.35 million by September 1931 and 6.13 million by February 1932. Especially hard hit were blue- and white-collar workers, who were among the first to be laid off, along with the small tradespeople and shopkeepers who depended on their patronage. Growing bands of embittered people, full of resentment toward a "system" that had failed them once again, thronged the cities and towns of Weimar Germany.

The social misery of the early thirties, like that of the early twenties, yielded a rapid polarization of the political landscape. This time, however, the political extremes exerted such a stranglehold on the center that parliamentary democracy suffocated and died. On the left, divided since 1919 between moderate Social Democrats and Communists, the latter made enormous gains in the Reichstag elections of September 1930, winning 4,600,000 votes and 77 parliamentary seats. On the other side of the political spectrum, the Nazis did even better, claiming 6.5 million votes and 107 seats. This represented a huge jump for the Hitlerites, who in the previous Reichstag elections of 1928 had managed only 800,000 votes and 12 parliamentary seats. The Nazis were now the second largest party in the Reichstag, ahead of the third-place Communists and only slightly behind the sagging SPD. In the next Reichstag elections in July 1932, which were held against a backdrop of long breadlines and bloody street battles between Communist and Nazi thugs, the KPD registered additional gains, but the biggest winners again were the Nazis, who polled 13.7 million votes and received 230 seats, thus allowing them to replace the SPD as the country's largest party. The Nazis actually lost some ground in the last Reichstag elections before Hitler took power, those of November 1932, no doubt because some of the Führer's followers had become fed up with his strategy of conquest by ballot box, but the Nazi Party (NSDAP) still polled the largest number of votes. It was on the basis of his status as leader of the largest party in the parliament that an increasingly impatient Hitler demanded to be named chancellor by President Paul von Hindenburg. The old president was no admirer of the Austrian firebrand, dismissively calling him "the Bohemian corporal," but he allowed himself to be convinced by fellow conservatives that the Nazi leader could be effectively used to fight off the resurgent Communists. The president's advisers also promised to keep Hitler under firm control so that he could not do anything rash. Hindenburg appointed Hitler chancellor on January 30, 1933.

The socioeconomic and political crises that brought Hitler to power were of course played out in cities and towns across the land, with virtually no locality too small to be affected. Flörsheim was no exception, despite its lack of a substantial Nazi movement before 1933.

Unemployment was on the rise in Flörsheim even before the American stock market crash, due primarily to layoffs at the nearby Opel plant in the spring of 1929. Following "Black Thursday" in distant New York, the stream of layoffs in town turned into a flood. In February 1930 the firm of Keramag, which made industrial ceramics, shut down part of its operations and laid off two-thirds of its workers. Between April and May of the same year Opel again cut its workforce, from 8,100 to 5,700, and then dropped another 1,100 workers in 1931. In mid-1932 Keramag shut its doors entirely, putting an additional 300 Flörsheimer out of work. By August 1932 the town had 632 people on its unemployment rolls, more than one-tenth of the total population. With so many of its citizens jobless, the municipal government was unable to pay full unemployment benefits, which left many families dependent on private charity for their sustenance.

Against this backdrop of dire emergency, Mayor Lauck turned to some of the wealthier citizens in town for additional help in feeding and clothing the destitute. Max Schohl was the first to step forward, which is not surprising given his readiness to help during the great inflation. In late 1929 he established a *Volksküche*, or "people's kitchen," which dispensed hot meals on a daily basis to the needy. To help folks heat their homes he turned over part of his plant's coal supply for residential use. His own workers—the vast majority of whom he kept on the payroll despite declining profits—were allowed to take whole carloads of coal home with them. In 1931, with the crisis worsening, the mayor again turned to Max, this time asking if he would help line up the local Jewish Gemeinde's charity organizations behind the cause of municipal relief. Max responded that the community's two principal charity groups stood ready to help. "I think I can assure you," he wrote the mayor on September 4, 1931, "that these two groups will be happy to assist in reducing the general misery." And so it was that, roughly a year before Hitler took power, Flörsheim's Jews, on the initiative of Max Schohl, came to the rescue of their neediest fellow citizens.

While Schohl and his colleagues were working to contain the pain caused by the Great Depression, others were working just as hard to take advantage of the misery for their own gain. Politically, the first to profit was the local branch of the KPD, which, just as it did on the national level, made significant gains by recruiting heavily among the ranks of the unemployed. In the September 1930 Reichstag elections the local KPD ticket won 607 votes, or 19.1 percent of the total, just 5 percentage points behind the SPD. Although the Flörsheim Communists engaged in occasional street and bar battles with Nazis in nearby towns, they focused most of their energy on trying to supplant the rival Socialists as the dominant force on the left. On April 17, 1932, a band of about 100 Communists, armed with brass knuckles and rubber truncheons, attacked a small contingent of Reichsbanner (the Socialist paramilitary force) on the Rathenauplatz. Yelling, *Do sinn se, die Arbeiterverräter, nixs wie druff* ("There they are, the betrayers of the workers, nothing but scum"), the Communists severely beat a number of Reichsbanner men. The only fatality, however, turned out to be one of the Communists, who died of a knife wound to the heart. Much to the dismay of the local SPD leadership, the Communists also defaced buildings and bridges in town with meter-high graffiti demanding that workers "Stand by the Soviet Union!" and declaring "The Red F.K.B. [Communist party army] Protects You!" and "Arm Yourself for Rebellion!" The SPD leadership appealed to Mayor Lauck to call in police from other towns to help keep the Communists in check (Flörsheim had only two police officers), but the mayor rejected the request. As for the Communist graffiti, it stayed in place until the Nazis came to power and made the Socialists and Jews clean it off.

In the waning years of the Weimar Republic the Nazi influence in Flörsheim was insubstantial compared to that of the Communists, not to mention that of the Catholic Center, which remained the town's largest political party. Until early 1931 there was no Nazi *Ortsgruppe*, or party cell, in town. On the other hand, neighboring villages like Wicker and Weilbach did have Nazi cells, evidence that the region was not entirely free of the Brown plague.

The founder of the Flörsheim Nazi Party chapter and local Sturmabteilung (SA) unit was a factory fireman named Heinrich Oesterling, who had moved to town from nearby Hoechst in 1929, determined to "launch a campaign for the conquest of Flörsheim for National Socialism." He went door to door hawking the Nazis' message of racial hatred. How ready the town was to hear this message is difficult to say with any precision. According to a September 1929 article in the *Flörsheimer Nachrichten*, "Der Antisemitismus in Flörsheim," some people in town were blaming the Jews for their misfortunes:

> There is a murmur going through our town. One person whispers it to another; every third person hears it somehow or someplace. Always it's the same story: the Jews are responsible for our troubles; the Jews have all the money in their hands. That artisan X has too little business is the fault of the Jews, as is the firing of worker Y. When farmer A gets one mark less for his corn, the Jews are behind it, and when railroad-man B doesn't get his bonus, here too the Jews are at fault. In short, a part of our population is infected with the bacillus of Jew-hatred, or anti-Semitism. The chief blame for this lies with certain political organizations in the Reich, which spread to the countryside the unhealthy propaganda that they have nurtured in the cities. Credulous people are to be found here [in the countryside] as well. Mostly these are politically immature people, and/or folks who are ignorant of the historical facts. . . . These Judenfresser [literally, Jew-eaters] must not be allowed to find a profitable arena of action in Flörsheim. We have to separate the true from the false. Our Jewish fellow citizens enjoy an excellent reputation and count among the finest sons of Flörsheim. We have to reject political dreamers and windmill-tilters who try to influence the population in their direction.

The author of this article, who used the pseudonym "Memphis," offered no concrete evidence for his assertions of widespread Jew-hatred and did not specify exactly who the "Judenfresser" in town were. One supposes, however, that he had Oesterling and company primarily in mind.

In addition to Oesterling, other pioneer members of the Nazi chapter in Flörsheim included Dr. Edmund Risse, a chemist; Risse's wife Thea; and the aforementioned Ludwig Stamm, the failed factory boss whom Max Schohl had supplanted as owner and director of the Electro chemical plant in 1919. Stamm joined the Nazi Party on June 1, 1932, on the advice of his son Hubert, who was already a member, and who convinced his father that getting in on the ground floor of the local Nazi movement would be good for the family fortunes. (And so it would prove to be, at least for a time.) Stamm quickly showed himself more adept at politicking than at business. He took over leadership of the local party cell and, exploiting the same social misery from which the Communists profited, began recruiting new members for the group. By the end of October 1932 he had brought the chapter strength up to eighteen—not exactly a mass movement, but nonetheless a small step toward Oesterling's goal of "conquering Flörsheim for National Socialism."

On July 18, 1932, the Flörsheim Nazi *Ortsgruppe* held its first town rally, with Stamm presiding. To advertise the rally the party published an advertisement in the *Flörsheimer Zeitung* containing the ominous warning: *Juden haben keinen Zutritt* ("No Entry to Jews"). The meeting came off without incident—no Jews tried to crash the gates—but two days later an indignant citizen wrote a letter to the paper protesting this slur against the Jews. The author of the letter did not identify himself, even with a pseudonym, but the tone of the missive resembled the earlier warning from "Memphis" about the spread of anti-Semitism in Flörsheim:

> It was certainly a great impertinence on the part of the local National Socialist leadership to include in its advertisement the provocative phrase, "No Entry to Jews." Crassly and openly displayed here is the racial hatred of certain local philistines, many of whom have perhaps been, and even remain, on the receiving end of assistance from the Jewish community. The disciples of the Third Reich ideology in Flörsheim will have no success with their admonition, "No Entry to Jews." Our Jewish fellow citizens are closely integrated with the adherents of other faiths and have always lived in peaceful harmony with the entire population. In Flörsheim there are no social differences between Jews and members of other faiths. Since the beginning of historical memory the Jewish residents of Flörsheim have taken an active role in local activities and events, in festivals of both secular and religious nature. Jews have also been active in the charity and welfare operations of local associations. The phrase "No Entry to Jews"

obviously means to defame these people and merits censure. Hopefully the leadership of the NSDAP in Flörsheim will in the future forgo such objectionable tactics; otherwise the party is likely to lose what little sympathy it has managed to find so far in this town.

Needless to say, the resident Nazis did not follow this citizen's well-meaning advice, and it would soon become evident that employing anti-Jewish slogans would hardly cost the Nazis much sympathy among the supposedly philo-Semitic burghers of Flörsheim.

"LET'S HAVE SOME DEEDS!"

Hitler's assumption of the chancellorship on January 30, 1933, did not generate widespread panic among the approximately 525,000 Jews living in Germany at that time. True, some 50,000 German Jews fled the country within the first few weeks after Hitler took power, but most of them had other reasons to flee aside from their Jewishness: They were Communists or Socialists, and thus stood at the top of the Nazis' initial list of targets for retribution. Most Jews apparently accepted the wisdom of a declaration issued by the Central Association of German Citizens of the Jewish Faith, which advised: "In general, today more than ever we must follow the directive: wait calmly." It made good sense to remain calm, the Jews reasoned, because Hitler's time in office would probably turn out to be short, like that of most of the Weimar chancellors before him. And even if he stayed in power for a while, the very fact of being in power would undoubtedly force him to act more "responsibly." Moreover, had not the conservatives who had helped bring him to power promised to "tame" him, to "keep him fenced in"?

In Flörsheim, where the Nazi movement had made relatively little headway in the Weimar period, the Jews seemed to have had even less cause for panic than their co-religionists elsewhere in the Reich. On January 30, 1933, the local Nazi Party chapter had twenty-four members, only a slight gain over its eighteen in October 1932. In the Reichstag elections of March 5, 1933, the first to be held under Nazi control, the NSDAP list in Flörsheim won 26.1 percent of the total vote. This represented a substantial gain from the 15 percent that the party had managed in the last "free" Reichstag elections of November 1932, but it was still significantly below the Nazis' national average of 43.9 percent. In Flörsheim the Center remained the strongest party, with 37.8 percent of the vote. Because in the Main-Rhine region, as elsewhere in the Reich, the Nazis focused their initial terror attacks on the Communists and Socialists, the first to flee the country from that area were prominent members of those parties. Among the early political refugees from Flörsheim was Jakob Altmaier, the Jewish Social Democratic activist. Knowing that he was on the Nazi hit list, he fled to Paris on April 1, 1933. His flight actually came as a relief to other Jews in town, who had worried that having a well-known political radical in their midst might bring unwanted attention to their community. Feeling relatively secure, the remaining Jews of Flörsheim, some fifty-two of them, preferred to follow the Central Association's advice to wait calmly in the Reich. Germany, after all, was *their* country, a nation to which they (rightly) believed they had a stronger claim than the Nazis. As one member of their community, Sali Kahn, liked to say, "I've lived in this country a lot longer than Adolf Hitler."

Famous last words. It quickly became clear that the Jews of Flörsheim had as much cause to worry about their future in Germany as did their brethren elsewhere in Hitler's Reich. Like other towns and cities across the land, Flörsheim soon took on a distinct Nazi look and feel. Rathenauplatz, the square honoring the Jewish foreign minister slain by nationalist fanatics in 1922, was renamed (what else?) Adolf-Hitler-Platz. On March 8, 1933, the swastika flag was hoisted above the Rathaus for the first time. Following new municipal elections on March 12, 1933, in which the Nazis won six seats (compared to seven for the Center, two for the SPD, and two for the KPD), the Nazi *Gauleitung*, or regional leadership, sent out a directive to all municipal and county governments advising them to purge their ranks of Jewish and Communist office holders:

In the newly elected county and town assemblies Jews and Communists are to be excluded from participation, if necessary with energetic measures. They are not to be allowed even to enter the assembly rooms for opening meetings. Sufficient SA and Schutzstaffel (SS) men are available to enforce this ruling. In a time of national revolution it is unthinkable that a representative or supporter of an un-German or Marxist tendency might be allowed to serve as an assemblyman, county deputy, mayor, town councilor, or lay assessor.

Flörsheim's newly elected town assembly met for the first time on April 4, 1933, minus the two Communist delegates, who were summarily expelled. No Jews needed to be purged because, in contrast to earlier assemblies, no Jews had run for office this time, much less been elected. Jakob Lauck still presided as mayor, but he carefully toed the new political line set down in Berlin. He opened the meeting with the declaration: "We stand behind the national movement . . . and will conduct all our business in the service of the new Germany." The assembly elected as deputy-mayor none other than Ludwig Stamm, the head of the local Nazi Party chapter. Not surprisingly, Stamm likewise declared that he would carry out his duties in the spirit of the new regime in Berlin. (In less than a year Stamm would be in an even better position to fulfill that promise, for he took over as mayor in early 1934 following the ailing Lauck's retirement.) Stamm's Nazi colleague, Dr. Risse, summed up the new assembly's mission by promising that the town fathers would always put "the common good before individual good." He concluded his peroration with a line from Goethe's *Faust:* "*Der Worte sind genug gewechselt, nun lässt uns endlich Taten sehen*" ("Enough of words, let's finally have some deeds").

Three days before this meeting, on April 1, 1933, the people of Flörsheim, along with the rest of the nation, had gotten a strong taste of what the Nazis meant by "the common good" and necessary "deeds." On that day Hitler's government orchestrated its first major operation against the Jewish population: a Reich-wide boycott of Jewish businesses and services. Although this action had been planned for some time, the Nazis sought to justify it by claiming that German Jews had inspired a series of articles in the international press that were critical of the new regime. The articles in question had called attention to brutal attacks against Jews in several German cities, attacks that in some cases had resulted in death. Labeling the critical reports deliberate fabrications, Joseph Goebbels, Hitler's head of propaganda, called on the people of Germany to make the Jews pay for their "lies" by hitting them in the place that hurt them most: their pocketbooks. To help people identify which stores and services to boycott, and to ensure that potential patrons stayed away, SA men across the Reich were ordered to paint anti-Semitic slogans on targeted businesses and to stand guard in front of them.

So it was also in Flörsheim. According to one witness, at 9:00 in the morning of April 1, "armed boys marched through town and stationed themselves in front of Jewish-owned businesses." The businesses they targeted included Hermann Altmaier's bakery, Julius and Benno Metzger's butcher shop, Sali Kahn's cattle brokerage, Joseph Birnzweig's men's clothing store, and David Mannheimer's textile store. The local press did not cover the boycott in Flörsheim, and it is unclear whether in this town, as in many other places, some citizens chose to thumb their noses at the Nazi intimidation and shop as usual. But however effective the Flörsheim action might have been, it certainly put local Jews on notice that they were no longer to be treated as "normal" German citizens. It was also very telling that this notice was served on the very day that Jakob Altmaier fled town—a move that led most of the local Jews to feel more secure about their future.

Max Schohl's factory was not among the businesses boycotted, perhaps because it was not a retail outlet where anyone would normally have shopped. In any case, Max was not intimidated by the boycott action. To his family he expressed nothing but derision for that "Austrian windbag," Hitler, who he believed would not remain in office much longer, for the German people would certainly soon come to their senses and throw the lout out. Max also believed that even if Hitler managed to stay in power a while longer and to further harass the Jews, he would surely exempt from this harassment Jews like Max, who had fought and bled for their nation in World War I.

In expecting special treatment from the Nazis because of his war service, Max was hardly alone. The Reich Association of Jewish War Veterans sent a number of petitions to their "fellow front-fighter" Adolf Hitler, stressing the group's loyalty and reminding him of the Jewish sacrifice in the last war. One of the petitions included a copy of the memorial book containing the names of all the 12,000 Jews who died in the war. Hitler's office acknowledged the petitions, and on his instructions the Nazi government exempted Jewish combat veterans from some of the new anti-Jewish legislation it was imposing. The exemptions did not last long, however, for in Nazi eyes Jewish blood was a form of pollution that could not be expunged by prior service to the fatherland or correct political views. Max Schohl may have thought that he had more in common with gentile nationalists than with leftist or pacifist Jews, but the Nazis believed differently.

In the spring and summer of 1933 Hitler's government, which had obtained dictatorial powers through the so-called Enabling Act of March 23, 1933, introduced a spate of laws designed to marginalize the Jewish population. Under the Law for the Restoration of the Civil Service (April 7, 1933), Jews were expelled from the public bureaucracy at all levels. A provision exempting combat veterans from this law was rescinded in July. Other laws forced Jews out of the national teachers' association, forbade kosher butchering, excluded Jewish physicians from the national insurance program, shut Jews out of the pharmacy business, restricted Jewish access to higher education, expelled Jews from national sport associations, banned Jews from public bathhouses and beaches, and forbade Jews to own farms.

Flörsheim did not have any beaches, but it had plenty of farms. Following a directive in September 1933 from the regional farmers' association instructing local farmers to eschew business contacts with Jews, Flörsheim-area farmers stopped having any dealings with Hermann Altmaier's bakery. Altmaier protested that he was a decorated war veteran, but to no avail; he was forced to lease his business to a gentile (and later to sell out entirely). In that same month a group of SA thugs pulled Altmaier from his house and forced him, along with two other Social Democrats and a Communist, to scrub away the Weimar-era KPD electoral slogans that remained legible on some local structures. During the course of this brutal action Altmaier, who had had one of his legs amputated in the war, suffered a mild heart attack and collapsed. The Nazis allowed him to return home, bringing in his brother-in-law, Robert Gerson, to replace him at the scrubbing task. A week later, however, they grabbed Altmaier again and made him finish the cleaning job. Reporting on this disgusting incident, the regional newspaper spoke of Altmaier's experiencing an "attack of nerves upon seeing the brown uniforms." The paper further noted: "Many townspeople witnessed this droll drama of [municipal] cleansing."

In another act of Jewish marginalization, the Nazi government in Berlin ordered the exclusion of Jews from the various social and cultural associations that played a crucial role in the lives of ordinary Germans, especially small-town Germans. Accordingly, in the fall of 1933 the clubs and associations of Flörsheim expelled their Jewish members. For Max Schohl, this meant exclusion from the Sängerbund, in which he had been a participant since his move to Flörsheim, and whose convivial evenings of beer drinking and singing were a cherished part of his routine. Expelled along with Max were Jakob Hermann, Ernst Altmaier (Hermann's brother), Josef Birnzweig, and Benno Metzger.

Painful as the Sängerbund exclusion was to Max's self-image as an upstanding and integral member of the broader Flörsheim community, it was a minor blow compared to his expulsion from the local chapter of the Kyffhäuserbund in November 1933. He regarded his service as an officer in the German army, after all, as the most rewarding experience of his life. Deeply wounded by his expulsion, Max wrote a letter to the national president of the organization expressing his incomprehension over the treatment he had been accorded. The letter speaks volumes about Max's state of mind and worldview in the face of this fresh calamity:

> Your Excellency!
>
> Pursuant to recent regulations, I have been expelled as a non-Aryan from the veterans and military association Kyffhäuserbund in Flörsheim am Main.
>
> If I turn to you today it is not—I want to emphasize—in order to try to have my membership in this association reinstated.

I see it as incompatible with my honor to belong to an association that chooses not to treat me as an equal member, [but which] at most might be willing to tolerate me as a second-class person.

In this regard I can with justice employ the same words that our chancellor and Führer used in his recent speech announcing our withdrawal from the League of Nations. [Hitler had said that the League was treating Germany like a second-class nation.]

I am turning to Your Excellency in my capacity as a retired German officer and as a comrade, because my whole sense of German comradeship has been deeply shaken.

When I entered the German Army as a young recruit in 1907, I was immediately inoculated, in body and soul, with the concept of comradeship. For me there was nothing higher than this comradeship in the German Army.

I have experienced and perpetuated this comradeship in war and peace, as an enlisted man, a non-commissioned officer, and, after I was accorded the honor of wearing the officer's tunic, as a commissioned officer.

In 1911, when by the grace of His Majesty the King of Bavaria I was promoted to the rank of lieutenant of the reserves, I experienced in the officer corps the same spirit of genuine comradeship that I had felt previously in the enlisted men's barracks.

In 1914, when I moved to the front with my regiment, I experienced once again what German comradeship really meant. And so it was also in all the battles of the World War in which I was allowed to participate. When in the course of leading my company in attack I was rendered a cripple by enemy fire, I saw once again what comradeship in the German Army was all about. I saw this as well when my two brothers were killed in the war.

I have described to Your Excellency very briefly my military career [to show that] it is inseparable from German comradeship.

But now I must ask myself: how can my comrades explain to me their current action? After all, these are comrades with whom I fought shoulder to shoulder in the war, with whom I was wounded in the mud of Flanders, with whom I once lay side by side in a military hospital.

When in the murderous Battle of the Somme artillery fire rained down on my company, none of the men under me, neither enlisted personnel nor officers, asked me if I were an Aryan or non-Aryan: all looked in comradely trust to their company commander.

And today should it be as if all this had simply not happened? Should this comradeship, proven in blood and suffering, simply evaporate into nothing?

I cannot and will not believe this, for to do so would rob my life of all meaning.

I joined the Kyffhäuserbund because I saw in it the truest representation of the—to me holy—front experience; no other group seemed better able to consecrate this experience.

I beg Your Excellency's pardon if I have taken too much of your valuable time, but I would be very thankful to you if you could give me your perspective on all of this.

Expressing my highest respect, I am Your Excellency's obedient servant,

Captain of the Reserve, Retired, Max Schohl

The president of the association did not bother to respond to Max's letter.

As Max's protest letter suggests, he now clearly understood that he was considered a second-class citizen, even among his former military comrades, yet at the same time he was unable to sever his ties entirely with a heritage that was so crucial to his self-understanding. Four years later, after suffering a host of additional injuries at the hands of Germany's and Flörsheim's new rulers, Max sent a valuable collection of negatives of photographs he had taken in World War I to the Bavarian

Army Archive in Munich. Along with the bequest went a letter documenting Max's continuing loyalty to his comrades of the front generation. This time Max did get a response: a curt note of thanks and a request for written identification of the negatives.

Shortly before being expelled from the community of German war veterans, Max had taken on a more prominent role in the community of Flörsheim Jews. On August 26, 1933, he had succeeded Sali Kahn as *Vorsteher*, or president, of the Jewish Gemeinde. (Since August 1927, Max had served as deputy-head.) Kahn had resigned this post in the wake of criticism of his leadership by other members of the community, in particular Hermann Altmaier. As Kahn complained in a letter to the Landrat of the Main-Taunus regional government, "These smear campaigns against me in recent days have led to great difficulties and conflicts within the Gemeinde." On Kahn's recommendation, the Gemeinde elected Schohl to represent it in relations with the regional government, presumably in the hope that a man of his stature would better be able to defend the community's interests in these trying times. In taking the oath "to loyally and conscientiously carry out the duties [of Vorsteher] according to the prevailing regulations," Max undoubtedly hoped to guide his community through its current travails with minimal further damage. He could not have known how difficult this assignment would be, or that he would have to spend much of his time contending with further assaults on his own status and livelihood.

On November 14, 1933, the Gestapo in Frankfurt sent a directive to regional and municipal governments asking them to supply a list "of all Jews and Freemasons" living in their districts, for purposes of assembling a national databank. The Jewish list, to be compiled separately from that of the Freemasons, was to include "women and children, as well as the illegitimate children of Jewish fathers and their mothers." The Gestapo also asked for information on the Jews' citizenship, religious affiliation (so as to include converts to Christianity), and political views. The broader object here was to prepare the way for the eventual mass arrest and/or deportation of the Jews, once the Nazi government came up with a specific program for rendering the nation "Jew-free." In his capacity as deputy-mayor, Ludwig Stamm sent a list to Frankfurt containing the names of the forty-three Jews still residing in Flörsheim. Included, of course, were the names of Max Schohl and his mother, wife, and two daughters. No commentary was provided regarding Max's political views, though Stamm was careful to note that Hermann Altmaier had belonged to the Social Democratic Party. "Had belonged" was the appropriate locution here, since all parties but the Nazis had been outlawed as of July 1933.

The fact that the number of Jews still living in Flörsheim had fallen from fifty-two in January 1933 to forty-three in November 1933 shows that at least some of the local Jews had decided that the time had come to get out. Max Schohl would not have accepted his new job as head of the Jewish Gemeinde had he been inclined to join the émigrés. Not only did he stay put, he also continued to operate his "people's kitchen," handing out free meals to all who needed them. In early 1934, however, following Ludwig's Stamm's takeover of the major's office, Max was forced to close down his charity. According to the Nazi perspective, it was unacceptable for any good German "to take even a crumb of bread from a Yid." In any case, the Nazi authorities claimed to have the hunger problem well in hand, so assistance like Max's was no longer needed. The reality was quite different: It took the Nazis considerable time to make up for the loss of private charities, and in the meantime many Flörsheimer were obliged to eat propaganda for breakfast.

In September 1935 the Nazis introduced their most comprehensive racial legislation to date, the notorious "Nuremberg Laws." Announced at the NSDAP's annual party rally in the northern Bavarian town of Nuremberg, these laws, divided into three subsections, officially reclassified German-Jews as "subjects" rather than as citizens, depriving them of basic political rights including the franchise. The "Law for the Defense of German Blood and Honor" forbade Jews to marry "Aryans" or even have sexual relations with them. As a further measure to keep the German blood "pure," no Jew could henceforth employ a female "Aryan" under the age of forty-five as his domestic servant. German "honor" was also to be protected by disallowing Jews from raising the national flag or showing the national colors of red, white, and black.

As announced at the rally in September 1935, the Nuremberg Laws applied only to "full Jews," that is, to Jews with three or more Jewish grandparents. At that point the Nazi government was still debating how it should deal with partial Jews, or so-called *Mischlinge*. Moderates within the government wanted to exclude from the law's provisions all the *Mischlinge*, and to include in that exempted category half-Jews with two Jewish grandparents (*Mischlinge* of the First Degree), while Nazi radicals insisted on considering the half-Jews as Jews for purposes of the law. Hitler, who hoped eventually to make Germany "free" even of partial Jews but who in the meantime also worried about provoking international sanctions against the Reich (including a possible removal of the impending 1936 Olympic Games from Germany), came up with a "compromise": Half-Jews would be treated as *Mischlinge* and not covered by the Nuremberg Laws, *unless* they had shown a personal preference for Judaism by marrying a full Jew or officially joining the Jewish religious community. (This inclusion of an element of personal preference constituted a slight deviation from the general Nazi practice of basing ethnic or racial identity exclusively on blood.) Supplementary decrees to the Nuremberg Laws announced on November 14, 1935, defined as Jewish all persons who had at least three full Jewish grandparents, or who had two Jewish grandparents and were married to a Jewish spouse or belonged to the Jewish religion at the time of the law's publication, or who entered into such commitments at a later date.

The purpose of the Nuremberg Laws was clearly to segregate the Jews from German society by placing them in a legal ghetto. Although the transformation of this legal ghetto into a physical ghetto was still some years away, the 1935 legislation certainly prepared the way for the more draconian policies by depriving German Jews of their political citizenship and hence of their full protection under the law.

Germany's Jews were understandably distressed by this codification of their second-class status, and some responded by migrating to foreign lands. Some 21,000 emigrated in 1935, followed by another 25,000 in 1936 and 23,000 in 1937. Ironically, however, the Nuremberg legislation also had a certain reassuring effect on many Jews, for it had been presented as a way of preventing further ad-hoc persecution, and Hitler had announced that the laws constituted a definitive legal solution to the Jewish question. Such assurances allowed Jews to hope that in the future they could live in a more secure, if highly circumscribed, legal environment. Clearly this was the view of the government-sanctioned agency representing German Jews, the Reichsvertretung der Juden in Deutschland, which issued a declaration on September 22, 1935, saying that while Jews in Germany were "troubled in the deepest way" (*auf schwerste betroffen*) by the new laws, this legislation would hopefully make possible "an acceptable relationship between the German and Jewish peoples" by bringing an end to "defamation and boycotts" against Jews and by guaranteeing their "moral and economic existence." The Reichsvertretung promised to help sustain a secure if segregated Jewish community in Germany by promoting the development of separate Jewish schools. To prepare those Jews who wanted to emigrate to Palestine (a goal the Nazi government endorsed), the Jewish schools would teach useful skills like agriculture, handicrafts, and Hebrew. The Reichsvertretung promised also to help Jewish emigrants liquidate their real property and transfer their liquid assets abroad. This declaration, acknowledging as it did the Nazis' legal definition of the Jews as non-Germans, constituted recognition, at least from the standpoint of the Jews' official representative agency, that the old dream of a "German-Jewish partnership" had come to an end.

We have no record of how Max Schohl responded to the Nuremberg Laws, but this new development must have unnerved him because of its implications for his family. Under the terms of the new legislation, his two daughters were now officially Jewish because they had two Jewish grandparents (his own parents) and were members of the Jewish community at the time of the laws' publication. Along with Max, the Schohl girls were thereby excluded from the German political community and would not be able to vote when they reached maturity. In the meantime, Hela and Käthe were expelled from the Opel Realgymnasium (preparatory high school) in Rüsselsheim; both girls transferred to all-Jewish vocational schools in Mainz. As for Max's wife Liesel, she was not considered Jewish under the new legislation (her inclusion in the Flörsheim Jewish census notwithstanding) because she had no Jewish grandparents. By marrying Max and converting to Judaism she had certainly documented a personal commitment to Judaism, but because she did not combine that preference with a certain quotient of Jewish blood she was still "Aryan" in Nazi eyes. She was an Aryan, however, of highly dubious standing, a virtual traitor to her blood. As far as the Nazis were concerned, the only way for such renegades to regain their status as "full Germans" was to divorce their husbands and to renounce their religious conversion. In fact, "Aryan" spouses of Jewish men had come under pressure to abandon their husbands even before the Nuremberg Laws. Starting in late 1933, some judges had begun granting quickie divorces based on racial differences. As a daughter of one such mixed marriage summed up the situation in 1934: "My mother could have gotten a divorce with the stroke of a pen." There was reason to expect further state pressure on racially mixed marriages after 1935, now that the Jewish husbands no longer held German citizenship. As of 1936–1937, racially mixed families no longer were eligible for the German Winter Relief, which provided food and fuel in the winter months. A new marriage law of 1938 made it possible to annul mixed marriages, after which the German woman could, if she made the proper declarations, "rejoin the racial community." Max Schohl could be reasonably sure that his devoted wife would never renounce him, but he could be just as sure that she would pay a price—how high a price was not yet certain—for remaining loyal to him.

The Nuremberg Laws had no sooner been passed than Max felt their force in his domestic life. As noted previously, he had employed since 1926 a domestic servant named Maria Caballo to help take care of his household. In the mid-1930s Caballo's help was all the more needed because Max's wife was quite ill and his seventy-four-year-old mother was bedridden. According to the above-mentioned law to "protect German blood," however, Jews could no longer employ Aryan women under forty-five as servants in their homes. A subprovision in the law stated that an Aryan woman already in the employ of a Jew might be allowed to retain her position if she had completed her thirty-fifth year of age by December 31, 1935, but her employer had to apply to the authorities for such dispensation, and the maid had to declare her own wish to stay on. As fate would have it, Maria Caballo was thirty-four in 1935, seven weeks too young to qualify for the exemption. Nonetheless, she desperately wanted to keep her job, and of course Max also wanted to keep her on, so he decided in early December to appeal his case to the regional authorities. To buttress his application, Max asked Mayor Stamm to provide a character reference for him. (Since he made this request through his "Aryan" wife, who was on much better terms with the mayor than he was, he had some reason to hope for a positive result.) In his application Max included a reference to the anticipated recommendation from Stamm, along with the required declaration from Caballo. These documents are worthy of quotation as little windows on the daily life of small-town Jews during the early phase of the anti-Jewish persecution. Max's application letter concluded with the lines:

> I enclose a declaration from our housemaid Maria Caballo, which shows that she is prepared to stay on in her position if my application is accepted. My wife has personally discussed this matter with the mayor of Flörsheim, Dr. Stamm, who will certainly provide additional information on the case. Because by law I am obliged to release my housemaid from my employment on December 31, that is, in a very short time, I humbly request that my application be dealt with as soon as possible.

Maria Caballo's statement read, in part:

> If I had reached my thirty-fifth year by December 31, 1935 I could have kept my position. However, since I won't reach that age until seven weeks after that date, namely on February 24, I am required to give up my job on December 31. Because Frau Dr. Schohl has been very sick for two years, having recently undergone three major operations, and because the seventy-four-year-old mother of Dr. Schohl is also very ill, the family is extremely dependent on my services. I therefore declare that I would be prepared to remain in the house of Dr. Schohl as a domestic servant if the relevant application by him is approved.

Mayor Stamm did indeed provide a character reference for Max, but although it supported his application it was not exactly glowing:

The following information is pertinent [to Schohl's application]: The personal data provided by the applicant in his appeal are accurate, in so far as can be determined by this office. According to local registration records, Schohl was born on November 15, 1884 in Pirmasens and moved here from Wiesbaden on October 8, 1919. His family consists of himself, his wife, his two daughters ages twelve and fifteen, and his seventy-four-year-old mother. No Jewish male other than the applicant resides in the Schohl home. During the time he has lived here Schohl has enjoyed a good reputation and has done nothing of a negative nature that has come to light. To my knowledge no legal punishments have been rendered against him. [In fact this was not the case, but Stamm might not have wanted to mention the court decision in 1923 that punished Max for paying his workers in hard currency.] With respect to their morals, the Schohl family and their maid can be classed as unobjectionable. A danger to the German blood in this case is completely out of the question, and for this reason I can recommend approval of the application for relief from the law.

Stamm's intervention notwithstanding, Max's application was turned down, and on December 30, 1933, Maria Caballo left the Schohl employ and moved to Mainz. Max got her a job there keeping house for his former dentist, who had also moved to Mainz. For several years thereafter, however, Caballo secretly returned to Flörsheim on weekends to help out at the Schohls'. She taught the girls how to cook, wash windows, and clean the silverware. Despite her official ouster, she remained very much part of the family.

The hope expressed by the Reichsvertretung der Juden in Deutschland that the Nuremberg Laws would put an end to state-sponsored economic persecution of the Jews proved, like all such hopes, to be an illusion. The Nazi regime had no intention of deviating from its campaign to strangle Jewish businesses through various forms of discrimination and harassment. Until 1938, the Nazis focused their attacks on small and middle-sized Jewish enterprises, for these were seen as least essential to the nation's prosperity. The pressure tactics employed by the regime included depriving Jewish-owned factories of necessary raw materials and supplies, ending all purchases by state agencies at Jewish firms, discouraging private business transactions between Aryans and Jews, and encouraging non-Jewish employees to quit their jobs at Jewish companies. As a result of these policies, Jewish enterprises began closing by the thousands, while thousands more were taken over by non-Jewish partners or sold at bargain prices to Aryans. Of the roughly 50,000 Jewish small businesses in operation in Germany at the time Hitler took power, only about 9,000 survived in July 1938.

Max Schohl's Electro chemical factory was among the firms that went under. The company had managed to survive the early years of the Depression with only minimal downsizing, but it could not survive the Nazis' policy of slow economic strangulation. After 1933 the municipal government of Flörsheim, like those across the Reich, officially registered the companies in its jurisdiction as "Aryan" or "non-Aryan." Potential patrons from outside the community typically sent inquiries to the mayor's office asking about a given company's racial status before deciding whether to do business with it. The mayor diligently provided such information, thereby determining which firms in town would continue to have customers and which would not. In the case of Flörsheim, for example, on August 16, 1933, the mayor's office was able to reassure the Kaiserslautern municipal hospital that the chemical factory of Dr. H. Nördlinger, previously under Jewish ownership, was now run by two gentlemen "of the Christian faith." The office noted further that Nördlinger's capital was invested with the Deutsche Bank in Frankfurt and Mannheim, and that most of its stock was "in Christian hands." (This blessing notwithstanding, the Nördlinger firm changed its name in 1935 to "Chemical Factory Flörsheim" because its old designation seemed to be causing too many doubts about its racial status.) There were many more such affirmations of racial acceptability from the municipal government in the following years, but also quite a few non-endorsements. Needless to say, when inquiries arrived at the mayor's office (especially after Stamm took over) about Max Schohl's Electro, the mayor did not hesitate to point out its "non-Aryan" ownership. The consequence was that the company won virtually no new customers after 1933, while some older customers, apparently fearful of guilt by association, began taking their business elsewhere. Profits dropped by 30 percent in 1934 alone. Electro's employees, meanwhile, also faced pressure from the local Nazis, including Stamm, to end their association with Max's company. In 1934 and early 1935 over one-half of Electro's workforce left its employ in search of greener pastures. By spring 1935 the firm had only twenty-four employees remaining on its payroll. Max tried desperately to keep the firm afloat by shutting down some of the production lines and cutting his own salary. However, with creditors closing in and no bank willing to provide an emergency loan, Electro was forced to seek bankruptcy protection on June 26, 1935.

During the bankruptcy proceedings ownership of the Electro passed from Max and his two Jewish partners to two young gentiles, both members of the Nazi Party. The young men in question, a Herr Schlegel and a Herr Hermann, had been trained as chemists by Max, and they promised him not only to keep the plant operating but also to give him a job in the company. They fulfilled neither of these promises. Max was summarily fired, and the Electro factory closed its doors for good on August 6, 1936, putting another twenty-four employees out of work. According to court records, the company was 78,000 marks in debt when it closed. The value of the plant's machinery and furniture was assessed as 700,000 marks, but none of the proceeds from the auction of these items went to Max or his original partners; all the money went to the new executors.

With the end of Electro an expansive if somewhat dilapidated set of buildings stood vacant on the edge of town. For some time the local Nazi Party leadership had been searching for quarters for its women's and youth branches, and it now looked to Max's old factory as the answer to this need. In June 1936 Mayor Stamm requested a subsidy of 1,600 marks from the Landrat in Hoechst to help refurbish some of the plant's buildings, which the municipal government took over as part of the bankruptcy settlement. In addition to making the necessary repairs, the municipality decided to blow up the plant's two hulking chimneys, which would hardly be needed in the facility's future life. According to the local press, the demolition, which took place on October 25, 1937, provided quite a spectacle for the townsfolk:

> At 1:15 there was a real sensation on the Haupstrasse. Experts blew up
> the huge chimneys of the former Electro chemical plant. Although this

action had not been announced to the public in advance, rumors about it had circulated among the public, and a large crowd was on hand to witness this rare spectacle. At 1:15 a signal sounded, then a second one and a third. What followed took only a few seconds. The two chimneys, which had stood for almost four decades, shook at their foundations as if hit by an unseen fist. One of the giants then made a partial turn and collapsed inwardly to the earth. Its somewhat smaller brother shook in its bones as well, made a little unwilling bow, and then tumbled to the ground. A huge cloud of dust rose up from the site and drifted toward the northwest over rooftops and houses. The windows of neighboring buildings and houses were all closed, [which was just as well], for small pieces of debris landed as far away as Brennergasse. But then everything was over. The two giants had come to rest on old mother earth according to the proscribed procedures and just as desired, while the public craned their necks to see what had become of them. The bricks from which the chimneys had been composed lay all around, but none had landed outside the factory grounds, and life soon resumed its normal course in the neighborhood.

In fact life hardly returned to "normal" in the old Electro neighborhood, for once the refurbishment of the facility had been completed the Nazis' Frauenschaft, Bund der Mädel, Jungmädel, Hitler Jugend, and Jungvolk moved in. Now instead of the banging of heavy machinery, one heard the tramp of marching feet and the trill of patriotic songs belted out by the Nazi youth groups of Flörsheim.

Max Schohl's life, it need hardly be said, also changed dramatically following the collapse and partial demolition of his factory. After being forced out at Electro he was not able to find new employment at any of the other chemical firms in the area—no one was willing to hire a Jew—so he set up a small laboratory in his own home, where he made a few simple products that he tried to market himself. For a while he managed to sell some pesticides and detergents around town, but even this small-scale enterprise provoked the ire of the local Nazis, who insisted that no Aryan should buy anything from a Jew. After a year or so, Max shut down his in-house lab for want of clients. His sole financial resource was now his savings account, upon which he began to draw heavily to support his family.

Meanwhile, the atmosphere in town was becoming increasingly hostile toward the remaining Jews. In spring 1938 local Nazis painted anti-Semitic slogans on several Jewish homes and businesses. An informal boycott forced a number of Jewish-owned enterprises to close, including Jakob Kahn's shoe store and Sali Kahn's cattle brokerage. Unidentified arsonists burned down a warehouse belonging to Hermann Herzheimer. In June 1938 vandals desecrated the Jewish cemetery outside town. True to the Nazi dictum that not even dead Jews should know any peace in the new Germany, the thugs smashed grave markers and monuments, throwing headstones and even bones into a small stream nearby. When they were finished, not a single grave was left unmolested. Furthermore, several stores in Flörsheim now sported signs saying, "Jews unwelcome." When Max's friend Fritz Wolf entered one such store, thinking that he might be served despite the warning, a Hitler Youth member who happened to be in the shop threw him out. Later that day the head of the local Hitler Youth and two other young thugs paid a visit to Wolf's home, where they severely beat Wolf and his seventy-three-year-old father, who subsequently died of his injuries.

It was profoundly galling for Max, as president of the local Jewish community, to witness such outrages and to be able to do nothing to prevent them. How galling, too, to look across the street from his home and see his former factory serving as a center for much of the thuggery that was going on in town. In the end, it must have been as difficult for him to come to grips with the growing callousness of his neighbors as it was for him to comprehend the collapse of "German comradeship."

Max had never been partial to the idea of leaving Germany, even when his nation had done so much to make him feel unwanted, but in the wake of Electro's closing he came under increasing pressure from his wife to take his family to safety outside the Reich. Liesel Schohl was as patriotic as Max, but she had come to identify more with the persecuted people of her chosen faith than with the "Aryan race" of which she was still technically a member. She was especially distressed that one of her own brothers, Fritz, was now a member of the Nazi SA, having joined the local NSDAP immediately after Hitler came to power. (Liesel's father, who despised the Nazis, was even more distressed than she was; he beat his son bloody when he came home in his brown-shirted Storm Trooper uniform.) Liesel socialized less and less with her former gentile friends, who in turn seemed to want to have less and less to do with her. Village ladies whom she had once entertained now crossed the street to avoid talking to her. With strict food rationing in place for Jews, she had to depend on under-the-table dealings with some of the local tradespeople to keep items like meat and butter on the family table. The family for which she had to care was also now larger by one, for Max's aged mother Johanna, having suffered a stroke in 1935, had moved into the Schohl home and lived on the top floor. In urging Max to consider emigration, Liesel was following a common behavioral pattern in Jewish households. In the words of one authority on the subject: "As emigration became more and more crucial, women usually saw the danger signals first and urged their husbands to flee Germany."

In this case the wife had help from her children, who were increasingly facing their own problems in Nazi-dominated Flörsheim. Having always had primarily Christian friends, the girls felt out of place in their all-Jewish school in Mainz. But at the same time they also felt more and more isolated at home, where some of their former friends had begun to shun them. Hela suffered somewhat more from the isolation than Käthe; being three years older than her sister, she had already found a steady boyfriend in the person of Josef Braumann, a young Catholic fellow who pledged his eternal love. However, once Hitler came to power and made it clear that "Aryan" boys must have no truck with Jewish (even half-Jewish) girls, Braumann disappeared from Hela's life. Besides missing her erstwhile boyfriend, Hela missed going with her Swiss nurse (no longer in the Schohls' employ) to services at the local Catholic Church, which of course was now closed to her. Hela's and Käthe's obvious loneliness weighed on Max, who in a valiant effort to cheer them up threw an impromptu party for them in the basement of their house. Since the party in question was to be a *Bauernball* (farmers' ball), Max converted the basement into a "barn" by bringing in rustic furniture he had borrowed from a pub and positioning a fragrant compost pile, replete with pitchfork, at the door. The "farmers" at this particular ball, however, were all students from the Schohl girls' Jewish school in Mainz; no locals attended. The girls appreciated Max's gesture—it afforded the only fun they had had in years—but in the end it seemed only to reinforce their sense of social isolation in Flörsheim. Their former Christian friends were now pointedly asking them why they bothered to stay around at all. The Schohl girls began to ask themselves the same question: Why are we still here?

But if the Schohls were to leave Germany, where should they go? Palestine, the goal of many of the early Jewish émigrés, held no attraction for any of the Schohls. Max in particular was a militant anti-Zionist. Closer to home, France offered a possible refuge, but Max felt no affinity for that country despite the fact that his former company had maintained a branch office in Paris. For him, France was first and foremost the *Erbfeind* (hereditary enemy) of Germany, having been the Reich's opponent in two major wars in the past seventy years. Max was more partial to Great Britain, where he had business contacts, and whose language he had learned in school. Moreover, he admired the British Empire and saw London as a bastion of refined elegance. Unfortunately, however, it was increasingly difficult for Jews to get visas for settlement in Britain, especially if they had no relatives there, which Max did not. The potential sanctuary in which Max *did* have relatives, of course, was the United States, and it was to America that his wife and daughters were trying to persuade him to consider moving. But, like many German conservatives, Max was no fan of America, which he considered culturally primitive and hyper-materialistic. He also believed it to be deeply racist. "I would never go to America," he told his family flatly. "Once they've finished with the Negroes they'll start in on the Jews."

And yet, as time went on, Max found himself reconsidering not only his opposition to emigration in general but his resistance to America in particular. The deciding factor in prompting his reassessment of emigration was his dawning recognition that he would never find work in a Germany run by Hitler, and that Hitler was not likely to go away any time soon. Without work he would be unable to support his family for very long. Of course, in addition to his family Max had obligations toward the Jewish community of Flörsheim, but that community was rapidly evaporating through emigration, and in any case he knew he was powerless to do much to protect the few Jews who remained. Max's reassessment of America as a possible sanctuary was simply a matter of practicality. There was work to be had there, he believed, for men of his abilities, and he had relatives in the country who could help him clear whatever immigration hurdles had to be cleared. When, in June 1938, he finally reached out to his relatives in that distant land, he knew that the matter was becoming urgent. The problem was, he did not know just how urgent it actually was.

CHAPTER THREE

Paper Walls

No Safe Haven

The land to which Dr. Max Schohl desperately sought entry in 1938 was no longer "an asylum for mankind" (in Thomas Paine's hopeful phrase of 1776); it had long ceased to put out an unqualified welcome mat to the world's "homeless, tempest-tossed"; and it was strongly disinclined to throw open its doors to the new wave of refugees from Hitler's racial and political oppression in the 1930s. Indeed, America actually admitted far fewer immigrants from Nazi Germany than it could have done under the law. The annual quota for immigrants from Germany did not come close to being filled until 1939.

America's first national restrictionist immigration law, passed in 1882, was aimed primarily at the Chinese, but it also barred lunatics, idiots, convicts, paupers, and any persons "likely to become a public charge" from admission to the United States. The idea that America could and should exclude certain racial categories, along with the impoverished and the infirm, received crucial backing from the soon-to-be influential eugenics movement, which held that America's own racial health depended on keeping out "inferior elements." In his best-selling book, *The Old World in the New* (1914), Edward A. Ross, a University of Wisconsin sociologist and leading advocate for immigration restriction, warned that America would go the way of the Roman Empire if it did not stop admitting the uncouth hordes of new barbarians from southern and Eastern Europe that were descending upon its shores. Ross singled out Eastern European Jews as especially menacing, for they were, in his horror scenario, "infecting entire metropolitan areas" with the diseases and vile practices that they had brought with them from the Old Country. Endowed with an "inborn love of money-making [that] leads them to crowd into the smallest quarters," the Jewish immigrants, claimed Ross, were sure to become permanent infestations of "dirt, disease, and poverty." Anticipating language that the Nazis would apply to the *Ostjuden*, Ross argued, "East European Hebrews have no reverence for law, . . . pursue Gentile girls . . . and lower standards wherever they enter."

Ross and his ilk were unable to do much to stem the tide of non-Asian immigration to the United States, which in the decade before World War I averaged more than 900,000 newcomers a year, about 10 percent of them Jewish. However, the world war, bringing with it an upsurge in American nativism and bigotry, opened the way for new restrictionist policies that also embraced the Caucasian lands. In 1921, and again in 1924, Congress passed legislation imposing strict limits on immigration from the European countries. The 1924 measure, the so-called National Origins Act, which was scheduled to take full effect in 1929, allowed an annual immigration of only 153,714 from the entire European area. Of these, 120,000 places were reserved for immigrants from Great Britain, Germany, and Scandinavia, the northern and western European region whose stock was deemed most likely "to preserve the basic stream of our population." By reducing immigration from southern and Eastern Europe to a trickle, the law effectively shut out what Kansas Congressman J. M. Tinches termed "Bolshevik Wops, Dagoes, Kikes, and Hunkies."

The Immigration Act of 1924 gave visa-granting authority to the U.S. State Department and its consular officials abroad. In the 1920s and 1930s the State Department, called "a pretty good club" by one of its members, was still dominated by "Christian gentlemen" from America's top prep schools and Ivy League colleges. Some of the department's consular officials, it is true, came from middle-class families and had degrees from public universities, but they tended to compensate for their unfortunate backgrounds by acting "more Grotty" than the men from Groton. Because genteel anti-Semitism belonged to the unwritten statutes of this Christian club, very few Jews worked at the State Department, and those who did were shut out of the better assignments. The chief of the Consular Service in the twenties and thirties, Wilbur J. Carr, went so far as to assign positions within the service according to whether one's name *sounded* Jewish. A gentile named Goldman was pretty certain to spend his entire career stamping passports in Africa. Contemplating the prospect of large numbers of Eastern European Jews immigrating to the United States in the early 1920s to escape persecution at home, Carr spoke contemptuously of "Russian or Polish Jews of the usual ghetto type . . . filthy, un-American, and dangerous in their habits." He advocated caution in admitting them, because "it is impossible to estimate the peril of the class of immigrant coming from this part of the world and every possible care and safeguard should be used to keep out the undesirables." Although Carr and his colleagues were concerned primarily about the influx of Eastern European Jews, their vigilance could be, and later was, extended to cover all Jews trying to gain access to America.

Restrictive as the 1924 law was, it seemed much too generous once America entered the Great Depression after 1929. With as many as 15 million citizens unemployed across the land in the early 1930s, and almost 30 percent of the adult population out of work in some industrial areas, America was in no mood to hold its doors open to more jobseekers from abroad. Pressure to shut those doors, or at least to reduce their opening, came from a variety of quarters, including organized labor, nativist groups, and patriotic associations. In response, President Herbert Hoover issued a directive on September 8, 1930, instructing

consular officers "before issuing a visa . . . to pass judgment with particular care on whether the applicant may become a public charge, and if
the applicant cannot convince the officer that this is not possible, the
visa will be refused." Hoover's instructions regarding the Likely to Become a Public Charge (LPC) clause turned a regulation originally designed to keep out mental defectives and the totally indigent into one
that could be used to exclude anyone with financial difficulties. At the
same time, by ordering strict adherence to the Alien Contract Labor
Law of 1885, which forbade immigrants from securing jobs in advance
of their arrival in the United States, Hoover made it impossible to use
prospective employment as proof of financial viability. In the president's eyes, anyone who *needed to work* seemed likely to become a public charge. On top of this federal regulation, many individual states
imposed their own restrictions on the economic activities of aliens following their admission to America. For example, in Massachusetts no
alien could secure a peddler's license or fish for lobsters; work as a
pharmacist, accountant, lawyer, doctor, or undertaker; be employed by
the street railway or in public works; or join the State Police, State
Militia, or Civil Service. Ohio prohibited aliens from owning or operating a pool hall. Montana banned aliens from working as teachers, ac-
countants, auctioneers, mine examiners, or fire bosses. Aside from job
protectionism, the reasons behind these restrictions included old-
fashioned nativist paranoia: Who knew what evil an alien running a
pool hall might perpetrate? Also at work here was the conviction that
aliens made unreliable employees. As the president of one of America's
largest automobile concerns put it: "We have found that the alien is a
shifting labor entity endowed with less of the qualities of dependability
and intelligence than is the native-born or naturalized citizen of the
United States." What this meant, in practice, was that only visa applicants with significant resources of their own, or with guaranteed access
to resources put up by relatives or other backers in the United States,
could expect favorable action. The famed lines on the Statue of Liberty
might have been rewritten to say, "To hell with your huddled masses,
send me your prosperous and well-connected, your stockholders, remittance men, and prospective heirs."

The number of visa applicants who could clear Hoover's high admission hurdles being understandably small, immigration totals dropped from 241,700 in 1930 to 97,139 in 1931, and to 35,576 in 1932. The number of German immigrants (including Jews) fell from 48,468 in 1929 to 10,100 in 1931, and to 1,320 in 1932. This represented a small percentage of the annual German quota of 27,370. Bizarrely, President Hoover attributed this decline in immigration to an alleged end of political persecution in Europe rather than to his restrictionist policies. In October 1932 he announced: "With the growth of democracy in foreign countries, political persecution has largely ceased. There is no longer a necessity for the United States to provide an asylum for those persecuted because of conscience."

Hitler's seizure of power the following January made a mockery of Hoover's pronouncement. The Nazi government not only opened a new chapter in state-sponsored persecution, especially of Jews, but simultaneously made emigration from Germany more difficult by limiting the amount of funds an emigrant could take out of the country. In 1933 emigrants could take with them 75 percent of their income after taxes. This amount declined yearly, dropping to 10 percent in 1938, the year Max Schohl applied to leave. After that it declined even further, so that by 1940, the year the Schohls actually left Germany, emigrants could take with them a grand total of 10 marks a piece. The reason for this policy was not to discourage Jews from leaving Germany—on the contrary, the Nazis urged them to go—but to augment the national treasury at the Jews' expense and to make their resettlement abroad more disorderly. The Nazis reasoned that the challenge of trying to accommodate small armies of impecunious Jews would make the receiving nations more sympathetic to German anti-Semitism and perhaps also help to destabilize the host nations. In the eyes of Hitler's government, the mass export of German Jews was an important weapon in its campaign to weaken potential enemies.

For the new administration of President Franklin Roosevelt in the United States, which took power about the same time that Hitler assumed the chancellorship in Germany, the prospect of another tide of immigrants surging toward its shores was alarming. Although other European countries, along with Palestine, were the primary migration targets for German Jews in the first three years after the Nazi takeover, applications for visas to the United States started to rise dramatically in mid-1933. George Messersmith, America's consul-general in Berlin from 1933 to late 1934, predicted that the number of emigrants hoping to come to America would continue to rise if Germany persisted in foreclosing economic opportunities to its Jews.

The question of how to frame U.S. immigration policy with respect to Germany's persecuted Jews inspired a protracted debate within the Roosevelt administration. As is well known, FDR had several Jewish political associates and confidants. He appointed more Jews to high office in his administration than had any previous chief executive. His cabinet included Henry Morgenthau at the Treasury Department and David Niles at the Department of Commerce. These men, along with close friends like banker Bernard Baruch, Supreme Court Justice Louis Brandeis, Harvard Law Professor Felix Frankfurter, and Judge Irving Lehman, urged the president to pressure Congress to liberalize America's immigration laws, or at the very least to throw out restrictive policies like Hoover's 1930 directive, which, as Judge Lehman told the president, "presented obstacles to a liberal and humane application of Immigration Law." Secretary of Labor Frances Perkins, the first female cabinet member in American history, pushed for a relaxation of the LPC regulation for Jewish visa applicants. FDR's combative wife Eleanor also argued for a more compassionate policy on Jewish refugees. For most of the 1930s, however, the State Department opposed any alterations that would allow significantly higher levels of immigration, including Jewish immigration. Secretary of State Cordell Hull, Assistant Secretary of State Wilbur Carr, and Undersecretary of State William Phillips all argued that taking in larger numbers of Jews would not be in America's best interest, and that Congress would oppose such an effort anyway. Roosevelt, who hardly needed instruction on what was politically expedient, allowed himself to be convinced that the Hoover-era restrictions should stay in place, at least for the time being. He speciously insisted that there was no need to make any special provisions for "political refugees" because Germany's immigration quota remained unfilled. Commenting on FDR's position, Louis Brandeis wrote dejectedly to Felix Frankfurter in April 1933: "FD [Franklin Delano] has shown amply that he has no anti-Semitism. . . . But this action, or rather determination that there shall be none, is a disgrace to America and to FD's administration."

Roosevelt's decision in April 1933 did not end the debate over the admission of would-be Jewish immigrants, for the anti-Semitic persecution in Germany that prompted Jews to want to leave sharpened over the course of the 1930s, with a minor lull during the Berlin Olympics of 1936. The positions in the American debate, however, remained fairly constant, with the State Department arguing against any effort to change the immigration laws, which the agency insisted it was enforcing fairly and impartially, and FDR making do with limited liberalizing actions within the existing quota structure.

The administration also decided against lodging any formal complaints with the German government regarding its treatment of the Jews. As Carr put the matter in May 1933: "Even if the United States were to make representations to Germany on the ground of humanity, it is likely that instead of causing a more considerate treatment of the Jews, it would probably have the opposite effect and incite further activity against them." Worried that America's emissary to Germany, Ambassador William Dodd, an outspoken liberal and reputedly something of a loose cannon, might embarrass Washington by denouncing Berlin's racial policies, Undersecretary of State William Phillips specifically warned Dodd not to say anything in public "which could be reasonably interpreted by the Germans as criticism of their own governmental and social systems." Dodd accepted this stricture, though he railed in private to the president about the "dangerous Jewish persecutions" carried on by the German government.

The day-to-day task of limiting the number of immigrants to the United States fell to the consular officials of the State Department. The Department maintained thirty consular offices in Germany, but only three of them—in Berlin, Hamburg, and Stuttgart (and, after the Anschluss, in Vienna)—were authorized to issue immigration visas. Although they enforced rather than made policy, the consuls had tremendous influence because of the LPC rule, which was vague enough to allow them considerable latitude in determining a visa applicant's financial viability. Although the State Department denied any bias on the part of its officers, there can be no question but that some of the consuls and vice-consuls went out of their way to be hard on Jewish applicants, at least in the early to mid-1930s. Many of these officials, after all, had studied at the Georgetown University School of Foreign Service, whose dean, the Reverend Edmund A. Walsh, taught them that "the Jew was . . . the entrepreneur [of the Bolshevik Revolution], who recognized his main chance and seized it shrewdly and successfully." According to Vice-Consul William Ware Adams in Berlin, the consuls had to be especially vigilant with Jewish visa applicants because all too many of them were secretly lining up employment prospects in America before departing Germany, thereby violating the contract labor provisions of the immigration law. Adams warned that "nine out of ten Jewish immigrants" would obtain immediate employment in the United States and thus "displace from employment a corresponding number of residents of the United States." He also complained that German Jews expected "preferential treatment" from the American consuls because of Nazi racial policies. Cecilia Razovsky, director of the National Coordinating Committee (a group that facilitated Jewish immigration), reported in July 1935 about a "very painful" visit in Berlin with Vice-Consul Prescott Childs, who was openly contemptuous of Jewish visa applicants, saying they were "full of worry when there is nothing to worry about." "If you haven't broken any laws," Childs insisted, "you do not get into trouble. If you are supposed to keep your mouth shut you have no right to talk." According to Razovsky, Childs discussed "case after case [of immigration applications] in a very sarcastic, unsympathetic way." Another Jewish visitor to the consulate in Berlin complained in a report received by Max Kohler (an expert on immigration issues) that there was a clear anti-Semitic bias among some of the officials there. "It is not a feeling but a fact that the officials at the Consulate do their best to discourage emigration to the States on the part of Jewish applicants," wrote this observer. "Affidavits of U.S. citizens to the effect that the would-be immigrant will not be a burden to the community are of no use whatsoever. Such an affidavit does not even enter the least bit into the decisions made by Messrs.

Woodford or Hugh Charley Fox, both of them vice-consuls. The aspirant has to show a substantial amount of money (at least a few thousand marks) should he be considered at all." George Messersmith, the American Consul-General in Berlin, was not known to be anti-Semitic, but he too could be dismissive of Jewish anxieties, and he tended to put smooth relations with Germany above accommodating desperate German Jews. On one occasion he refused to listen to a Jewish physician's report of "atrocities" against Jews at a Berlin hospital, declaring: "You Jews are always afraid for your own skins. We consular officials are here to preserve friendly relations between the two countries." Shortly after his transfer to the U.S. consulate in Vienna in 1934, Messersmith blithely claimed in a letter to an American Jewish official that anti-Jewish sentiment was not a serious problem in that city, and that the racial tensions that did exist there derived primarily from public complaining on the part of "a small minority of Jews." Messersmith could reassure the official that "the situation here is developing very satisfactorily and . . . is not one to give cause for concern to us at home."

Whether or not it was motivated by the bureaucratic mindset, prejudice, or ill will, the decision-making process at the American consular offices was certainly arbitrary. As one report noted, "even in the same office, no two Consuls interpreted instructions from the State Department in the same way." A striking example of this occurred in 1934 at the Stuttgart office (the one to which Max Schohl applied four years later). A nineteen-year-old German Jewish student named Herman Kilsheimer went to the consulate to apply for an immigration visa. A sister who had already immigrated to America and returned to help him with his application accompanied him to the office. Kilsheimer was armed with three affidavits, one from his sister's husband, one from a first cousin, and one from another cousin's husband. Alas, cousins were not considered close relations according to the consuls' regulations, and the money that Kilsheimer's sponsors put up was not impressive. Consul Charles Taylor accordingly rejected the application. As Kilsheimer and his sister were leaving the consulate in tears, however, a vice-consul to whom the sister had taught German in Washington spotted the pair and invited them back into the building. Upon reviewing Kilsheimer's documents, the vice-consul gave him a visa after all (presumably with the approval of Consul Taylor). Although the consuls generally favored candidates with affidavits of support supplied by close relatives, they would sometimes accept pledges from nonrelatives if enough money were involved. For example, the banker Felix Warburg had no trouble obtaining a visa for an academic acquaintance because he was able to list assets in his affidavit of over $1 million and an annual income of over $50,000.

Even if they did not immediately turn down an immigration candidate on the basis of the (arbitrarily interpreted) LPC rule, the consuls could strangle the application in red tape. The rules required of all would-be immigrants to America a vast array of documents, including a valid passport; a police certificate attesting to the applicant's good conduct in the past; a statement from the Public Health Office guaranteeing that the applicant was not suffering from "any loathsome or contagious disease or from an illness or physical handicap that might make him a public charge"; duplicate records of birth, marriage, and divorce certificates; and complete bank records. If any of these documents was missing or illegible, the consuls could, and often did, simply sit on an application. As the German writer Alfred Polgar ruefully observed (after escaping to America by the skin of his teeth): "Hitler was quicker than the consuls on whose moods depended the visas that could save us."

As visa applications to the United States mounted from 1933 to 1936, the American consuls in Germany seemed to be in competition to see who could approve the fewest number of them. In 1935, however, word came down from Washington to proceed somewhat more leniently with the Jewish applicants. Under constant pressure from Jewish organizations to bring in more German Jews, the Roosevelt administration decided to try to increase the number of Jewish immigrants without altering the quota system or challenging the immigration laws. The administration could thereby make a humanitarian gesture without, as Consul Messersmith put it, "provoking painful discussion." In January 1937 the State Department formalized this order by amending the way in which consuls across Europe were directed to interpret the LPC rule; now they were told to deny entry only if an applicant was "probably" going to become a public charge, not merely if it was "possible" that he or she might do so. The result was a significant increase in European immigration to the United States, above all in immigration from Germany (about 90 percent of which was now Jewish). In fiscal 1936 some 6,798 German applicants (36.9 percent of the German quota) received visas; in 1937 the figure jumped to 12,532 (43 percent of the quota); and in 1938 it increased to 20,301 (66 percent). Yet, to be fairly assessed, these numbers must be measured against the number of people trying to get out of Germany, which went up considerably faster than the acceptances. Waiting lists for admission to the annual quota pools now lengthened rapidly. At the Stuttgart consulate a low-level employee apparently accepted bribes to move people up the waiting list; he was fired for this action. It is significant, moreover, that the German quota (which after 1938 was combined with the Austrian quota) remained unfilled until 1939, despite the increasing number and desperation of would-be immigrants. In the end, the only way fully to have accommodated the large number of visa applicants would have been to expand the German quota, or better yet, to have eliminated it entirely, but this the State Department effectively advised against.

The State Department was not the only influential voice in the American establishment opposing any change in immigration law to accommodate the Jews. Influential figures within the officer corps of the U.S. Army, which had a long tradition of anti-Semitism, took the position from the outset of the Third Reich that getting along with Hitler's government was more important than helping the German Jews. Some of the officers stationed in Germany also argued that if America provided a refuge for Germany's Jews, this would only transplant "the Jewish problem" to America. Taking the lead in this argument was the American military attaché in Berlin from 1935 to 1940, Captain Truman Smith, a Yale graduate and scion of the old American elite. Smith and his wife Katherine admired most of what they saw in Nazi Germany, especially the "cleanliness" and order of its cities. Katherine complained that American newspapers stressed only "Jewish troubles and warlike preparations," while ignoring the fact that German cities were safe once again because "all the drunks, bums, homosexuals, etc. had been put in concentration camps." In addition to pushing for appeasement of Hitler, Smith counseled patience with the Führer's Jewish policy, whose "excesses" he lamented, but whose basic motivation he could understand owing to what he, Smith, considered a genuine Jewish threat to Germany's welfare. Retailing standard German anti-Semitic prejudices, Smith claimed in a report to Washington that the Jews possessed "financial and industrial strength far in excess of their numerical strength" and that they had added insult to injury by "display[ing] their wealth throughout Germany's years of misery (1921–1924) in anything but an unostentatious manner." Furthermore, said Smith, the Jews had played a leading role in the German Communist Party and were now active in Communist subversion worldwide. Given the depth of anti-Semitic feeling in Germany, argued the captain, it would be folly for the United States to try to change the Nazis' racial policies. He did not advise specifically against allowing more German Jews to enter the United States, but this advice could be easily inferred from his comments about their allegedly nefarious Jewish role in Germany. Moreover, he believed that the forces of international Jewry had already extended their influence to America, establishing considerable "control" over American society.

In parroting the anti-Semitic nostrums of Hitler's Germany, Smith was simply echoing prejudices that were widely disseminated within the American public in the 1930s. Some 3.5 million Americans tuned in regularly to the weekly broadcasts of the Catholic radio-priest Father Charles E. Coughlin (a forerunner of the right-wing televangelists of the late twentieth century), who fulminated against "Jewish communists" and other aliens who were allegedly robbing natives of jobs and spreading subversion throughout the land. Mass organizations like the Crusaders and the Sentinels of the Republic, both underwritten by major American corporations and business tycoons, denounced (in the words of Sentinel President Alexander Lincoln) "the Jewish brigade Roosevelt took to Washington" and insisted that the war to save Western civilization could be won only "if we recognize that the enemy is worldwide and that it is Jewish in origin." Fearing that the Roosevelt administration was considering a "relaxation of immigration laws to admit refugees from persecution in Germany," the Paul Reveres ("A Society for Americans Who Will Ride and Spread the Alarm") reminded the president that "many of the Jews whom Hitler is trying to get rid of are Communists," and therefore "letting down existing barriers to refugees will . . . expose us to the entry of undesirables whose Communist affiliations cannot be detected by cursory examination." The Daughters of the American Revolution concurred, protesting against any "opening of our gates to those who would destroy our private property rights, our monogamous homes, our racial purity, and our belief in a spiritual Creator."

Private citizens, too, issued dire warnings regarding the "Jewish threat" in hundreds of letters to Roosevelt and to members of the State Department. In one such communication, an indignant resident of Maine fulminated:

> [The Jewish] race came here unasked, arrived unwelcomed and in the main have proved themselves highly undesirable. Moreover, their national patriotism is not prominent. If they had been desirable citizens of Germany that nation would not now seek to evict them. Their very eviction is their curse. American Jews are taking the improper course of making this a national issue when it strictly concerns their race only. Nothing prevents them from buying Palestine tracts sufficient to harbor all those evicted. We don't want them here. We are already Jewed to death.

Another "concerned citizen of American stock" claimed to speak for "the VAST MAJORITY of American citizens, both native and of foreign origin," in warning FDR against "letting down the bars to Jewish Communists," every one of whom "would of necessity take the bread out of the mouth of some American unemployed," not to mention "accentuate the growing dislike of real Americans against the rat-like qualities of the lower-type Ghetto European Jews—racketeers, chiselers, bootleggers, kidnappers, adulterers of foods and drugs, insurance swindlers, thieves and murderers." The chairman of the German Department at Vanderbilt University protested in a letter to Cordell Hull against "an organized effort to place German Jews, refugees from a land that is trying to strengthen itself by making some of its harmful elements impotent, on the roster of American universities," an action that could "only do harm to American education and to America's friendship with Germany." These were not the phobias of a few isolated cranks; according to public opinion polls conducted in the later part of the decade, three-fifths of the respondents attributed negative traits to the Jews, such as selfishness, dishonesty, greed, and clannishness. Between one-third and one-half of the people surveyed agreed that Jews had "too much power" in America. Seventy-two percent opposed any increase in the number of Jewish refugees admitted to America.

JEWISH DISCORD

Faced with strong public and congressional opposition to a liberalization of American immigration law, Jewish organizations in the United States could not come up with a unified or coherent campaign to change national policy. Some groups hesitated to push too hard in the public sphere for fear of exacerbating anti-Semitic sentiments. Yet—and this needs to be emphasized—it is highly doubtful that a more unified drive by Jewish groups to alter American policy in this matter would have been successful. Jews accounted for less than 3 percent of the nation's voters. Although they had considerable influence in some northeastern states and cities, especially New York, they were never in a position to dictate policy to any American national leader, including FDR. The Jews needed "their friend" in Washington more than he needed them, and both sides knew it.

The lack of a common Jewish front in the face of the challenges of Nazism reflected older divisions within the American Jewish community, divisions that in many ways mirrored the rifts among the various Jewish factions in Germany. Broadly speaking, there was a historical social divide between the well-established, highly assimilated Jews of Germanic stock and the more recently arrived, less-integrated, and poorer Eastern European Jews. Very different cultures and political perspectives were in evidence here. The German Jews tended to favor reform Judaism (if they were religious at all), support liberal (as opposed to socialist or communist) political ideals, and reject Zionism. The Eastern European Jews were typically more conservative in their religious practices and/or more mili-

tant in their politics; if they were secular, they often championed the socialist and Zionist ideals that they had embraced in the old country.

Each of these camps had a specific lobby organization in America.
Jews of Germanic background dominated the American Jewish Committee, which was established in 1906 by wealthy Jews who used their
influence to court America's top office holders. Russian and Polish Jews,
feeling almost as alienated from the domestic German-Jewish elite as
from the gentile American establishment, founded the American Jewish
Congress in 1915 to articulate and defend their own perspectives. Reflecting their divergent backgrounds and social composition, the two
camps favored very different tactics in their campaigns to influence
American policy. The American Jewish Committee preferred discreet,
personal interaction between its own well-connected leaders and highly
placed personages in the American ruling class. The American Jewish
Congress, by contrast, favored noisy and visible public protests such as
mass rallies, boycotts, fasts, and demonstrations.

Initially, the two groups sought to adopt a common response to the
related challenges of Nazism and Jewish immigration, but this aspira-
tion quickly collapsed in the face of the American government's unwillingness to take a firm stand against Nazi racial persecution or to change
its own immigration policy. To the embarrassment of the American
Jewish Committee, and to the horror of the State Department, the
American Jewish Congress sponsored a mass rally on March 28, 1933,
in Madison Square Garden to protest Nazi actions against the Jews.
Here Rabbi Stephen Wise, the Hungarian-born head of the Congress,
demanded that the Hitler government immediately end its anti-Semitic
measures, and called upon the U.S. government to exact reprisals
against Germany if Berlin did not comply. Believing that such public
protests would only make matters worse for the German Jews, State
Department officials, after consulting with equally alarmed representa-
tives of the American Jewish Committee and the B'nai B'rith, sent a reassuring telegram to Wise for presentation at the rally. The telegram,
which Wise duly read, declared that the mistreatment of the Jews in
Germany "may be considered virtually terminated," that Hitler had instructed his followers "to maintain law and order," and that the State

Department would "watch the situation closely, with a sympathetic interest and with a desire to be helpful in whatever way possible."

The hollowness of such reassurances became evident a few days later when the Nazis launched their Reich-wide boycott of Jewish businesses. In response, the Jewish War Veterans of America, joined later by the American Jewish Congress, called for an international boycott of German products and services. Speaking in Prague before the World Zionist Congress, Wise declared that as long as Germany continued its anti-Semitic policies, "decent, self-respecting Jews cannot deal with Germany in any way, buy or sell or maintain any manner of commerce with Germany or travel on German boats." Although leaders of the American Jewish Committee were as appalled by the Nazis' anti-Jewish boycott as were members of the American Jewish Congress and the Jewish War Veterans Association, they believed that a counter-boycott would be not be productive, and they deeply resented Wise's claim to speak for all "decent, self-respecting Jews."

With the pressure to admit more Jews to the United States rising in tandem with Germany's campaign to force Jews—minus their fortunes—out of the Reich, American Jews could agree only on the need for a liberalization of domestic immigration policy; the question of *how* this should be implemented once again divided the ranks. The American Jewish Committee tried repeatedly to exert friendly persuasion at the top; committee leaders like Cyrus Adler, Joseph Proskauer, and Morris Waldman made personal appeals to FDR, Cordell Hull, and William Phillips. Frankfurter, who was close to the committee, also continued to raise the immigration issue with Roosevelt, only to be brushed off with assurances that the American government was doing all it could under the circumstances. Though frustrated by his inability to move FDR, Frankfurter put the blame not on the president but on the State Department, which he believed was tying his friend's hands. The American Jewish Congress, meanwhile, along with the American Jewish Labor Committee, organized more demonstrations and pressed on with its boycott campaign. Wise, too, managed to meet with FDR in 1936, but like Frankfurter he was unable to convince the president that the situation in Germany merited a fundamental reappraisal of American policy on political refugees. Unlike Frankfurter, Wise *did* blame the president (along with the State Department), but he also chastised the American Jewish Committee for not joining with the American Jewish Congress in exerting more pressure from below. This internal feuding and finger pointing within the American Jewish community undoubtedly weakened the Jewish campaign, but it cannot be held responsible for the fact that little significant change occurred. The chief causes for that sad reality were the priorities and perspectives of American policy makers, attitudes in the U.S. Congress, and, underlying all of this, the prejudices and fears running through American society as a whole.

ANSCHLUSS TO EVIAN

On March 12, 1938, shortly before Max Schohl made his first request for help to his American relatives, German troops marched into Austria, bringing that small Alpine nation "home to the Reich," as the Austrian native Adolf Hitler put it. Three days later Hitler delivered a speech before a huge crowd in Vienna's Heldenplatz. "We thank our Führer," shouted the mob. Austria's Jews, of course, had nothing to be thankful for. For them the Anschluss—as Germany's annexation of Austria was called—brought immediate persecution by local Nazis, who had long been panting for the chance to show that they could be even more ruthless in this domain than their brothers in Germany. In Vienna and other cities, Jews were robbed, beaten, and subjected to humiliating tasks, such as scrubbing anti-Nazi graffiti from sidewalks with toothbrushes. The suicide rate among Jews in Vienna rose to 200 a day. In the weeks after the Austrian takeover more than 30,000 people lined up at the American consulate in Vienna, hoping to get a visa to the United States. Officials estimated that 95 percent of them were Jewish.

The American press, which in the past had rarely made persecution of the Jews the central theme of its reporting on Nazi Germany, covered the anti-Jewish terror in Austria fulsomely and with unrestrained indignation. "Adolf Hitler has left behind him in Austria an anti-Semitism that is blossoming far more rapidly than it ever did in Germany," opined the *New York Times*. Many papers commented extensively on the abusive treatment of Sigmund Freud, whose home was raided (as one paper put it) "by thugs cloaked in the law's vestments." Yet with respect to the refugee issue, now becoming even more acute, the American press as a whole maintained the position it had taken from the beginning of the Third Reich: namely, that America should not change its laws to admit more Jews.

Shocked by reports coming out of Vienna, and aware that the persecutions there and elsewhere in the Reich were heightening the demand by Central European Jews for refuge in the United States, FDR mused to his cabinet on March 18: "America was a place of refuge for so many fine Germans in the period of 1848. Why couldn't we offer them again a place of refuge at this time?" The question was rhetorical, and FDR himself knew the answer. The depression had deepened in 1937–1938, dashing hopes for a recovery following the election year of 1936. According to the American Federation of Labor, unemployment in 1938 stood at 11 million, or about 20 percent of the workforce. In that same year, a Roper poll showed that only 4.9 percent of the respondents believed that America should change its laws to admit more victims of Nazi persecution; 18.2 percent said that the country should admit as many refugees as the law allowed; and a staggering 67.4 percent said that the government should "keep them all out." The extreme restrictionists were not all Christian nativists: 20 percent of the American Jews responding to a poll on immigration in July 1938 favored a rigid exclusionist policy. Vice President John Nance Gardner (known now only for his pithy observation that the vice presidency wasn't "worth a bucket of warm spit") told FDR that if the question of expanding national quotas were to be left up to a secret vote in Congress, *all* immigration would probably be stopped. Meanwhile, Father Coughlin was warning his huge American audience that Jewish internationalists were plotting to push the United States into a war with Germany to reap windfall profits for Jewish financiers.

Not surprisingly, FDR was getting a very different perspective on the immigration issue, and specifically on the likely impact of increased Jewish immigration on the national economy, from various Jewish experts and the pro-immigration faction in his cabinet. These experts provided data suggesting that admitting more immigrants with professional and business skills—the profile of most of the Jews now applying for visas—would ease rather than compound America's unemployment problems. Rather than competing with unskilled native labor, these immigrants would bring much-needed technical and entrepreneurial skills to the American marketplace, thereby expanding job opportunities for all Americans.

Whether or not he himself was convinced by such arguments, FDR knew that they would not overcome restrictionist sentiment in Congress or in the public at large. At the same time, however, he wanted to make some kind of public gesture to show that he and his government were not indifferent to the fate of the Jews, as many critics were suggesting. By proposing that the president summon an international conference to discuss the refugee crisis, Undersecretary of State Sumner Welles adroitly addressed FDR's need for just such a public gesture. Welles did not say, "Let's cover our lack of action with a lot of talk," but this was the thrust of his plan. Roosevelt readily agreed to Welles's proposal, and France consented to host the conference at the spa town of Evian-les-Bains. (That a meeting to discuss the plight of an oppressed people was held in a posh resort was not unusual in those days, nor has it been since.)

To facilitate preparations for the Evian meeting and to coordinate the immigration efforts between U.S. groups and a planned Intergovernmental Committee on Refugees, the Roosevelt administration established the Presidential Advisory Committee on Political Refugees (PACPR). The group's membership included the Jewish leaders Paul Baerwald and Stephen Wise, but the PACPR was weighted in favor of men with no particular commitment to the Jewish cause. One of the committee members, Hamilton Fish Armstrong, chairman of the prestigious Foreign Policy Association, turned down the committee chairmanship on grounds that his interest was "after all [more] international relations than relief or philanthropy as such." At the committee's first full meeting, on May 16, 1938, George Messersmith, who had since become assistant secretary of state, made it clear that no one should expect too much from the upcoming Evian meeting or the proposed

Intergovernmental Committee on Refugees. His unvarnished confidential memorandum stated, inter alia:

> I think we must frankly face certain facts at the outset and the most important of these is that, although many of the countries represented on the Committee are deeply moved by humanitarian instincts, none of them is approaching the problem with enthusiasm and very few with the disposition to make sacrifices. The replies which we have received from most countries indicate that they approach the problem and the Committee with much reserve. It is to be feared that some of the countries have agreed to be represented on the Committee only because they did not wish to appear before international opinion as completely standing aside. . . . There will be a tendency on the part of all countries to render lip service to the idea of aiding the refugees accompanied by an unwillingness, however, to do anything to ease existing restrictions of the admission of immigrants. So far as the Untied States is concerned, our present quotas are such and our visa practice is such that little positive action can be expected. On the other hand, the liberal attitude which we now have in admitting immigrants and the liberal attitude we have towards them after they enter our country can serve as an example and incentive to other countries. If the other major countries would show anything like the attitude which we show it will go far towards relieving the situation.

Although, as Messersmith made clear to his colleagues, the United States had no intention of changing its immigration laws or expanding its German quota, the country had for some time been employing a more "liberal" selection policy within the quota system, and in anticipation of the Evian meeting FDR announced that henceforth the combined German-Austrian quota would become "fully available" for refugees. This was a significant change from the previous practice of holding immigration levels well below the quota limits. Combined with the earlier "leniency" in visa-granting practices, this step did increase the number of immigrants admitted to the United States, allowing the German-Austrian quota to be filled for the first time in 1939.

The belated "liberal attitude" that America displayed by filling its German immigration quota in a time of crisis did not, contrary to Messersmith's hopes, have any appreciable effect on the other thirty-one nations attending the Evian conference. One delegate after another professed his nation's "concern" for the plight of the refugees but excused that government from raising the number of immigrants it could accept. The British representative said that England was already overcrowded and that considerations of climate, race, and "local conditions" ruled out most of London's overseas empire as receiving areas for new migrants from Europe. "Local conditions" referred primarily to Palestine, where, in light of fierce Arab opposition to the steady influx of Jews, the British were already trying desperately to curtail further Jewish immigration. The French delegate lamented that his country had already reached "the extreme point of saturation as regards admission of refugees." Australia said it could not tolerate much new immigration because, "as we have no real racial problem, we are not desirous of importing one." With the exception of the Dominican Republic, all the Latin American countries claimed that high unemployment in their lands mandated keeping immigration levels low. Before adjourning, the conference approved Washington's proposal for a new Intergovernmental Committee on Refugees, whose twofold mission was to search for "opportunities for permanent settlement" for refugees and to negotiate with the German government to let emigrants take more of their resources with them when they left Germany. The conference participants knew that neither of these aspirations was likely to be fulfilled, especially the latter. Germany's foreign minister, Joachim von Ribbentrop, had recently reaffirmed Berlin's refusal to allow Jewish capital to leave the Reich, adding that German Jews would be further penalized by any anti-German propaganda at Evian. (For this reason, Germany, whose policies were the main reason for the conference, was hardly referred to at all during the proceedings.) Summing up the conference's accomplishments, a reporter for *Newsweek* quoted the American delegate's opening appeal for prompt action on the refugee crisis, adding: "Most governments represented acted promptly by slamming their doors against Jewish refugees."

"A More Friendly State":
Max Schohl Opens His Immigration Campaign

The shortcomings of American immigration law, the inability of feuding American Jewish groups to do anything much to change that law, and the failure of the international community to come up with practical measures to relieve the refugee crisis certainly clouded the outlook for would-be escapees from Germany like Max Schohl and his family. Yet what was primarily on Max's mind in the summer of 1938 was not the broad shape of American and international refugee policy but the narrower problem of his own effort to gain admission to the United States, a campaign he now mounted in earnest.

Max directed his first calls for help to his aged aunts, Lina and Therese. Writing in German, he asked his aunts if they, in tandem with Lina's grown son and daughter, could provide affidavits guaranteeing that the Schohl family would be provided for financially if admitted to America. Max instructed that the documents be sent to the American Consulate in Stuttgart, which had visa-granting authority for Flörsheim. At this point the chemist specifically requested visas only for himself and his older daughter Hela; once he was safely established in America and working, he would bring over his wife, Liesel, and his younger daughter Käthe. His closing words betrayed a mixture of hope and barely disguised alarm: "I have complete confidence in all of you and hardly need assure you of my gratitude if you are able to help us in our hour of need. I plead with you not to delay, for it is becoming harder by the day to get to America. This year's emigration quota will soon be filled, and [if we can't come now] we will have to wait another entire year before reaching our turn. You cannot imagine with what impatience I await your response."

To Max's consternation, only Aunt Therese responded to his initial call for help. While offering words of sympathy and encouragement to her nephew, she insisted that she was too old and infirm to be of much assistance in getting the Schohls to America. She advised Max to focus his efforts on Aunt Lina and her children. After waiting six weeks without a response from Lina's side of the family, Max returned to his typewriter and, on two fingers, beat out an anguished SOS addressed to

Lina's daughter Norma and her husband Grover Kaufman, who lived near Lina in Charleston, West Virginia. Max had never met the Kaufmans, but he believed that they, along with Lina's son Julius Hess and another pair of American cousins, Charles and Ferdinand (Ferd) Midelburg, were in a good position to help him. (Max had met Ferd Midelburg in Germany and knew him to be a very wealthy man.) Because these younger relatives knew no German, Max was obliged to write to them in English, a language he had not used in years. To complicate matters further, he had to make the seriousness of his predicament evident without maligning the people who were responsible for it; Nazi censors monitored most outgoing mail sent by Jews. The resulting missive, written with linguistic help from daughter Käthe, delivered a clear enough message despite the impediments, but it must have been deeply shaming for Max, a man of immense pride and dignity, to go begging for help to distant relatives whom for the most part he had never met.

August 3, 1938

My dear cousins Grover and Norma,

About six weeks ago, I have written to Your mother, my aunt Lina; but till today I have not received any answer. The same day I wrote to our aunt Therese. She answered me, we should have a good hopeness, that we could come to USA. But it is clear, our aunt Therese is too old and she cannot do anything for us.

I regret very much that I didn't more knew so much English, that I could declare You our situation. But when Your mother has translated my letter of June 22, You will know all exactly. My situation is so that I cannot have any possibility in this country to find an occasion to work. So I must go out of this country, to find a more friendly state, what I here cannot have.

The situation in USA may be not good to come. But I am a chemist, who has learned many things and with many experience. I am sure, when I am in Your country, I will find a position for me. Some weeks ago a business friend of Milwaukee I have seen here and he promised to me, when I came to USA, he would give me a position in his factory. Another friend of mine in Franklin (PA) wrote to me, he would do what he could do, to help me to a position. He is a manager in a great petrol refinery, where chemists are occupied. Then the best friend of my wife, who has a factory in lady hats in Chicago wrote, she would always have a place for our girls.

You see, we are not without any chance in Your country. But the most important thing is, that we have not an "affidavit." I wrote to my aunt Lina, that I hope my cousins will do that for me. I think when You, the children of my aunt Lina and my cousin Ferdy Midelburg help together, it will not be difficult for Your this affidavit, to give. I have not the address of cousin Ferdy and I beg You, to communicate with him and to declare our situation. I am sure, when You all would know the real situation, You would not wait a day, to help us. I have the opinion, at first to go out with my elder daughter Hela (18) and later my wife will come with my younger girl, aged 15. I need only an affidavit for me and my daughter and when I am in the USA I am sure I can give myself the affidavits for my wife and my other girl. . . .

Excuse, please, my bad English. Several years ago, I spoke quite good. But to time I have no more practice. I am sure, when I am in USA, in a few months I speak all what I need. Many thanks for your kindness and best regards,

Max Schohl

Two weeks later, on August 26, 1938, having heard nothing from the Kaufmans or Ferd Midelburg, Max wrote a second letter (again in German) to his Aunt Therese. Although indignant over the prolonged silence from his younger relatives, he refused to believe that they would do nothing to help him if they fully understood the situation. Moreover, as he reminded his aunt, he was only asking for help so that he could help himself:

Flörsheim, 26.8.38

Dear Aunt Therese

You answered my last letter promptly, for which I thank you. From this I see that you still have an interest in your relatives, and your kind words helped a lot. Naturally I understand that you, with your advanced age, cannot be expected to do everything to help us in our need. But I know that you have an appreciation for our terrible situation.

I have now written three times to Charleston without receiving an answer, which I cannot understand. I will not and cannot believe that Aunt Lina and her children, who are prospering, wish to remain oblivious to our plight. After all, I have not asked for money, but simply that all the relatives get together to vouch for my older daughter and me so that we can come to America. Once I am over there I will ensure that my wife and younger daughter can follow us. But of course I have to get there first. I asked Aunt Lina to approach Ferdy Midelburg, but have heard nothing of this. Will you, dear Aunt, talk to Ferdy? And please send me his address. Perhaps you could also talk with the other Charleston relatives and ask them why they don't write to me. . . .

[What I'm asking] requires no great sacrifice, since thousands of American Jews have sent affidavits to their distant relatives [in Germany] and even to complete strangers. As the president of the Jewish community here, I have frequently seen this with my own eyes. There is certainly no risk entailed, for we all are willing and able to work and will present a burden to no one. I have very great prospects to get a good job as soon as I'm over there. And therefore, dear

Aunt Therese, do what you can to get us an affidavit. Perhaps you might speak with your nephew, Herr Friedman, who seems to have his heart in the right place and might be able to give us some advice.

Again, I cannot imagine that our relatives in the USA would let us go under, but we can expect no other fate in the long run if we continue to stay here. . . .

In spite of everything we do not despair, for we tell ourselves that in America there are people with good hearts who will not let other people go under whose desperate plight is not of their own making. So there, dear Aunt Therese, I've written to you what is in my heart and I plead with you to do all that you can, within the limits of your capacities, to help us. I am certain that your nephew can advise you on how best to proceed. Stay healthy and be assured of the warmest greetings from all of us, and especially from your nephew,

Max

JULIUS

What Max did not know at that time was that his appeals to his aged aunts had resulted in some practical measures being taken on his behalf. Aunt Therese had contacted her nephew Charles Friedman, a lawyer in Toledo, Ohio, who in turn had dispatched a translated version of Max's letter to his aunt to the chemist's American cousins—the Midelburgs, the Kaufmans, and Julius Hess—asking them on behalf of Therese to do what they could for Max Schohl and his family. On the basis of what Max had written, Friedman felt confident that the Schohls would present no burden to their American relatives. "The letter from him seems to indicate a man of culture and energy, who, with his daughter, some eighteen years of age, should before long be self-sustaining in this country," Friedman wrote. "It appears that what he now seeks is the necessary documents which will enable him to emigrate to this country and without which he cannot take that step."

Even before contacting Friedman, Therese had personally spoken to the Kaufmans and to Julius Hess about Max's situation. Hess persuaded

Laurence Kaufman (Grover's brother) to write a letter to West Virginia's senior senator, Rush D. Holt, asking him to use his influence on the Schohls' behalf. As a member of the Senate Committee on Education and Labor, Holt was very familiar with American immigration policy and was in a good position to pull strings should he be inclined to do so. In this case, however, Holt merely sent an inquiry about the Schohl visa application to Ambassador Hugh Wilson in Berlin. (Wilson had replaced Dodd as American ambassador in 1937.) On September 9, Holt informed Kaufman of the step he had taken, adding "as soon as information is given to me on the cases, I shall get in touch with you and Mr. Hess."

Ambassador Wilson did not reply to Holt; he simply passed Holt's letter on to the American Consulate in Stuttgart, which had jurisdiction in Max's case. It is not surprising that Wilson should have confined himself to such perfunctory action. Upon being named ambassador to Berlin, Wilson had established himself as an arch-appeaser of Hitler, some of whose policies he genuinely admired. He was particularly impressed by the Nazis' *Kraft durch Freude* (Strength through Joy) program, which organized vacations and recreational activities for German workers as a means of keeping them loyal to the regime. He compared the director of this program to "a Hull House worker under Jane Addams," and equated the group's labor camps "to the efforts we were making in the CCC [Civilian Conservation Corps]." Wilson made it his mission to prevent the growing anti-Nazi sentiment in America from burdening U.S.-German relations. "Certain elements," he wrote in 1938, are working "frantically to bring the United States into war, and with motives which do not appeal to the vast majority of the American people as a real cause for war." By "certain elements" Wilson meant primarily German and American Jews, and he believed that the more German-Jewish refugees that reached America the harder it would be for people like him to keep America and Germany from eventually coming to blows. There is no record of his ever having gone out of his way to facilitate the emigration of Jews to the United States.

Julius Hess, the instigator of Laurence Kaufman's letter to Senator Holt, responded to Charles Friedman's letter by assuring him that he had "personally assumed the responsibility of signing affidavits for Dr. Max Schohl and his daughter." He also noted that he had talked to

Charley Midelburg, who had "assured me that I could rely on him to do his part," and that Ferd Midelburg (to whom he had not yet spoken) "fully knows the situation." In short, Julius was doing "all in my power to get [the Schohls] over."

It soon became evident that Julius Hess was virtually the *only* one of Max's American relatives willing to make a concerted effort to get Max and his family to the United States, whatever the Midelburgs may have promised. The sad irony here is that Julius was in some ways the least likely among the American cousins to be able to achieve this goal. At the same time, however, his act of stepping forth to help a man he had never met was by no means out of character. If he had certain practical disadvantages as a guarantor of the Schohls' visa applications, he possessed in abundance the "good heart" that Max hoped and expected to find on the other side of the Atlantic.

Julius Hess was born on August 13, 1897, in Greenup, Kentucky, a small town on the Ohio River near the Ohio and West Virginia borders. His family moved to Charleston, West Virginia, when he was a child. Julius's grandfather, David Hess, fought for the South in the Civil War and worked for a time as the manager of a hotel in Charleston. Little is known about Seymour Hess, Julius's father, save that he was a harness maker and that he married Lina Schohl, Max's aunt, shortly after her emigration to America.

Julius grew up without much money, and his financial circumstances remained constrained throughout adulthood. Along with his sister, Norma, he attended local schools in Charleston but never went to college. Too young to serve in World War I, he went to work at age sixteen for Harry Smith Clothiers, then worked for a time as a teller at Citizen's National Bank, and in 1928 landed a position as a clerk at Kaufman Brothers Department Store, owned by Norma's husband Grover. He eventually became manager of the men's department, earning a salary of $86 a week. With time he was able to purchase a one-quarter partnership in the business. He also worked part-time as a life insurance agent. (Incidentally, Julius's practice of writing "agent" on the heading of his letters to Max greatly alarmed the chemist, who thought that this meant his cousin worked for the FBI.)

Julius and his wife Beatrice (Bea), who did not work outside the home, enjoyed a modest but comfortable existence. They shared a three-bedroom house with Bea's parents on Charleston's West Side, a good distance from the Kanawha River Valley mansions inhabited by the local coal barons and across town from the precincts of Charleston's wealthier Jews, including Charley Midelburg. (Ferd Midelburg lived in Logan, West Virginia.) Bea's father, a salesman of baby clothing, helped with the household expenses, but Julius was never able to save enough money to pay off his mortgage, nor did he feel that he could afford to own a car until the last years of his life.

His one indulgence was membership in the Southmoor Country Club, Charleston's preeminent Jewish social organization. (The toniest country club in town, Edgewood, did not officially exclude Jews, but it found ways to make them feel unwelcome.) Founded by four business-men of German-Jewish descent, the Southmoor Club had a nine-hole golf course and swimming pool. Here Julius played golf regularly and enjoyed a weekly Scotch-fueled poker game with his closest male friends, all fellows who made considerably more money than he did. Julius apparently did not begrudge them their higher salaries; by all ac-counts he was content with his modest circumstances. He was happy in his marriage, too, enjoying nothing more (save perhaps his card games with the guys) than going dancing with Bea. His one regret in his mar-riage was that he and Bea were not able to have children.

When it came to matters of religion, Julius, rather like Max, let his wife do the heavy lifting. He was a member of Charleston's Virginia Street Temple, but in contrast to Bea, who worshipped at every Sabbath, Julius attended services only on high holidays. He was also a member of Charleston's chapter of B'nai B'rith, but he rarely went to meetings.

Like his friends at the Southmoor Club—indeed like most Jews across America—Julius was a Democrat and an admirer of FDR. He did not, however, take an active role in politics at any level; that would not have been his style. Nor did he get caught up in the mass protests over Nazism that roiled the larger Jewish communities in America, especially those on the Eastern Seaboard. He attended no rallies, marched in no demon-strations, joined in no public fasts. He seems to have been unconcerned with the political and tactical quarrels between the American Jewish Committee and the American Jewish Congress, neither of which had a presence in Charleston. He was, however, quite aware of the internecine battles among American Jews over Zionism, which was a subject of heated discussion in the Hess's social circle. Interestingly enough, without exactly championing the Zionist ideal of a separate Jewish state, he and his wife expressed support for the Jewish settlement of Palestine. Since all of the Hess's friends were strongly anti-Zionist, this mildly pro-Zionist stance provoked some comment. Mrs. Hess became known as the "Queen Bee of Zionism."

In matters of temperament Julius was undoubtedly very different from the distant cousin in Germany he tried to help—he certainly lacked Max's dynamism, charisma, assertiveness, and ambition—but in one respect the two were strikingly similar: Julius, in his fashion, was every bit as generous as Max. He became known around town as a soft touch, someone who would give away money to just about anyone who asked for help. He donated to most of the local charities. He lent money to hard-up friends and did not press them for repayment. The result was that he fell badly into debt himself; when he died he owed $20,000 to various creditors.

How different was the situation of Julius's cousins, the Midelburgs! Charley Midelburg owned a car dealership, a movie theater (the "Capitol"), and an ice skating rink in Charleston. Ferd Midelberg owned several valuable properties in and around Logan, West Virginia, his hometown. Ferd, the wealthier of the two, had a large house, several cars, and two servants. Unlike Julius, who virtually never traveled, Ferd regularly sailed to Germany, replete with family, servants, and chests full of supplies. On these trips the Midelburgs often stayed for days or even weeks with Max Schohl in Flörsheim. Max proudly showed off his factory to his lordly cousin from America. Ferd may or may not have been impressed by Max's factory, but Liesel Schohl was emphatically not impressed by the fact that the Midelburgs insisted upon sleeping on the silk sheets they had brought along from America rather than on the lowly linens supplied by their hosts.

Ferd's sizable (and ostentatiously displayed) wealth definitely made an impression on Max, convincing him that Ferd might be of help to him even before the issue of his own possible immigration to America arose. In the mid-1930s Max toyed with the idea of getting his older daughter Helene out of Germany by sending her to school in America. He wrote Ferd to ask if his daughter might not live with the Midelburgs while attending school in Logan. Ferd wrote back with the question: "What kind of work can your daughter do?" Indignant over this response, Max swore never to ask another favor of Ferd. He cannot have been oblivious to this vow in 1938, when circumstances forced him to think of his wealthy cousin once again as a possible source of assistance, this time for himself as well. If it was painful for Max to turn for help to relatives like Julius Hess whom he had never met, it must have been doubly painful to include Ferd in that appeal.

The affidavit that Julius submitted in September 1938 in support of Max's visa application listed an annual income of $4,500 from all sources. Julius also registered assets valued at $10,000 (presumably the store partnership), an insurance policy for $23,500, and real estate worth $15,000, with a mortgage on it of $8,500. He indicated that he had no savings in the bank. All in all, this was a relatively weak financial statement. It would have helped greatly if Julius had been able to secure additional guarantees from the other relatives to buttress his own resources. It would also have helped—though neither Julius nor Max could have known this—if Julius's relationship to Max had been closer than that of cousin. The American consuls interpreting the Public Charge clause tended to regard distant relatives like cousins as less reliable sources of support than immediate relatives. Even President Roosevelt took the view that support from a close relative was worth more than from a distant relation. As he wrote to New York Governor Herbert Lehman, who was pushing him for a more liberal stance on Jewish immigration: "A promise of support made by a close relative will naturally be given more weight than one from a distant relative upon whom there may be no legal or moral obligation to support the applicant, and whose feeling or responsibility towards the applicant will not ordinarily be as great as in the case of a close relative." Of course, FDR did not know Julius.

In addition to submitting affidavits for Max and his daughter to the American consulate in Stuttgart and persuading Laurence Kaufman to write to Senator Holt on behalf of the Schohls, Julius sent his own personal appeals to Holt and to Joseph L. Smith, the U.S. congressman from Charleston, asking for help in getting the Schohls to America. In these letters he laid out Max's intellectual assets and praised his work ethic. Julius was full of confidence that these steps would be sufficient to get Max in. After all, the various officials would readily see that Max had valuable skills to offer and that he was a hard worker. Was not hard work and making a contribution what America was all about? (Obviously, poor Julius did not realize that professional talent and a willingness to work were actually strikes against potential migrants to Depression-era, job-protectionist America.) Sure that he would soon be meeting his illustrious cousin on American soil, Julius dispatched the first of his "Dear Cousin Max" letters to Germany on September 13, 1938:

Mr. [sic] Max Schohl
Florsheim, Germany

Dear Cousin Max:

It is with much pleasure that I can write you this letter to inform you that I am doing everything in my power to arrange for your coming to this country. No doubt by the time you receive this letter you will have already have heard from Mother, informing you that I have signed affidavits and that they should be in the American Consul's hands before you receive this letter.

I have requested two of our most influential men, Hon. Rush D. Holt, United States Senator, and Hon. Joseph L. Smith, United States Congressman, to write the American Consul for his help, and I am assured that both of them will do what they can to help us.

From what I understand, you will be notified by the American Consul at the proper time regarding your passports. Be sure and let me hear from you in English just what takes place. You might also write me the names of your friends in Milwaulkee [sic] and Franklin so that I may get in touch with them and let them know when you expect to arrive in this country.

I sincerely hope it will not be long before you are on your way here and that in a very short time it will be possible for your wife and younger daughter to join you. If I were but a rich man you and the whole family would have been on their way here without any worries as to the future, you may rest assured though that together we will be able to bring them over in a very short time.

Trusting I shall hear good news from you within a short time, and with lots of love to you and the family, I am,

Devotedly your cousin,

Julius Hess

Understandably elated by this positive—and so very hopeful—response from America to his call for help, Max replied to Julius on September 25, 1938:

My dear cousin Julius,

I thank You from all my heart for Your letter of 13th and especially for Your good words and the good news, which You have given to me.

Now I can hope again, to come over in Your country, where I can live as a respectable man; and I am sure, that I will find any job for me, so that I can live there with my family. I know exactly, that my wife and my children too must work with me, to earn, what we need for our life. But we all will do that with pleasure. We know too, that in the States will be worked very hard; but that is nothing against the bad position, which we have now here.

I write that for knewing [informing] You that we have no illusions, when we come over. We will work and I know, I can work [because] I have learned a profession, which can be used in the States too. Now I give you the addresses of both firms, with which I have had a correspondence:

Mr. Charles H. Arlsberg, 1446 Elk Street, Franklin (Pa), a jew too, is one of the oldest friends of mine; he is since 28 years in the States and the technical manager of a great petrol raffinery in Franklin. He has written to me, he would do what he could do, to get a job for me. He has spoken [to] the first manager of his big firm in New York, to find out a position for me; he is a very good man and I am sure, he would do what he can do. I add that I had helped him with money, when he emigrated before 28 years and I think he has it not forgotten.

Mr. William Pohl, a German subject too (but not a jew), 25 years in the States, is the owner of a big chemical factory. His address: "Kepec" Chemical Works, Milwaukee. His firm has in Germany a great department and I know him good as a concurrent [competitor] of my own factory, which I have had some years ago. Before 4 months I have seen Mr. Pohl in Frankfurt and he meaned [opined], that it were possible that I can work in his firm in Milwaukee. Some weeks ago he wrote me he would see, that he can give me a job in his firm.

When you will write to the both gentlemen, I think, that will be good and I believe I can get any job here or there. I find, it has been very clever of You, that You have spoken with two influential men, of whom You have written. When these men would write some words to the American Consulate in Stuttgart, that would be very good for me, then it was not necessary for me to wait for a long time before I could emigrate. When these men would write that Mr. Dr. Schohl from Florsheim-am-Main should come as soon as possible to the States, because he know a lot of very interesting things for American chemical industry, I am sure I get my American Visum for me and my daughter at once; they can write Mr. Schohl is a special-chemist in leather-colours with great experience and these colours are used in a great quantity in the States. Then I hope all will be good and when I can soon emigrate, I know, I must thank for this great affair only to You and Your efforts.

To day I can only thank with some poor writed words to You, [but] I am always thankful to Your real good doing, my dear Cousin. To Your mother I wrote to day too. I beg You, give please to all relations my best regardings and for Your I will remain always Your grateful cousin,

Max

Shortly after sending this letter, Max learned that his joy might be premature. He heard (incorrectly) from other applicants for American visas that the quota for 1938 was already filled, and that he might have to wait a long time for his visa. Full of concern, he wrote Julius on September 29, pleading with him to have his "influential friends" put special pressure on the consulate in Stuttgart:

My dear cousin,

My letter of the 25 Sept. will You have received. I think, You will have understood my thankful feeling for all what You have done for us. When I to day write again, then therefore, because I have heard that it will take yet a very long time till we can come over; perhaps two years. The cause is the fact that the emigration of german subjects has a certain number and this number is reached for this year so that the others, who will emigrate in the next year or in two years have their turn. You understand that is a long time and I cannot believe that we can that time live in this country. I write to You, my dear cousin, because I believe that it will be possible to help me that I can come quicker.

I have seen You have good friends and that is a great thing in such affairs. When You will speak with Your influential friends that they do anything, from what I have written to You, I believe the American Consulate in Stuttgart let me go at once. A chemist with my experience can do a good work for Your country, I am sure. When your friends write some words in such manner, then is done the most, I believe it certainly.

Give me please the answer, if You believe the same, when You have spoken to Your friends.

You can think we have not a good time [at this] time; I cannot write [more], but You will understand me . . .

I remain always Your thankful cousin,

Max Schohl

Before sending this letter, Max received a form letter from the American Consulate in Stuttgart, which had duly received his application and Julius Hess's affidavits. The letter confirmed Max's worst fears. It told him that he and his daughter could not be included in the present year's immigration quota for German citizens, and that his application was on a waiting list for the quotas for future years. Max's number on the waiting list was 24,792. The letter also mentioned the Non-Quota Immigrant Class, indicating that applicants for this category must obtain special forms from the United States Labor Department, to be completed and returned to that department. Max attached a copy of the consulate's formulaic response to his September 29 letter to Julius, along with the following distressed addendum:

My dear cousin,

When I had finished the enclosed letter, I received from the American Consulate, Stuttgart, a printed letter (in German), which I send to You in original. I think, You know any persons who can translate for You it. I would have translated it, but there are so many technical expressions, that I fear, You cannot understand me. You shall know, that some weeks ago I have written to the American Consulate and I have asked for the affidavit You had sent for me and my daughter. This printed letter is the answer to my letter but it does not content any answer to my questions. To Your information I tell You, that I have the number 24,792, what the consulate have written me some weeks ago. The printed letter of the consulate speaks of favoured persons, which shall not wait a long time till comes their turn. For these persons two formulars, Nr. 575 and 633 shall be sent to the Department of Labour; these formulars are to get in the States.

Perhaps You can speak this affair with Your friends or with Your advocate [lawyer], who doubtless know any way to help me. I hope, You have understood my bad English and You can do anything that I can get the permit soon as possible.

I thank You from all my heart my dear cousin.

Yours truly, Max

Here matters stood at the beginning of October 1938. To his extreme consternation, Julius did not get another letter from Max until mid-February 1939, though he received a letter (since lost) in early December from Max's daughter Helene. It was in the interval between Max's last communication in September 1938 and the letter from Helene that the huge state-sponsored pogrom known as Kristallnacht, or "Night of the Crystals," took place in Germany. Julius undoubtedly read about this new wave of terror, which swept across the Reich on the night of November 9–10, in his daily newspaper, the *Charleston Gazette*, and Helene seems to have informed him that the Schohls' own situation had thereby become much more desperate, as their home had been vandalized and Max arrested. It would be years later, however, before Julius learned what had actually happened to Max and his family during that horrific night and in the weeks that followed.

CHAPTER FOUR

"The Night of the Crystals"

"Now the People Will Act"

In the fall of 1938 the Nazi government was anxious to step up its campaign against the Jews still remaining in Germany. In the regime's view, the Jews' continued presence was an affront to the dignity of the Reich. As early as January 1937 the *Sicherheitsdienst* (SD), the security arm of the SS, had recommended the purposeful use of violence as a way of achieving this aim. During the summer of 1938 there were sporadic attacks on synagogues, including some in Munich and Nuremberg. Before launching any systematic terror, however, the regime preferred to have a pretext that might help it justify this action to the world and the German public.

That pretext was delivered on November 7, 1938, by a seventeen-year-old Polish Jew named Herschel Grynszpan, who shot a German diplomat in Paris to protest the deportation of his parents from the Reich in October. Even before the diplomat, Ernst vom Rath, had expired from his wounds, Nazi thugs began vandalizing Jewish houses and businesses in various parts of Germany, primarily in Anhalt and Hesse. The major onslaught, however, came in the immediate aftermath of vom Rath's death on the afternoon of November 9. The news that Rath had died reached Hitler in Munich as he was preparing to address party leaders gathered for the annual commemoration of the Beer Hall Putsch of November 1923. The Führer went into a hasty conference with Goebbels and then abruptly left the hall, ceding the floor to his propaganda minister. After relating the news of vom Rath's death to the party leaders, Goebbels announced, in reference to the violence that had already taken place, that Hitler did not want any demonstrations to be "organized" by the party, but insofar as the actions erupted "spontaneously," they were "not to be hampered." According to one witness, Goebbels's audience understood his remarks as a clear call for more violence, and they signaled their enthusiasm for this prospect with wild applause. The next morning Goebbels wrote an entry in his private diary describing his conversation with Hitler and his address to the Nazi meeting: "I report the matter [of vom Rath's death] to the Führer. He decides: demonstrations should be allowed to continue. The police should be withdrawn. For once the Jews should get the feel of popular anger. That is right. I immediately give the necessary instructions to the police and the Party. Then I speak in that vein to the Party leadership. Stormy applause. All are instantly at the phones. Now the people will act."

What "the people" did during the next thirty-six hours was to engage in a Reich-wide torrent of violence against Jews and Jewish property. Major cities like Berlin, Munich, and Frankfurt were especially hard hit— nine of Berlin's twelve synagogues were destroyed, as were all of Frankfurt's—but smaller towns and villages were affected as well, with some of them using the occasion to become *Judenrein*. The chief perpetrators were SA, though in some cases ordinary citizens joined in. The *New York Times* correspondent in Berlin reported seeing looters handing out goods stolen from smashed Jewish stores, shouting to passersby: "Here are some cheap Christmas presents. Get yours early!" More often, however, people simply stood by and watched, some of them grinning, others shaking their heads in disapproval at the "rowdiness" of the assailants. "The German people do not approve of such treatment of the Jews," insisted one man to the *Times* correspondent. Pursuant to their instructions, the police did not intervene to stop the vandalism, though in some instances they tried to discourage looting. The fire brigades stood by with their hoses coiled as Jewish shops and synagogues burned, going into action only to prevent the fires from spreading to "German property." By the time the action was halted, 267 synagogues had been destroyed and some 7,500 businesses had been vandalized. Hundreds of Jewish cemeteries had also been desecrated or wrecked. The broken glass alone, some of it colored lead-crystal, was valued at millions of marks.

The attacks against property, ugly as they were, were not the worst of it. Some Nazis took this opportunity to beat or even kill Jews they encountered in the streets. There were also cases of premeditated murder: prominent Jews hacked to death in their homes or executed in secluded spots after being dragged from their dwellings. The Austrian Nazis, anxious to show that they deserved their recent inclusion in the Reich, proved especially brutal. An SS squad in Innsbruck stabbed and beat to death the leaders of that town's Jewish community. Throughout the Greater German Reich, some ninety-one Jews were killed during the pogrom. Suicides among Jews increased to 1,000 a month.

It seemed for a time as if the Jews of Flörsheim might be spared the wave of terror sweeping across Germany. The town remained quiet on November 9, and early on the morning of November 10 the local police received a radio message from the regional government in Wiesbaden instructing them "to prevent assaults against Jews, including damage to Jewish property." A short while later, however, another message carried quite different instructions: "In revision of the previous instructions, personal assaults and looting are to be avoided, [but] otherwise there is freedom of action against Jewish property. In order to maintain law, order, and security, all Jewish shops are to be closed before the beginning of the business day."

Whether the police actually passed this green-light signal on to the local Nazis is unclear. Apparently the SA leadership in Wiesbaden had telephoned the Brownshirts in Flörsheim during the night to find out what was happening there. The answer was nothing much, so far. That changed abruptly at 10:00 in the morning of November 10. According to testimony by Robert Gerson at postwar hearings on the events of that day, a group of four SA men entered the feed store belonging to his brother-in-law, Martin Altmaier, and thoroughly vandalized it. Gerson, who observed the action without being attacked, recognized one of the vandals as a worker from the nearby Opel plant at Rüsselsheim. He guessed that the other assailants were also from Rüsselsheim. Armed with hammers, picks, and an ax, the men spent approximately twenty minutes wrecking Altmaier's store. During the entire proceeding they uttered hardly a word.

If Nazis from Flörsheim were apparently not involved in the vandalism of Altmaier's property, they certainly had a major part in the next anti-Jewish operation that day: the destruction and looting of the local synagogue. The action began at 11:30 in the morning, when a dozen men, most of them local SA members, showed up at the building armed with picks and crowbars and commanded the janitor, a Christian named Johann Willewohl, to let them in. Once inside the men smashed all the windows and broke up much of the furniture. One of the vandals climbed up on the roof and dismantled the six-pointed Star of David, which he tossed down to the street. Before leaving, the men gathered up various sacred and valuable objects, including Torah rolls, prayer shawls, candelabras, tapestries, and rugs. These they loaded on to a Jewish *Totenwagen*, or hearse carriage, which they had pulled from its shed next to the synagogue and parked in the street. Shortly thereafter one of the SA vandals returned to the building with a group of local children and demanded of Willewohl that they be admitted and shown the wreckage. When Willewohl demurred, the man smashed in the front door with an ax and let the children enter. The kids then proceeded to trash what had not already been wrecked, making, according to Willewohl's later testimony, "a complete end" of the place. Some of the kids donned prayer shawls and went howling through the streets. Willewohl repeatedly called for help from the police, whose station was located nearby, but no officers appeared. Nor did anyone intervene later that day when SA thugs, accompanied by some children and other townspeople, returned to the scene and pushed the booty-laden hearse through the village to the banks of the River Main, where they burned some of the religious objects and threw the rest into the river.

Sali Kahn, who had headed the Jewish Gemeinde in Flörsheim before Max Schohl took over, observed the destruction of his community's sacred patrimony from a window in his house. It was too much for him. A war veteran like Max, Kahn still possessed the banner that his fellow citizens had hung over the main street to greet him upon his return from the First World War; it read, "You Are Assured of the Thanks of Your Fatherland." Kahn now retrieved this banner, along with his military helmet, from storage, and as soon as night fell he took these objects down to the river and tossed them in.

That same evening an order went out to the local SA to "go after the Jews," meaning the private homes of prominent Jewish citizens. The order probably came from the SA office in Wiesbaden, since a Brownshirt from that office showed up at the meeting of the local SA at their tavern headquarters where the action was discussed. Heinrich Oesterling, chief of the Flörsheim SA, was apparently not present at this meeting (he had recently moved back to Höchst), nor was Mayor Ludwig Stamm, the local Nazi party boss. According to his wife's exculpatory testimony after the war, Stamm was away at his small country house during these crucial hours, enjoying his favorite pastime of hunting wild stag. This of course was a convenient alibi for the mayor, and it is possible that Stamm, not wanting to bear responsibility for anything too dirty, had left town on purpose.

Before setting out on their evening's rampage against Jewish homes, the Flörsheim SA men were joined by a group of workers from the Organisation Todt, a Nazi construction outfit that was building a section of the new *Autobahn* nearby. The Todt men had a flatbed truck at their disposal, as well as an assortment of tools such as sledgehammers, picks, and wrecking bars. A local SA member who worked for the *Reichsbahn* (national railway) apparently supplied the group with additional wrecking equipment from railway supplies.

For their first victim that night the vandals chose Hermann Herzheimer, whose large home lay just down the street from the SA's informal tavern-headquarters near the train station. Arriving at 9:30, the men broke in through the front door and, over the course of the next half hour, systematically destroyed everything in the house. Moving from room to room, they broke all the windows, pried apart the furniture, sliced open mattresses, smashed crockery and mirrors, and demolished a beautiful grand piano. They pulled clothing from drawers and pitched it out the broken windows, festooning the surrounding trees and hedges with articles of the Herzheimers' underwear. The Herzheimers themselves were not molested, but as they cowered in one of the upstairs bedrooms they understandably feared for their lives. When the vandals finally left they took away money, jewelry, silverware, and even some of the family papers. (A few days later, a local high school teacher read the love letters between Hermann Herzheimer and his wife to his classes.) As the demolition was proceeding the neighbors watched from their windows but did not venture outside. The police also made no effort to intervene, and no arrests were made in subsequent days even though some of the perpetrators were well known to the authorities.

Max Schohl's stately home in Albanusstrasse was next on the Nazis' hit list that evening. The cry "On to Schohl" rang out as soon as the demolition at Herzheimer's was completed. Arriving by truck at a little after 11:00, the thugs, about thirty in all, used their construction tools to break down the heavy outer gate and then goose-stepped across the courtyard to the house itself. Max, having been in Frankfurt the day before and seen the destruction there, was worried that something similar might happen in Flörsheim. He did not, however, believe that any private homes would be attacked, least of all his own. At 8:00 he had told his family that he was going to bed, and he had advised them to do the same.

As soon as the vandals broke into the house, they began breaking windows and smashing furniture on the first floor. In the living room they tipped over an enormous bookshelf, spilling volumes of Goethe and Schiller across the floor. Max, accompanied by his wife and older daughter Hela, rushed downstairs, leaving Käthe with her aged grandmother in an upstairs bedroom. While Max tried to remonstrate with the intruders, some of whom he recognized as patrons of his now-closed soup kitchen, Liesel Schohl subjected the thugs to indignant questions. "What do you think you're doing here?" she asked. "What do you people want of my family and me?" One of the men paused long enough from his wrecking work to reply: "You shouldn't have married a Jew, you dirty sow." In her own postwar testimony, Liesel Schohl claimed to have known at least four of the intruders by name and to have recognized a few others without knowing exactly who they were. She noticed that the axes they were carrying all had brand new handles, which suggested to her that the action must have been planned. When one of the men tried to go upstairs, presumably to wreck the rooms up there as well, she blocked the stairway with her body. "Is it not enough," she cried, "that my husband's aged and sick mother is likely to die of shock?" Thereupon the man on the stairs pulled a railing from the banister and struck her with it in the chest, injuring her badly enough to require medical attention. The vandals retreated from the stairway, however, and contented themselves with completing their wreckage of the lower floor. Hela Schohl, meanwhile, ran into the courtyard to see if any fires had been set around the house; establishing that there were none, she set off down the street in search of the police. Needless to say, she could find no officers in the vicinity. After about twenty or thirty minutes, a man stationed outside the house blew a whistle, whereupon the vandals promptly exited the Schohl residence, climbed into their truck, and drove away.

"When I returned to the house," recalled Hela Schohl in her postwar testimony, "I found nothing left intact" on the first floor. Her younger sister Käthe recalled a similar scene of complete devastation. All the furniture, including big heavy wooden tables and chairs imported from Italy, lay scattered about in pieces. So did a huge grandfather clock, a Schohl family heirloom that Max had delighted in winding every day, but now would wind no more. On the ceiling and walls gaping holes revealed where light fixtures had once been attached. Hanging askew was a painting of Max in his military officer's uniform, its surface slashed by an ax blade. In the kitchen bits of food littered the floor, mixed with glass from broken crockery. According to Käthe, who ventured downstairs after the vandals had left, Max said nothing as he surveyed the mess, save to tell her to go over to the next-door neighbors to get milk for her grandmother. Fearing to go into the street, she climbed over the courtyard wall to the neighbors, the Hoffmanns, who gave her the milk, adding, "We are so ashamed."

The Schohls' neighbors may indeed have been ashamed, but, like those living next to the Herzheimers, they were careful to keep their heads down during the vandalism. As one of the Albanusstrasse neighbors reported in her postwar testimony: "At about 10:00 o'clock we heard noise [at the Schohls'], one could clearly hear windows being broken and furniture smashed. We went to the window and saw the tumult at the Schohls'. A large crowd [almost a hundred in all] had gathered outside the house. I could see that several people were vandalizing the interior. People were going in and out. I watched for a few minutes and then went to bed, completely in shock." Another neighbor reported: "We saw a crowd in the street in front of the Schohl house. One could hear glass breaking. I didn't watch for very long, since the whole thing seemed too terrible."

Reporting the next day on the anti-Semitic violence in Flörsheim, the local paper employed the same self-righteous justifications and whitewashing terminology adopted by the Nazi-controlled press across the Reich:

A people has defended itself. When on Wednesday the news of the death of the German representative in Paris, vom Rath, became known, there arose here in Flörsheim a storm of indignation, just as in the rest of the Reich. Once again a Jew had committed murder. One had to expect an explosion of the folk-soul, and it was not long in coming. On Friday morning people began venting their anger in demonstrations. Curses were repeatedly leveled at this people [the Jews], who operate through murder and slander. All day long the rage fermented, finally boiling over during the night. And yet not a single Jew suffered any injury to his person—only inanimate things took the force of the people's frustration. The time has clearly ended when 99 percent of the population will allow themselves to be terrorized by a few. The Jew has played out his hand in Germany.

If the Flörsheim residents who participated in the destruction of Max Schohl's house during Kristallnacht seemed to have forgotten the chemist's generosity to his hometown, their memories proved equally faulty when they faced legal proceedings after the war for their actions on the night of November 10. Virtually to a man, the defendants testified that they could not recall doing anything untoward that night, nor could they remember any other individuals by name who might have done anything more than break a window or two. One of the defendants, Josef Hoffmann (no relation to the Schohls' neighbors), claimed that he had entered the Schohl house only to protect Max's aged mother, whose bedroom door he allegedly barred to the intruders. He further claimed to have seen no Flörsheimer among the vandals, only outsiders. Another defendant, Georg Kohl, testified that he had heard something at the SA meeting that evening about an impending "*Judenaktion*," but had neither taken part in the action himself nor known of any other Flörsheimer who had. One Josef Hartmann admitted to having seen someone tip over the Schohl's bookcase, but he could not say who that person might have been. The man who, according to Liesel Schohl, had called her a "filthy sow" claimed to have entered the house only out of "curiosity" and to have heard *another man* exchange words with Max's wife. In an intriguing and creative variation on this theme, another defendant, Heinrich Kraft, claimed to have done no wrecking at the Schohls' because the previous demolition at the Herzheimers' had filled him with "revulsion." In response to Liesel Schohl's accusation that he had smashed up her home with a crowbar, Kraft protested that he could not have done so, "because for most of the time that I was in the Schohl house Frau Schohl held me so tightly I could not move." Claiming innocence for himself, Kraft further insisted that "most of the destruction was done by strangers." The publican who ran the tavern that served as the SA's headquarters claimed to have heard nothing about a "*Judenaktion*" or stand-down by the local police; meanwhile, a former policeman insisted that the police had offered "protection" to the Herzheimer family. In his own postwar testimony, former mayor Ludwig Stamm insisted that he had undertaken an "energetic investigation" into the violence upon his return to town, only to come up empty with regard to any local participation in the affair. The court accepted Stamm's astounding claim at face value, as it did the testimony of half of the other defendants charged with crimes during the Kristallnacht pogrom. Of the eighteen defendants, only nine were found guilty on any of the counts leveled against them; they were sentenced to small fines or to light prison terms of between seven and twelve months.

On the morning following the demolition of their house, the Schohls' neighbors, the Hoffmanns, brought over breakfast and again expressed their shame over what had happened. A little later a policeman appeared and informed Max and his family that they would have to clean up the mess in the street outside their house by themselves, per orders from the Führer. (In fact, the Nazi government ordered Jews across the Reich to clean up all the wreckage from Kristallnacht on the grounds that they had brought this destruction upon themselves.) After delivering this message, the Flörsheim policeman assured Max that he and his colleagues had known nothing about any impending action against the Jews and had been caught completely off guard by the action. Max said nothing to the cop, but he muttered to his family: "This is not my Germany any more."

In addition to cleaning up the mess left by Nazi vandals during the Kristallnacht pogrom, Germany's Jews were ordered by the Hitler government to pay the costs of restoring their homes and businesses out of their own pockets. The Reich would confiscate any payments made by insurance companies. Furthermore, the Jewish community as a whole was ordered to pay an "atonement fine" of 1 billion marks to compensate the German government for the costs and difficulties sustained during the "people's rage." This sum was to be amassed by collecting from individual Jews across the Reich 20 percent of their total fortunes, payable in three installments on December 15, 1938, February 15, 1939, and August 15, 1939. Currency and stock certificates were the only acceptable forms of payment. Realizing that many

Jews might need to sell off personal valuables like jewels and art-works to raise their contributions, the government established a buy-ing office in Berlin to purchase such items. Purchase prices were set by government-appointed experts.

Meanwhile, armed with brooms and shovels, the Schohls dutifully cleared the street outside their house of the shattered remains of their property. While they were doing so, a car with Danish license plates drove slowly by. Suddenly the car stopped and the driver got out and took pictures of this curious scene. Max was elated. "Now *das Ausland* [the world abroad] will see what has happened here and take action," he predicted confidently to his daughters.

"THE CIVILIZED WORLD STANDS REVOLTED"

The rest of the world was indeed shocked and appalled by what tran-spired in Germany during the "Night of the Crystals." Politicians and opinion makers around the world, especially in America, rushed to re-buke the Nazis for what almost everyone saw as a relapse into bar-barism. Active heads of state, on the other hand, generally waited a while to comment publicly on the issue, and then calibrated their prac-tical responses very carefully.

Typical of the initial condemnations from America was the response of Thomas Dewey, the ex-governor of New York, who fulminated: "The civilized world stands revolted by a bloody pogrom against a defenseless people. Every instinct in us cries out in protest against the outrages which have taken place in Germany during the last five years and which sank to new depths in the organized frenzies of the last few days." For-mer President Herbert Hoover said that the leaders of Nazi Germany "are taking Germany back 450 years in civilization to Torquemada's ex-pulsion of the Jews from Spain. They are bringing to Germany not alone the condemnation of the public opinion of the world. These men are building their own condemnation by mankind for centuries to come."

Newspaper editorials across America, in large cities and small, picked up on this theme of neo-barbarism. The *New York Times* spoke of a "wave of destruction, looting, and incendiarism unparalleled in Germany since the Thirty Years War, and in Europe generally since the Bolshevist revolution." The *Washington Post* said that only the St. Bartholomew's Day massacre in France in 1572 had equaled Kristallnacht in primitive fury. The *St. Louis Dispatch* declared: "Reprisal against a whole people for the crime of an overwrought youth is a throwback to barbarity." The *Charleston Gazette*, Julius Hess's local paper, put Louis P. Lochner's graphic Associated Press stories about the pogrom on its front page for several days running; it also reported extensively on the post-pogrom fines imposed on Germany's Jews, condemning them as an effort to drive a whole people into poverty and exile.

The European papers, too, bristled with indignation, and sometimes with calls for active protest against the inhumane policies of the Reich government. Declared the Danish *Nationaltidende* on November 12:

> There happen in the course of time many things on which one must take a stand out of regard for one's own human dignity, even if this should involve a personal or national risk. Silence in the face of crimes committed may be regarded as a form of participation therein—equally punishable whether committed by individuals or nations. . . . One must at least have the courage to protest, even if you feel that you do not have power to prevent a violation of justice, or even to mitigate the consequences thereof. . . . Now that it has been announced that after being plundered, tortured and terrorized, this heap of human beings [the Jews of Germany] will be expelled and thrown over the gate of the nearest neighbor, the question no longer remains an internal one and Germany's voice will not be the only one that will be heard in the council of nations.

The newspaper reports and editorials helped inspire popular demonstrations against the Reich in many cities in Europe and America. In London and Paris large crowds protested outside the German embassy buildings, and there was an anti-German rally in Copenhagen. According to *Time* magazine, American feeling had not been "so outraged since the sinking of the *Lusitania*." Anti-German sentiment ran so high in New York City that Mayor Fiorello LaGuardia felt compelled to provide police protection for the German consulate there. Stealing a leaf from

Theodore Roosevelt, who as police commissioner for New York had once used Jewish policemen to guard an anti-Semitic German preacher, LaGuardia appointed an all-Jewish detachment of police under the command of a Captain Max Finkelstein to guard the German consulate.

Berlin was taken aback by all the fuss. Even Goebbels had to admit that the pogrom, with whose organization he had had so much to do, was giving the Reich a black eye abroad. "The foreign press is very bad, especially the American," he confided in his diary on November 12. Hoping to stem the tide of hostile commentary, he invited the Berlin-based foreign correspondents to his office and "explained the whole thing to them."

Goebbels's "explanations," however, had little impact on the foreign press, which remained almost universally hostile. Yet condemnation of the pogrom was one thing, demands for significant practical retribution quite another. Even the most outraged papers typically called for only the most modest of retaliatory measures, and many papers counseled against antagonizing the Nazi Reich at all.

Horrified though they were by the Nazi pogrom, America's main Jewish organizations also adopted a cautious stance, limiting their public response to interfaith worship services and their private activities to the usual jawboning with the president and his advisors.

The counselors of caution need not have worried about an overreaction on the part of the world's policy makers. Governmental leaders in Europe and America, although as shocked as anyone by the events of November 9–10 in Germany, were not about to let this incident dictate their policies either on relations with Berlin or on the thorny question of Jewish immigration.

In Britain Prime Minister Neville Chamberlain, whose name was already becoming synonymous with appeasement of Hitler, and who privately acknowledged that he found anti-Jewish prejudice "understandable," feared that the Nazi pogrom would complicate his efforts to work with the Nazi leader. The British government, in its eagerness to limit the possible damage to Anglo-German relations, put forth the view that Nazi violence against the Jews had peaked with the November events and could now be expected to abate. Chamberlain rejected proposals from some members of the House of Commons to pressure Berlin to modify its racial policies, claiming that Britain was "not in a position to frighten Germany." Chamberlain's government also continued to insist that Britain was not in a position substantially to increase its intake of German-Jewish refugees. Berlin's refusal to let emigrating Jews remove most of their assets made them "undesirable immigrants" for a financially strapped Britain. A proposal from Winston Churchill that Britain might settle Jewish immigrants in some underdeveloped colony like British Guiana also went nowhere. Opening up an undeveloped tropical colony for immigration, said Chamberlain, was "a long and expensive business." Rather than making room for substantial numbers of new immigrants, London decided in mid-November to show its concern for the plight of the Jews by expanding possibilities for Jewish children to come to Britain for temporary refuge from persecution. This set the stage for the famous *Kindertransport*, or transport of children, which between December 1938 and the outbreak of World War II brought thousands of Jewish children to safety in Britain. Yet valuable as this program undoubtedly was, it did nothing for all the adult Jews seeking permanent settlement abroad. Their needs, London asserted, could best be accommodated by traditional receivers of large-scale immigration like the United States, Canada, and some of the South American countries.

In America the consequences of Kristallnacht in terms of practical policy were no more substantial than in Britain; indeed, they were arguably weaker. In reporting on America's *Lusitania*-like outrage over the Nazi pogrom, *Time* magazine proposed that FDR now had a "mandate from the people" that he "would undoubtedly translate into foreign policy." But FDR was not at all convinced that he had any such mandate to revise America's policy toward Nazi Germany or, for that matter, to change U.S. policy on Jewish immigration. Certainly he was aware of the widespread popular revulsion over Kristallnacht, and he fully shared in this himself, but he did not believe that this moral outrage significantly altered the American public's reluctance to alienate Germany or to help solve Hitler's "Jewish problem" by taking the Jews off his hands. As a way of registering America's displeasure with the

German government without over-antagonizing Berlin, therefore, FDR limited himself to recalling Ambassador Wilson "for consultation," adding a rebuke of the Reich to his announcement of the recall:

> The news of the past few days from Germany has deeply shocked public opinion in the U.S. Such news from any part of the world would inevitably produce a similar profound reaction among American people in every part of the nation. I myself could scarcely believe that such things could occur in a twentieth century civilization. With a view to having a first-hand picture of the situation in Germany I asked the Secretary of State to order our Ambassador in Berlin to return at once for report and consultation.

The president was careful to offer no more than this time-honored gesture of official displeasure. He admitted at his news conference announcing Wilson's recall that no formal protest had been made to the German government. To a reporter's question if he would "recommend a relaxation of immigration restrictions so that Jewish refugees could be received in this country," FDR replied, "That is not in contemplation; we have the quota system." In mid-November, when the British government offered to give up the bulk of the 65,000 places allotted to British immigrants to the United States under the American quota system, so that these slots might be added to the German quota, the State Department, with FDR's approval, rejected the proposal out of hand. With respect to the plight of endangered Jews, the president's sole concession was to recommend to the Labor Department that the temporary visas of some 12,000 to 15,000 German nationals, most of them Jews, presently in America working in colleges and in similar positions, be extended indefinitely so they would not have to return to the Reich. "As I understand it," FDR carefully added, "these visitors cannot apply for American citizenship."

The press and popular response to FDR's recall of Wilson and his other limited measures tended to confirm that the president had read the public mood correctly. While applauding the ambassadorial recall as a gesture of America's revulsion over Kristallnacht, most papers cautioned against doing anything to interfere in Germany's internal affairs. There was considerable relief that America had not severed diplomatic ties with Germany and had confined itself to actions showing that, as one paper put it, the American people had "no desire to go to war with Germany." Although some liberal papers argued that the ambassadorial recall was too weak and that America should now liberalize its immigration policies, most major dailies insisted that Washington should keep its barriers intact. Even the *New York Times* editorialized against enlarging the quotas, stating, "The United States . . . cannot be expected to perform today . . . the historic service it has previously performed." Public opinion polls taken in the aftermath of the Nazi pogrom showed that most Americans were still opposed to any significant changes in immigration policy. Pity the German Jews yes, but keep them the hell out of America, was the message of the day.

"Protective Custody"

Max Schohl was not following the foreign response to Kristallnacht. He was one of approximately 30,000 Jews who were forced to spend the weeks immediately following the pogrom in temporary "protective confinement" in concentration camps at Dachau, Buchenwald, and Sachsenhausen. The arrest order, issued by SD chief Reinhard Heydrich on November 10, encompassed all physically fit male Jews between eighteen and sixty years of age, "especially the well-off." The horror of a concentration camp experience, following upon the terror of the pogrom, was meant to convince Jews remaining in Germany to emigrate as soon as they were released. By reducing the prominent and wealthier Jews to utter helplessness, the confinement also offered more opportunities for plunder and theft.

In the late morning of November 11 a Flörsheim policeman appeared at the Schohls' wrecked home with a warrant for Max's arrest. Max was ordered to pack a small suitcase and accompany the policeman to the train station, where he was to catch the next train for Frankfurt. Exactly where he would go from there, and how long he would be gone, was not specified. As he was preparing to leave, his wife advised him to take along his heavy overcoat and gloves. "I won't need them," said Max. Liesel Schohl also urged her husband to take his war medals, but Max insisted that he had no need for them either. Undeterred, Liesel put Max's medals in the pocket of his overcoat and threw the coat over his shoulders as he went out the door. Like Max, she had no idea where he was going or when he might return. Shortly after his departure, the mailman came by and told Frau Schohl that he had heard that Max and some other local Jews were being sent to a camp called Buchenwald, near Weimar. The Schohls knew nothing of this place. "It's like Dachau," said the mailman.

Max, along with four other Flörsheim Jews—Martin Altmaier, Theodor Birnzweig, Jakob Kahn, and Sali Kahn—arrived just after noon in Frankfurt. They were immediately loaded on to a truck and driven to a large exhibition facility, the Festhalle Frankfurt. The men were detained at this facility for a day before being sent by train to Weimar, and from there on to the Buchenwald concentration camp a few miles away.

Established on the magnificent grounds of the former princely Turn und Taxis estate in August 1937, the Buchenwald camp had been enlarged in the summer of 1938 to accommodate infusions of new inmates. Jewish prisoners already there were told that the new inmates would be Jews. Near the middle of the camp stood a tall oak tree under which Goethe had come to meditate and admire the view of a nearby beech forest and gently rolling hills. "I often came here," Goethe wrote, "to look out at the world's richness and splendor. . . . It is a place where one can feel great and free."

Max did not compose a written account of what happened to him during the four weeks of his "protective custody" in Buchenwald, and during his absence he was able to send his family only one cursory postcard. For obvious reasons, this communication could not contain any details about what was actually going on. It said simply:

My dear wife and children,

I am sitting here and doing well. I am not allowed to receive mail. Please do not write to me or send anything. Also,

please do not address any questions to the headquarters
here.

Hearty greetings,
Your father

From the graphic accounts of other survivors of this experience, we
know quite a bit about what Max must have gone through during his
trip to the camp and in the camp itself, and we now know also that this
first mass incarceration of Jews amounted to a horrific foretaste of what
was to come in the labor and death camps during the war.

One of Max's fellow detainees in Buchenwald, a resident of Wiesbaden named Hans Berger, penned the following description of conditions in the detention hall in Frankfurt and the train trip to Weimar:

A howling mob received us at the entrance to the Festhalle. Jeers, rocks
thrown—in short, the atmosphere of a pogrom. We ran into the hall and
immediately got a taste of what was in store for us. Just opposite the entrance laid a corpse. The fellow seemed to have suffered a heart attack.
In the cavernous hall thousands of people, divided into small groups,
each watched over by SS men in black uniforms or civilian clothes, performed various physical exercises. Others sat on the floor resting, or
stood at tables to be registered by SA men or police. The exercises were
meant to help keep the new arrivals occupied, in so far as they were not
being registered. . . . I saw how one man had to do deep knee-bends
with his face pressed to the wall. Naturally he fell backwards. Every time
he did so the SS thug standing behind him struck him with a riding
whip. This process repeated itself perhaps one hundred times, until the
poor man was no longer capable of standing. . . . Later we were driven in
groups to the south train station in Frankfurt, where, again at a running
pace, we were forced to go through a gauntlet of yelling, stone-throwing
men. One of the men tripped me, sending me sprawling lengthwise to
the ground. At the station we were loaded into an unheated special train
with locked doors, and as soon as the train filled up we moved off under
armed guard into the night, toward an unknown destination. Along the

way came the command, "Take off your coats!" so that we would more keenly feel the cold.

Upon arrival at the train station in Weimar, the detainees were subjected to more mistreatment. Wrote Berger:

> We had to get off the train in groups and, under a hail of blows with steel rods and rifle butts, run along the platform and down some stairs into the underpass. Woe be to him who collapsed or fell down the stairs. . . . In the underpass itself we had to stand in rows of ten, the first guy in line with his face pressed against the wall; the guards ensured that we were packed together like sardines. The poor sods who stood at the tail end of the rows had to endure blows and kicks designed to compress the lines. I stood in the middle and eventually found it hardly possible to breathe; and all the while whip blows rained down on our exposed heads.

Describing this same nightmare odyssey from the detention center in Frankfurt to the train station in Weimar, another (unidentified) survivor reported that the police in Frankfurt collected the detainees' valuables and placed them in large envelopes, as if for safekeeping. Many of the prisoners never saw these envelopes again, or if they got them back they found that the packets had been pilfered. During the train trip to Weimar SS guards made the Jews do more exercises in the crowded aisles. The guards also forced the Jews to hold their suitcases in front of them at arm's length for agonizingly long periods of time; to ensure that the men did not lower their burdens the guards held their daggers just below their captives' outstretched arms. Prisoners who wished to go the bathroom were required to stand at attention and phrase their request in a precise formula; anyone who deviated from the ritual had to stand in the aisle until he soiled himself. Prisoners who fell asleep were slapped back into wakefulness. According to the same witness, only one of the captives escaped molestation. "This man sat with his coat thrown over his shoulders, Napoleon-fashion. In his eyes was a look of horror, and his face had the pallor of a corpse. On his coat were affixed the ribbons of the Iron Cross and the Bavarian Service Medal. He sat entirely immobile throughout the night. Perhaps the watchdogs thought he was dead." One cannot help wondering if this corpselike creature was Max Schohl.

Despite its recent enlargement, the Buchenwald concentration camp lacked sufficient quarters to accommodate all the new arrivals, some 10,000 in number. Additional emergency barracks had to be hastily erected, a task that fell to the inmates themselves. Berger reported:

> These emergency barracks were a story unto themselves. They were essentially large huts thrown together out of raw pine boards, their few narrow windows affording inadequate ventilation, and their small doors hardly big enough for two men to stand in. The interiors of the barracks were broken up into four levels of compartments stacked on top of each other like wall-units in a store. The compartments were not high enough for a man to sit up in, but just long enough to stretch out in. Here we had to lie at night, on the bare wood without straw or blankets, and in the clothes in which we had been arrested. For our bodily needs we used an area outside the barracks next to the place where the dead were collected, a large pit with a bar over it, a rather doubtful latrine. . . . We could only use this latrine before the barracks were closed for the night; the death penalty awaited anyone leaving the barracks after the closing hour.

Primitive housing and sanitary facilities, of course, were not the only indignities that the Jewish detainees had to endure in Buchenwald. Ewald Blumenthal, the banker-father of Michael Blumenthal (a Jewish immigrant to America who became President Jimmy Carter's secretary of the treasury), was among the 10,000 Jews shipped to the camp in the wake of Kristallnacht. As related by Michael in his captivating family memoir, Ewald and the other detainees went through an "arrival ceremony" at Buchenwald even worse than their ordeal during the intermediary stop at Weimar. After being made to run at top speed through an iron gate bearing the inscription "To Each His Own," the prisoners were greeted by vicious guards who struck them repeatedly with steel rods and whips. Those who fell down in the rush were often trampled or beaten to death. Some of the prisoners were forced to beat each other for the amusement of their tormentors. Dozens died from the brutal "welcome" they received.

The inmates' daily routine at Buchenwald, as in the other camps, included four "roll calls": endless periods of standing at attention in the cold and wet while the guards ascertained that all were accounted for, alive or dead. Again to amuse themselves, the guards often made the men perform the "Saxon salute": stand ramrod straight with arms behind their heads for hours at a time. Anyone who faltered was beaten. Following the first roll call and a meager breakfast the prisoners were sent off to do twelve to fourteen hours of hard labor in a nearby stone quarry. It was not long before the striped uniforms that the prisoners had been issued in place of their street clothes started to hang loosely off their battered frames. The uniforms of the Jewish inmates (there were other detainees in the camp as well, including political prisoners and common criminals) were marked with identification numbers and triangular yellow patches, precursors to the tattooed numbers Jewish inmates later wore in the death camps and the yellow stars that all Jews, starting in 1941, were forced to wear whenever they went out in public. Those prisoners who managed to hold on to a little money could secure small favors through bribes to the guards, and the camp loudspeakers announced repeatedly that "rich Jews" who signed over their assets to the SS would receive better treatment, perhaps even early release.

Release from this hell was undoubtedly a constant preoccupation for Max Schohl, as it must have been for all the inmates. Fortunately Max's earliest possible delivery from Buchenwald was also a priority for his resourceful wife, Liesel. Even before learning exactly where Max had been sent, Liesel wrote a letter to Emmy Göring, the wife of Hermann Göring, pleading with her to ask her husband to intervene in favor of the Reich Marshal's highly decorated "war comrade," Max Schohl. Liesel turned to Emmy Göring because she had heard that the Reich Marshal's wife disapproved of the anti-Jewish persecution and was at bottom "a good soul." Emmy Göring's response to Liesel Schohl has not survived, but daughter Käthe recalls that her mother received a "nice" letter from Emmy informing her that in principle she did not interfere in her husband's political affairs. Emmy advised Frau Schohl to write directly to

Göring. This Liesel promptly did, emphasizing in her letter Max's distinguished military record and passionate love of country.

Göring never replied, and Liesel had to assume that the Reich Marshal was unwilling to help her husband. This does not seem to have been the case, however. At the beginning of his fourth week at Buchenwald, Max was suddenly called in to see the commandant, who asked him, "What is your connection to Göring?" When Max replied that he had none, the commandant held up a piece of paper, explaining that it was a letter from the Reich Marshal ordering the release of "Retired Captain Max Schohl." Looking Max up and down, the commandant added, "I'm sure you'll tell the Reich Marshal that you've been treated well." Shortly after this meeting, Max was given his release, making him one of the first Jewish detainees to leave the camp. Unbeknownst to him, Reinhard Heydrich had also issued an order for the early release from the camps of "front fighters" of the First World War. Whether Max's early release resulted from the specific intervention by Göring or from the more general order from Heydrich is impossible to know.

When Max, and a few days later three of the other Flörsheim Jews who had been sent to Buchenwald, returned to their hometown, their appearance was a shock to the townspeople. "Their treatment must have been extremely bad," reported one resident in his diary. "They are physically and mentally completely broken. When one asks them [about their experience] they do not answer. They are martyrs for their belief. Martin Altmaier is still not back."

Although he returned slightly earlier than the others, Max was as broken as they were. His younger daughter recalls that when he appeared at the door he was so changed that she hardly recognized him. He had lost a great deal of weight and seemed barely capable of standing. Indeed, he was so weak that his wife had to carry him up the stairs and put him to bed. She called in the family physician, a Catholic named Wilhelm Hamel, who continued to treat Jews when many other gentile doctors would not. Dr. Hamel told the Schohl women that Max did not show signs of having been beaten, but he was severely malnourished. Max himself refused to tell the doctor anything about his experiences in the camp, and this for good reason: upon their release the Jews were warned that if they talked about what had happened to them they would be sent back.

"I Wouldn't Want to Be a Jew in Germany!"

Even as Max Schohl and his fellow Jewish prisoners languished in Buchenwald, Hitler's government drafted additional measures to plunder Jewish assets, ensuring that any Jews remaining in the country would have few resources to sustain themselves. On November 12, 1938, the same day that Göring ordered Jews to pay the billion-mark "atonement" bill for Kristallnacht, the Reich Marshal also announced a "Law for the Exclusion of Jews from the German Economy." As of January 1, 1939, most Jewish business activity was to cease. Jews were to be excluded from the "operation of retail stores, pawn shops, mail order houses, and the independent exercise of handicrafts." They were also banned from trading at public markets, fairs, and exhibitions. Jews were prohibited from holding positions as foremen or supervisors in any factory or company.

In Flörsheim this economic "Aryanization" had relatively little impact, since the remaining Jewish businesses—those of Hermann Herzheimer, Jakob Kahn, and Martin Altmaier—had already been so decimated during Kristallnacht that they were considered virtually worthless. Mayor Stamm, ordered by the regional government to ensure "the quickest possible transfer of Jewish businesses to Aryan ownership," could find no gentile takers for the remains of what had once been prosperous businesses. Max Schohl, of course, had no business left to "Aryanize," and to raise money for his contribution to the Jewish "atonement fine" he had to sell off some of his books and other personal items that had survived the Nazi vandals on November 10. He also gave up his car, which in any case he would not have been able to continue to drive, since as of December 3, 1938, Jews were banned from owning automobiles and required to turn in their drivers' licenses.

Following an order from Berlin in early 1939 to liquidate or Aryanize Jewish religious properties, cultural foundations, and Jewish Gemeinde-owned charity institutions (with the exception of those that furthered emigration), the Flörsheim Gemeinde, with Max as executor, sold the Jewish community house adjoining the gutted synagogue to Johann and Barbara Willewohl, who had already been living in the house for two years. (Johann Willewohl had tried in his capacity as janitor of the synagogue to protect the building during the November pogrom.) The Willewohls stayed on in the community house, but most of the synagogue was torn down in spring 1939. Only the wall facing the street and a rear wall of the upper story of the building remained intact. This rear wall was hastily stuccoed-over, so as to hide the religious paintings and Hebrew inscriptions that decorated it. The name of the street on which the building stood, Synagogengasse, was changed to Mälzergasse.

As soon as he was able to get back on his feet, Max was ordered to report weekly to the Gestapo in Frankfurt, which insisted upon keeping abreast the of the Schohls' plans to emigrate. He was told that if he did not leave soon, he could expect further punitive measures, including the possible incarceration of his entire family in a Jewish-only "ghetto." (Hermann Göring had proposed the creation of Jewish ghettos right after Kristallnacht, but Heydrich had opposed this idea on the grounds that the ghettos might become "hiding places for criminal activities," and the question of ghettoizing the Jews was put off for the time being.) Hoping to expedite Jewish emigration, Reich Minister of Economics Walther Funk instructed the nation's chambers of commerce and industry to provide letters of recommendation to Jews preparing to emigrate.

As if it had not already done enough to convince Jews to leave Germany, the Hitler government imposed yet another raft of discriminatory measures in late 1938 and early 1939. These regulations were designed to further seal off the Jewish community from the rest of the nation. Henceforth, Jews could no longer own radios. In Flörsheim the radio ban affected Robert Gerson, Siegfried Weill, and Max Schohl. Jews were also prohibited from attending theaters, cinemas, concerts, and art galleries. For the Schohl girls, this meant forgoing their periodic trips to the movies in Frankfurt and Mainz, and for Max it meant no more excursions to the Frankfurt region's symphony and opera houses, theaters, and art museums. On November 15 the central government ordered the expulsion of all Jewish children from the regular public schools. Henceforth, they would be obliged to attend Jewish-only schools. Explaining this action, a Nazi education official insisted that after vom Rath's assassination, "one could not demand of a German teacher that he teach Jewish children," nor could it be expected that "German children [would be willing] to sit in the same classroom with Jewish children." The Schohl girls were not affected by this order because they were already attending Jewish schools in Mainz. As of 1938 they were learning skills that were meant to make them more attractive as immigrants. Hela was studying to be a seamstress, while Käthe was learning cosmetics. Summing up the Reich government's latest spate of discriminatory legislation, Hermann Göring exclaimed, "I wouldn't want to be a Jew in Germany!"

Whether or not they *wished* to remain in Germany—many Jews stayed on only because the Hitler government made it economically impossible for them to leave—Jews holding out in the country after Kristallnacht had to face still more persecution in the coming months. As of January 1, 1939, adult Jews had to append the names "Israel" (for men) and "Sara" (for women) to their given names in all public correspondence. Some members of the Nazi government, including Goebbels and Heydrich, wanted to go further and make Jews wear a uniform or badge, but Hitler rejected this idea for the time being, arguing that such stigmata might encourage Germans to beat up Jews in the streets. The Führer, of course, had nothing in principle against the beating of Jews in the streets, but in late 1938 and early 1939 he was still hoping to secure a large loan from the international Jewish community to help finance Jewish emigration, and he believed that the public pummeling of Jews in the Reich was not likely to advance that cause. (As it happened, Jews were not required to wear the infamous yellow stars in public until September 1941, when any hope for international assistance in getting the remaining Jews out of Germany had long been abandoned.) Pending the imposition of more far-reaching measures to segregate the Jewish community, the name-changing regulation was humiliating enough for Jews who still thought of themselves as primarily German. Max Schohl, for one, profoundly hated having to use the designation "Max Israel Schohl" in all his correspondence with official agencies.

Of course, Max hoped that he would not be conducting much more correspondence with the German authorities. Despite the setbacks he had encountered in his campaign to emigrate to America, he still hoped to gain entry to that country in the not-too-distant future. For this reason he made no effort to try to find sanctuary in Shanghai, the one place in the world that in late 1938 and early 1939 imposed no entry barriers to Jewish refugees. Thousands of Jews, including two families from Flörsheim, managed to find refuge in the teeming Chinese metropolis before it finally closed its doors to further immigration in September 1939. Even during its days of open admission, however, Shanghai was regarded by most German Jews as "the worst place of all" to seek sanctuary, a totally alien environment plagued with horrid diseases and inedible food. Having no interest in Shanghai or any other "exotic" places of refuge, Max continued to press his faithful cousin in Charleston, Julius Hess, to help him pry open the doors of the world's greatest democracy.

CHAPTER FIVE

High Hopes and Hot Tears

COLLEGE TRY

On November 18, 1938, Julius Hess wrote his cousin an upbeat letter, reaffirming his optimism regarding Max's prospects but at the same time urging his cousin to resume contact with Charleston:

Dear Cousin Max,

I was more than glad to receive your last letter but was rather disappointed at what you had to say regarding your visa. Well, all I can tell you is do not be discouraged for we are now doing everything possible to get you out under the Non-Quota Immigrant Class and I feel that we will be able to do so very shortly.

Of course I do not know just how matters stand since the time you wrote me your last letter but I sincerely hope that you and your family are still well and all together.

I have today written to the Department of Labor to obtain from them the forms you mentioned in your letter, namely Form #575 and Form #633. As quickly as I receive these I shall fill them out and send [them] off at once. In the meantime as I said before I shall ask my influential friends for their assistance in this manner [and] I believe for sure that it will not be long until you and Helaine will be on your way over here.

I hope that by the next time I write you I will have some positive news and good news to write and that it will be very soon. Please write to me often as we are always pleased to hear from you as to how you all are getting along, and above all do not worry about your English as we all think it is quite alright [sic], and as I said before love to receive your letters.

Again I beg of you not to worry or be discouraged as I surely believe everything will be alright [sic] in the near future. With lots of love to you all and hoping to hear from you real soon again,

Sincerely your cousin, [Julius]

On the same day he wrote Max, Julius sent a letter to one of his "influential friends," Senator Holt, requesting his assistance in the Schohl matter. This was Julius's first letter to Holt, though as we have noted, he had had Laurence Kaufman contact the senator on Max's behalf earlier. Julius's letter to Holt reflected his awe of Max's educational and professional attainments, along with his conviction that America would be fortunate indeed to get such an extraordinary man:

Dear Senator Holt,

On September 8th last, I had Mr. Laurence Kaufman write to you for whatever assistance you could give us in bringing to this country my cousin Dr. Max Schohl and his daughter Helaine Schohl who are now existing if I may put it that way, in Florsheim, Germany.

You very promptly answered his letter stating you were writing the Hon. Hugh R. Wilson, Ambassador to Germany and that as soon as you heard from him you would get in touch with us. To date we have not heard from you and feel that in some way he might have failed to answer your letter. Will you please let us hear at your earliest convenience?

I realize that you are very busy and no doubt are requested by hundreds to do the very same thing I am asking, but I beg of you to kindly note the type [of] man and his daughter that I am trying so hard to get over here.

This man is a very learned man, a college graduate, having a Doctor degree in Chemistry, who before this crisis took place was in the Chemical Manufacturing business having a factory of his own and dealt extensively with concerns in this country. He has FORMULAS that would be of great value to this country and could be used much to our country's advantage in the Tanning and Dyeing Industry. One Chemical Plant here in this country have been trying to capitalize on his knowledge and have been after his formulas and service for some time, this was one of the concerns he dealt with before his place of business was taken from him.

You can easily discern from what I have written that this gentleman and his daughter are by no means just ordinary immigrants, but should be classed in the Non-Quota class and are surely deserving of your most kind consideration.

Assuring you of my deepest appreciation of whatever you can do for my cousins, I am,

Sincerely, [Julius Hess]

On November 27, 1938, Max received a curt reply from Holt, similar to the one the senator had sent Laurence Kaufman in September:

Dear Mr. Hess:

I have your letter of November 18.

I took the matter up at the time I received a letter from Mr. Kaufman and have been waiting for a reply. You may be sure of my interest and as soon as information comes to me, you will be advised.

Sincerely, [Russ D. Holt]

While waiting to hear from his "friend" in the Senate, Julius learned more about the Non-Quota Immigrant Class. He discovered that it was reserved for specific groups of individuals, namely "ministers, professors, their wives and unmarried children under eighteen, and students at least fifteen years of age." Technically, Max did not fit into this category, being neither a minister nor a professor, but Julius believed, not without reason, that the chemist's background qualified him to teach at an American college. After all, many professors, especially in the technical and business fields, owed their appointments primarily to their practical experience outside academia. Proud of Max's accomplishments as an inventor and professional chemist, Julius was convinced that his cousin could perform well as a professor and that American students would profit immensely from his expertise. The only problem was to get a college or university to take an interest in Max and make him an offer of employment.

As it happened, Charleston had an institution of higher learning of its own, Kanawha College. Founded in 1932, the school was a junior college with 200 full-time students and a faculty of twenty-five. Specializing in technical and business education, it had strong ties with the regional chemical and coal-mining industries, where many of its graduates found jobs. Its faculty members, especially the chemists, took on research projects for the area's industrial plants. Kanawha College, in other words, seemed made to order for Max, although it was hardly on a par with the great German institutions in which he had been trained. (Teaching at a backwoods American college, of course, was the lot of many an illustrious émigré from Europe during the 1930s and 1940s).

Getting Kanawha College to take an interest in Max proved to be no problem for Julius. He knew the college's amiable president, L. S. McDaniel, who lived kitty-corner to the Hesses on Charleston's west side. Through the Southmoor Country Club Julius also knew a local chemical factory owner named Bernard Jacobson, whose business drew on the expertise of Kanawha College's chemists, and who was anxious to bring fresh intellectual talent to that institution. Upon learning about Max from Julius, Jacobsen urged McDaniel to hire the German chemist, as did, of course, Julius himself. Convinced from these conversations that Max would indeed be a stellar addition to his institution's chemistry faculty—"Kanawha College's own Einstein"—and a valuable resource for local industry, McDaniel readily consented to offer Dr. Schohl a job. Per instructions from Julius, who was becoming an expert in such matters, President McDaniel sent notification of the job offer post haste to the American Consulate in Stuttgart:

> December 12, 1938
> American Consul
> Stuttgart, Germany

Dear Sir:

Will you please communicate with Max Schohl, and extend to him for us an offer of a position on our faculty, teaching chemistry and related subjects.

We do not ordinarily offer a man a position without seeing him first, but certain local people in whom I have confidence are recommending him.

We will arrange about salary after we have seen his work. It may seem low to him, but we will guarantee it to take care of his living expenses in the station suitable for a college professor.

> Very truly yours,
> L. S. McDaniel, President

Elated that he had gotten Max a job offer, and convinced that this would gain him Non-Quota Immigrant status and hence rapid admission to America, Julius hastened to relay the good news to Flörsheim. Unsure of Max's present location or condition, he addressed the letter to Hela in hopes that she would pass it on to her father:

December 13, 1938

My Dear Cousin Helaine:

I am indeed sorry that I could not answer your letter sooner, but I wanted to wait until I had some good news to write you and now I believe I have excellent news for you all.

Please be sure and get this information to Cousin Max if it is possible as it will prove very important to you all.

Today a letter was mailed to the American Consul at Stuttgart, Germany, requesting him to contact Cousin Max offering him a position as professor of Chemistry at Kanawha College, here in Charleston, W. Va. USA. This means that all of you will be able to come over immediately providing no unseen circumstances come up. I was given to understand that this was the only way I could get you all over here without waiting a terribly long time.

I shall enclose a copy of the letter that was written to the American Consul that you will be familiar with it if you are questioned regarding same. If you do not receive word from the Consul within a certain length of time you should find out definitely if he received this letter.

It is useless to tell you how worried we are regarding you and family and how much it affects us all when we think of the predicament you are in, but there is little we can do to alleviate your untold misery. This offer of the Kanawha College is the one bright spot in the future for helping you all.

Now Helaine please do me the favor of writing us just as often as you can as we must keep in touch with each other, keep up your courage and everything will turn out alright [sic] if we keep on fighting together.

Be sure and extend our love to the whole family and anxiously awaiting your reply to my letter I am, devotedly,

Your cousin [Julius]

Hela was more than happy to pass this good news on to her father. Like Käthe, she was desperate to get out of Germany. Always a voracious reader—a childhood accident had left her with a limp, and books, along with boys, had taken the place of sports as her primary passion—she read every book she could find on the United States. She saw herself studying at an American university and becoming a cultured intellectual like her father.

Julius heard nothing from any of the Schohls for the next two months, but he did, finally, receive a response from Senator Holt containing a copy of a letter that Holt had received from the American consul in Stuttgart. As the consul's letter made clear, Julius's elation over the job offer for Max was premature:

American Consulate
Stuttgart, Germany
February 8, 1939

My dear Senator Holt:

I have your letter of December 30, 1938, enclosing a copy of your letter to the Consulate dated September 9, 1938, to which you have apparently received no reply. You ask to be informed as to the status of the visa applications of Max and Helene Marianne Schohl, residents of Floersheim, Germany.

There is enclosed a copy of the Consulate's letter to you of October 6, 1938. It now appears that the aliens named above are registered on the waiting list of intending immigrants at this office under the number 24,792, and it is not anticipated that their turns will be reached before January, 1944.

You may be sure, however, that these cases will be given every consideration possible consistent with the proper administration of the immigration laws and regulations.

I am, my dear Senator Holt,

Sincerely yours,

Samuel W. Honaker

American Consul General

Shortly after receiving the copy of the consul's letter to Holt, Julius received a missive directly from the consul, explaining the additional steps that would have to be taken to allow Max to be placed in the Non-Quota Immigrant Class as a college professor. It was not enough, said the consul, for Max to have a job offer from a college. He also had to have a signed contract replete with salary terms. Furthermore, he had to show proof that he had two years' teaching experience at a European institution of higher learning.

Frustrated but undaunted, Julius now got Kanawha College to send Max a signed contract and salary terms by registered mail on February 15. The next day, Julius communicated the information he had received from the consul to Hela Schohl, along with another plea for news regarding the family's current situation:

February 14, 1939

My Dear Cousin [Helaine],

On December 13th, 1938, I wrote you a letter pertaining to your father and the rest of the family to the affect [sic] that I was doing all in my power to get all of you over here. I sent the letter registered mail with return receipt requested. I received the return receipt some three or four weeks ago but as yet I have not received a line from any of you.

Due to this fact you have us very much worried and we would surely like to hear from you to reassure us that you are still alright [sic].

In my letter I wrote you that one of the colleges here had offered your father a position as professor and director of research in chemistry, this was sent to the Consul at Stuttgart. We received a reply today from the Consul which outlined a technicality we will have to eliminate. For you all to get out under the Non-Quota Immigrant Class as the family of a professor, the college has to send a signed contract stating the salary your father is to receive and he in turn has to have at least two years teaching behind him. The salary part is very easily taken care of but the two years teaching may prove a stumbling block. The College is going to send the signed contract and instruct the Consul to eliminate the two year teaching part if they will, as the College is telling them that it is not one of their requirements for a professor or instructor to have any previous experience.

I am telling you all of this so that if the occasion ever presents itself you will be familiar with all of it, and also to let you know that I am doing everything possible to get you over here.

If I but knew that you were all alright [sic] I would feel very much better so Dear Cousin please answer this letter immediately upon receipt of same.

With much love to you all from all of us, I am devotedly,

Your Cousin, [Julius]

As it happened, Max and his family, like Julius Hess, had been kept in the dark by the American consulate for many long weeks regarding the Schohls' immigration status. It was not until mid-February 1939 that Max learned that he was currently number 24,792 on the wait list and that he would have to wait until 1944, at the earliest, to come to the United States. At that point he had still heard nothing about his application for Non-Quota Immigrant status. Believing that an additional four or five years' wait in Germany was akin to a death sentence, on February 16 (before the arrival of Julius's letter of February 14 to Hela), Max returned to the typewriter to draft an anguished appeal to his American cousin.

16 February 1939
Mr. Julius Hess, Agent

My dear Cousin,

I have not written for a long time, because we all have believed, to come in a short time in your country. Your registered letter from December 13th to our daughter Helen has been a great hope for us, especially, when we had read the copy of Mr. L. S. McDaniel's letter to the American Consulate at Stuttgart. We are all so thankful to You for all what You have done for us and we feel You as a very good friend and cousin. After receiving this fine letter, we have been waiting day for day for an answer from Stuttgart; but we heard nothing from there. I have written twice to the American Consul and asked him for any replay at Mr. McDaniel's letter; but I did not get any answer.

You, my dear cousin, can think, so we are in a very bad position, than our great hope, that we could start in cause of Mr. McDaniel's letter, has become smaller and smaller from day to day.

Indeed, today we do not know, what we can do, to come away from here; it is a despaired situation for us. Perhaps You can speak again Your good and learned friends in these affairs, will You, my dear cousin? May be that Mr. McDaniel writes directly to a department of American Government, that he need me for teaching chemistry and related subjects. It is sure, that I can get my visum by the American Consul, when the American Government has given the permission.

What do You think of this propose? Perhaps You and Your friends find another and a better one! That would be very good for us. You see, that is our situation: In this country we could no more remain for a long time; I cannot write, why.

We wish from all our heart to come out, but we do not know the right way. Our registered number at the American Consulate in Stuttgart is so high (Nr. 24792), that we cannot await to get a visum before three or four years, when we live at that time.

I beg You, write us soon again, then we are in a very bad situation and we are waiting for Your answer and we hope You can give us any hope again.

Many, many thanks for all what You do for us. I hope, soon I can show You, that all Your trouble were done for a real good purpose and for men, who will ever be thankful to You.

With our best regards for You, Aunt Lena, sister and brother-in-law, I am devotedly,

Your cousin,

[Max]

Three weeks later, having still heard nothing from the American consul regarding his Non-Quota Status application, but having just read Julius's letter to Hela, Max wrote his cousin once again. As always, he had to use elliptical language to convey the seriousness of his predicament. Yet he continued to have faith in the reasonableness of American officials. If the *college* that wished to employ him did not insist on two years' teaching experience, why would the immigration authorities?

March 5, 1939
Mr. Julius Hess, Agent

My dear Cousin,

Today we received Your letter from Feb. 14th, for our daughter Helene Marianne; but I have seen, the content of this letter was determined for me and us all. I must always repeat, how thankful we are for all Your love and for all Your trouble in our affairs.

I hope, You will have received my letter from Febr. 16, in which I had written all the difficulties for us to come over. But in Your last letter I can see, You know exactly all these difficulties and it is true, that it is a stumbling block, that I cannot proof a teaching time of two years. May be, the American Consul at Stuttgart is content, when he hears from the College, that it is not a condition for teaching of two years behind me; we hope all, that the Consul will be content and gives us the visas. We think all, that will be a happy day, when we can hear, we get the visas; then we have many 'black' days behind us. I think You can understand me, my dear cousin. Now we are waiting for an answer in a good sense from Stuttgart and we hope day for day again. But you can understand that it is a terrible time for us, but not to change.

Now we hope again a few more, to come over and we all know, when we come, that only our dear cousin Julius has made true this wonder. Ever our hearty thank for all the good, which You have done for us. With much love to You all from all of us, I am devotedly,

Your cousin, [Max]

On March 14, Max finally received a formal notification from the American consul containing the stipulation that he had to have taught for two years to qualify for Non-Quota Status—something he already knew through Julius. On the same day, Max responded to the consulate, explaining that Kanawha College had sent a signed contract to Stuttgart and that the college officials did not require two years' teaching experience. If, however, the consulate still insisted on enforcing this regulation, Max pointed out that he had in fact done some teaching in his life, almost two years' worth. Along with this letter he sent a copy of his Ph.D. dissertation as proof of his qualifications as a researcher. (One can imagine the delight with which the consulate received Max's learned elucidation of auto-oxidation.)

March 14, 1939
To the American General Consul

Dear Sir,

I have the honour to inform you that the Kanawha-College in Charleston (W. Va.) has offered me a position in their faculty for teaching chemistry and related subjects. In December 1938 Mr. [Mc]Daniel, the President of the College, has informed you of this offer and to day I heard of your reply, in which you find fault with the formal side of the matter.

First it is urgent for me, to have a contract and, indeed, the College is going to send a signed contract with my salary; it may be possible that the contract has meanwhile arrived at the consulate. Further, I have been told, that a teaching time of two years behind me is one of the suppositions for your permit.

From October 1907 till December 1908 I have been an Assistant of Prof. Schultz at the Technical High-School [University] in Munich. In that time I had to teach and to support the students in their practical chemical works.

In 1918 I have been a teacher in chemistry and chemical technology at the 'Internierten Schule' in St. Gallen, Switzerland, for eight months.

So I have a teaching time of almost two years behind me. But it is of a greater importance that I have much and great practical experience in many parts of chemical technology. I have been over twenty years the leader of the laboratories in a chemical factory, where I had to teach and support many assistants.

Mr. [Mc]Daniel, I was told, would inform you that it is not one of the requirements of the College to have a teaching time behind me. For a chemist the practical experience as an instructor is more valuable than the experience of teaching.

But to show you that I am able to work in scientific-chemical research too, I send with this letter a dissertation, written by me many years ago.

I hope that I can convince you, to consider me able to take over that position at the Kanawha-College in Charleston.

In reference to the above mentioned reasons, I beg you to tell me, if it is possible to get a non-quota-visa. I may point out that I should like to come to Stuttgart at any time you wish me to.

Hoping to get soon a favourable answer, I remain,

Yours truly,

[Dr. Max Schohl]

On the day that Max sent the above letter and dissertation to the American consulate in Stuttgart, he sent another copy of his thesis to Julius, along with a carbon of his letter to the consulate. He asked Julius to pass the dissertation on to President McDaniel, "because he is interesting in such scientific works." Rarely can so much hope have been invested in a document like this, whose usual purpose is to secure an academic degree, not to save a life.

To Julius Hess, who received the dissertation and copy of Max's letter to the consulate on March 23, the news that his cousin had in fact put in roughly two years teaching chemistry meant that the Schohls must surely have cleared the last hurdle on their odyssey to safety in America. Now, he thought, it could only be a matter of pushing the necessary paperwork through the busy bureaucracy, a task that might take "a few more weeks."

March 23rd, 1939

Dear Cousin Max;

I received today your letter and copy of the letter you sent the American Consul at Stuttgart along with the dissertation you wrote. The contents of your letter and the information you gave to the consul as per your letter has made me feel very happy.

Although it might take a few more weeks before you hear from the consul I feel sure now that everything is going to work out perfectly. Do not be discouraged or impatient if you do not hear from the consul just when you expect to, because I understand that they are so terribly busy it takes them weeks to answer their ordinary mail.

The contract that the Kanawha College mailed to the consul was sent registered mail with a request for a return receipt, and mailed on the 13th of February, the college did not receive the return receipt until just this last week, in other words it took more than a month to get a return receipt back from the consul. I shall get the college to write again today asking the consul to please do them the favor of pushing this matter along as they are very desirous of your services.

It will certainly be one of the greatest pleasures of my life to greet you and the rest of my dear cousins upon your arrival here in Charleston when the time comes, and if the good Lord is with us it should be not so very far off.

Cousin Max there is one thing we have not discussed and that is the condition of your finances relative to getting over here. Although I am personally not in the position to help you very much in this respect I have the assurance of our cousins Charlie and Ferdy Midelburg that they will come to my assistance whenever I call upon them, this is especially so with Charlie who tells me that he will do anything I ask of him in helping you. The reason I am telling you this is so that you will feel free to call upon me if you need a little help, and I am sure it will be forthcoming. I want you to know, and feel, that you can rely on me no matter what happens, and that I am doing all that can possibly be done to bring you over here, just as quickly as I can.

As I said before it will be the happiest day in my life when I accomplish this task of relocating you and your family here in Charleston.

Every day Mother [Lina] asks if I have heard from you and of the prospects of your coming, and as the days go by and I do not hear from you we all get worried, and then what a relief when we at last get a letter from you and we

know that you are alright [sic] once more. So please Cousin
Max write us often even if it is but a line just to let us know
you are still alright [sic].

With love to you all from myself and all the rest of the
family and hoping to hear from you real soon, I am,

Devotedly your cousin, [Julius]

Although Max's spirits were buoyed, as always, by the confident and
supportive lines from his American cousin, his experience with the U.S.
immigration officials in Stuttgart were teaching him to be less sanguine
than Julius about his prospects. He had come to doubt that the fastest
and surest route to America ran through the consulate in Stuttgart, and
he became even more pessimistic on that score after learning from a
friend who had recently visited the Stuttgart consulate that he could not
expect favorable treatment from that office. It would be advisable, the
friend had said, for Max to leapfrog the Stuttgart office and go directly
to Washington for his ticket of admission to America. This made good
sense to Max, who had always believed in "going to the top," and who
(yet again) hoped that one of Julius's "influential friends" in the government would buttress his case.

April 6, 1939

My dear cousin,

Today I have received your letter of March 23rd and I myself and my family, we thank you from all our heart for the
encouraging words, you have written, but for the love to us,
which is speaking out of every one your words, too. I have
seen, that you are thinking at all things for us and I have no
doubt, all will be going, when we have been coming over. I
am very grateful to our cousins Charlie and Ferdy Midelburg,
that they are willing to help us, when we need their help.
Sorry, I don't know the address of cousin Charlie; please give

me in your next letter this address; I will write him and thank him for his willing to help us. To cousin Ferdy I have written long time ago; but I have never received any answer; I cannot find the reason why.

But I know exactly, when it will succeed to come over, you alone, my dear cousin Julius, have realized this great affair for us; in all times we will be greatly to you for this love and this help in heavy times.

Referring to the answer of the consul in Stuttgart, which I have not yet received, I shall tell you the following: Some days ago I have seen a friend of mine who is coming back from Stuttgart and I was told that the consul cannot do anything in my affair; and therefore he has not yet written to me. My friend who is understanding these things quite good and who has good relations to the American consulate, has the opinion, the only and surest way, to come over, is not going by the consul directly, but by the government in Washington. He means, the best way is, when the College will write a letter . . . that it needs my service as an instructor in chemical research, especially for metal-and-leather-industry on the strength of my great experiences extending over many years. It would be still better when you had a friend with relations to the government who could support the desires of the College. When the government is willing to give me the permit, then it will give an order to the consul in Stuttgart and I can come over. I am hoping you can understand what I mean, dear cousin; but naturally I do no know, if it is possible to go this way. Pleas write me your opinion at this fact.

You can think how is our life in these trouble times and I will not say anything over it.

I am waiting for your reply, my dear cousin and send you and all relations, especially our good mother, our best regards.

In love I am devotedly, your cousin, [Max]

Even before mailing this letter, Max came up with another gambit to get him and his family through the thicket of American immigration regulations. He could obtain a visitor's visa through a different consulate, then secure permanent residency after proving his worth to Kanawha College and the American government. He would even promise to return to Germany following the expiration of his visitor's visa if the American authorities insisted on it. As he explained to Julius in an addendum to his letter of April 6:

Dear Cousin,

After finishing this letter I have thought to give you another idea to make possible my coming over.

I have heard that the American Consul in Francfort [sic] on Main [Frankfurt] (but not in Stuttgart) is able to give a so-named "visit-visa" for a visit for a certain time in the States. I am thinking so: The College could write to the Consul in Francfort [sic], that they need my service for an instructor in chemical researches, but they will make a trial with me of about three or four months; and the consul shall give me for that purpose a visit-visa. When the college was satisfied with my service, they will at the government ask for a permanent permit for me; if the college is not satisfied, then I could return at any time to Germany.

The American Board knows exactly that the returning of Jewish persons to Germany is generally impossible; but I make an exception; I can have by the German Board a letter, that I can return at any time without any difficulties. This fact may be important for the American consul in Francfort, because he can be sure that I can return, if it is necessary.

Hoping that you understand what I mean, my dear cousin. Naturally I have not the opinion [intention] to return when I am one time in the States; I believe I can settle all difficulties and my family could come over some months later.

I am hoping you have understood what I mean and I beg
you to give me soon as possible your reply.

Ever grateful to you, devotedly, [Max]

Max had very good reason to search for new angles in his immigration quest in the first months of 1939, for the plight of the Jews remaining in Central Europe was becoming more desperate by the day. On
January 30 Hitler made a shocking prophecy before the Reichstag: "If
international finance Jewry in and outside Europe should succeed in
forcing the peoples once again into a world war, the result would not be
the Bolshevization of the earth and the triumph of Jewry, but the destruction of the Jewish race in Europe." In March 1939 Hitler sent
troops into the rest of Czechoslovakia, breaking the promise he had
made at the Munich Conference to be content with absorbing the Sude-
tenland. This move added thousands more Jews to the pool of would-be
immigrants anxious to flee from the expanding Nazi Reich. Like all
these hopefuls, Max was increasingly living in a world of rumor and
speculation, where the latest hot tip might spell salvation.

We do not know what Julius thought about Max's visitor's visa
gambit, but in any event it was not really a viable option at that time.
While most German Jews and other German refugees already in the
United States on temporary visas could now get their visas extended
indefinitely, the consuls in Germany were severely limiting the number of visitor's visas they issued. Indignant that German Jews were
"misusing" their temporary visas to gain permanent residence in the
United States, the consuls would now grant a visitor's visa to a German
Jew only if he put up a high bond and showed proof that he had a residence outside America to which he could move when his temporary
visa expired. The German government, moreover, was increasingly
loath to allow Jews to leave the country for short-term visits abroad;
they had to get out for good.

Julius apparently did not bother to explore the temporary visa option
for Max, but he did continue to work hard to get him out under the
Non-Quota Immigrant provision. At his instigation, President McDaniel

of Kanawha College wrote a letter to Secretary of State Cordell Hull, asking for his help in securing the services of a valuable scientific talent. At the time he took this step, McDaniel himself was becoming thoroughly fed up with the Stuttgart consulate's foot-dragging, and his letter to Hull represented a valiant effort to go over the consul's head. What McDaniel did not realize, however, was that Hull almost never intervened in specific visa cases, believing that the consuls' authority in this realm should be sacrosanct. Nor did he know that the State Department as a whole was pushing hard to limit the number of immigrants admitted in the NQI class.

April 26, 1939
The Honorable Cordell Hull
Secretary of State

Dear Sir:

Will it be possible for you to help us get a visa for Dr. Max Schohl and family of Florsheim, Germany? Repeated communications, including a notarized contractual offer by us of a position to Dr. Schohl, have failed to get action from the American consul in Stuttgart.

We have been fortunate in securing the services of Dr. Schohl as a chemical laboratory supervisor and director of research especially for the metal and leather industry. Dr. Schohl has had a wide experience in these fields extending over many years and I am thoroughly satisfied with his ability and competence. Dr. Schohl is the more desirable to us in that his near relatives living in this community have practically underwritten the costs to the college entailed by his service.

Since the founding of the college of which I am the president, I have been constantly striving to build up our chemical research as well as our general chemistry department.

**Max Schohl (third from left)
as a young lieutenant in
World War I**
Schohl family collection

The dapper Max in Flörsheim, early 1930s
Schohl family collection

The Schohls' Albanusstrasse house as it now appears
Author photo

The Electro chemical factory in Flörsheim, 1934
Schohl family collection

Max (in white coat) presiding over his chemical factory
Schohl family collection

A display of goods produced by the Electro Chemical Company
Schohl family collection

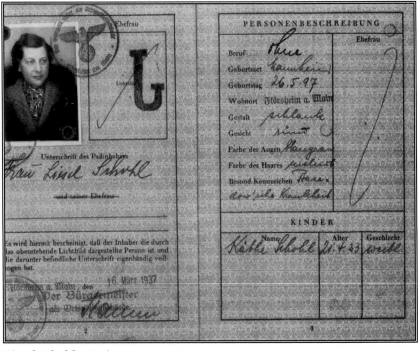

Käthe Schohl's Nazi-era passport, with the letter "J" stamped on it
Schohl family collection

Liesel Schohl's Nazi-era passport
Schohl family collection

The identification papers that Schohl began carrying in May 1939
Schohl family collection

Julius Hess in 1960
Schohl family collection

Julius and his wife, Bea, dancing at the Southmoor Country Club circa 1955
Schohl family collection

Ruma, Yugoslavia, in 1940
Schohl family collection

Käthe Schohl (left), Aunt Lina (center), and Norma Kaufman (right) in Charleston, West Virginia, in 1946 shortly after Käthe's arrival in America
Schohl family collection

Sign at the top of the small street in Flörsheim named in honor of Max Schohl
Author photo

Memorial in the Jewish cemetery near Flörsheim for Max Schohl, his mother, Johanna, his wife, Liesel, and his older daughter, Hela
Author photo

The exterior wall of the now-vanished synagogue in Flörsheim
Author photo

This I have done for the reason that this valley is rapidly becoming one of the chemical centers of the world.

Respectfully yours, [L. S. McDaniel, President]

President McDaniel also enlisted the support of the governor of West
Virginia on Max's behalf. The governor, Homer "Rocky" Holt (no relation to Senator Holt), had himself been a professor of mathematics and
law at Washington and Lee University and was a strong supporter of his
state's educational system. He was also determined to combat the lingering effects of the depression in West Virginia by doing all he could for
the mining and chemical industries that were central to the region's
economy. On May 1 McDaniel paid a personal visit to Holt at the stately
governor's mansion on Kanawha Boulevard, briefing him on Max's case
and stressing the benefits that would accrue to Kanawha College and
the state of West Virginia by bringing Dr. Schohl to Charleston. Apparently impressed by what he heard, Holt immediately dashed off a letter
to Cordell Hull echoing McDaniel's sentiments:

May 1, 1939
The Honorable Cordell Hull
Secretary of State

My dear Secretary:

Doctor L. S. McDaniels [sic], President of Kanawha College,
Charleston, West Virginia, has just been in my office with ref-
erence to his interest in securing the services of Doctor Max
Schohl of Florsheim, Germany, as a professor in Kanawha
College, giving attention particularly to the subjects of chem-
istry and metallurgy.

As you probably know, the Kanawha Valley is one of the
great chemical centers, not only of the United States but of
the World, and this, naturally, makes it especially appropriate

that the department of this college in this field be strength-
ened as far as is possible.

Though I do not know Doctor Schohl personally, I understand that he has been a professor in these subjects in Germany, and, more recently, has been the proprietor of rather
large chemical industries in that country.

Those connected with Kanawha College and others interested in Doctor Schohl are entirely responsible and I am sure
that if arrangements are made for the emigration of Doctor
Schohl from Germany to the United States, there is no likelihood whatsoever of his becoming a public charge in any
sense of the word.

If there is anything else that I might do in this connection
to assist you in arranging for Doctor Schohl's visa and for his
family (consisting of a wife and two daughters) to accompany him, I shall be happy if you will advise me.

Yours sincerely,

Homer A. Holt, Governor

Given Hull's hands-off stance in visa-granting matters, it is not surprising that the combined efforts of President McDaniel and Governor
Holt to induce an intervention by the secretary of state on Max's behalf
yielded no results. McDaniel did not receive a reply from Hull, and the
secretary seems not to have passed his and Governor Holt's appeals on
to the consulate in Stuttgart. (Max's file from the Stuttgart consulate
contains no copies of McDaniel's and Holt's letters to Hull.)

While McDaniel was pressing Max's case with Hull and Holt, the in-
trepid Julius was trying his own hand at personal diplomacy by visiting
the commissioner of immigration, James L. Houghteling, in Washington, D.C. Although Washington is not far from Charleston, Julius rarely
went there, and he had never set foot in a national government agency.
To improve his chances with Houghteling, Julius brought along a letter
of reference written by Mrs. Hannah G. Solomon, a Chicago grand
dame and leading figure in the American Jewish community. Julius had

gained access to her through a lawyer friend of his named Philip Angel, who was Mrs. Solomon's son-in-law.

April 28, 1939
Mr. James L. Houghteling
Commissioner of Immigration

My dear Mr. Houghteling,

This will introduce to you Mr. Julius Hess of Charleston, West Virginia, who wishes to bring to this country a cousin from Germany for whom he can secure a position as a research worker in chemistry. We who are in a position to know the dire distress of our co-religionists in Germany are eager to aid those who can come to our blessed shores, and so I take the liberty of giving Mr. Hess this letter to you with the hope that you can assist him.

Most sincerely yours,
[Hannah G. Solomon]

We have no record of Houghteling's response to Julius's personal appeal on behalf of Max, but in light of the commissioner's actions (or non-actions) on the Jewish refugee crisis in general it seems improbable that he would have been of much help. In February 1939, when New York Senator Robert Wagner and Massachusetts Congresswoman Edith Rogers introduced bills in their respective houses calling for the admission of 20,000 German refugee children on a non-quota basis over the next two years (a prospective U.S. version of Britain's *Kindertransport*), Houghteling kept his distance from the measure in hostile Senate hearings. Queried by Senator Robert Reynolds of North Carolina if he wished to see more immigrants coming to America, Houghteling replied, "Not under present circumstances." Asked if he therefore opposed the Wagner bill, the commissioner said, "I am not taking any position on that." Houghteling's wife, in what may have been an articulation of her husband's view of this legislation, confided to J. Pierrepont Moffat (chief of the Division of European Affairs of the State Department) at a Washington cocktail party that the trouble with the Wagner-Rogers bill was "that 20,000 children would all too soon grow up to be 20,000 ugly adults." Cold-shouldered by immigration officials like Houghteling, and bitterly attacked by restrictionists who claimed that the children would be the thin edge of a nasty alien wedge, the Wagner-Rogers bill was quickly killed. In sum, Houghteling, like Hull, was not a likely resource for German Jews and their American sponsors who were desperately trying to find a way around, or over, unsympathetic or unhelpful consular officials in Germany.

On May 4, 1939, in a letter from Consul Honaker to President McDaniel, the Stuttgart consulate put an unhappy end to the prolonged effort by Julius Hess, Kanawha College, and the governor of West Virginia to bring Max Schohl to America as a prospective college professor:

May 4, 1939

Mr. L. S. McDaniel, President

Kanawha College, Charleston, West Virginia

Sir:

The receipt is acknowledged of your letter dated February 21, 1939, with which you enclose a copy of a contract with Mr. Max Schohl, who desires to immigrate to the United States to accept the position of professor at Kanawha College, Charleston, West Virginia.

As you are aware, section 4 (d) of the Immigration Act of 1924 provides, inter alia, that an applicant for a visa as professor under that section of the law must have carried on the vocation of professor for at least two years immediately preceding the time of his application for admission into the United States.

It appears from your letter that Mr. Schohl has owned and managed a chemical plant for the past two decades and you believe that it would seem logical to consider his activities as an acceptable equivalent to the vocation of professor.

The Consulate regrets that as Mr. Schohl is unable to meet the requirements of the law, since he has not been a professor for the last two years, it is not possible to grant him a nonquota visa. It will, therefore, be necessary for him to wait until his turn on the waiting list will be reached, which may not be for several years.

Respectfully yours
Samuel W. Honaker,
American Consul General

Max Schohl, in other words, was denied a non-quota visa because he had not taught chemistry in the two years *immediately preceding* his application. Revealingly—and maddeningly for Max and Julius—the consul had not mentioned this additional technicality in his earlier correspondence regarding the non-quota class. It was as if he were stringing them along, putting up new hurdles every time they cleared the ones previously placed in their path. But apart from noting the unnecessarily protracted fashion in which this judgment was delivered, what are we to make of it?

First, we must concede that the law did read as the consul indicated; the relevant section (d) of the regulations specifically allowed non-quota consideration to "ministers and professors, namely immigrants who for at least two years continuously immediately preceding the time of their admission into the United States had been—and who sought to enter the United States solely for the purpose of—carrying on the vocation of minister of any religious denomination, or professor of a college, academy, seminary, or university, and their wives and unmarried children under 18 years of age accompanying them or following them." However, the individual consuls had considerable leeway in interpreting these regulations and could certainly waive minor technical restrictions if they so chose. By 1939, moreover, the consuls were certainly aware of what it meant for German Jews to be denied the chance to escape Germany because of some technical problem with their visa applications. Under instructions from Washington, they had finally approved enough applications (primarily from Jews) to fill the German immigration quota. On the other hand, the consular officials were also under orders from the State Department's Visa Division not to allow the crisis in Germany to yield an immigration rate that transcended the yearly quotas or cast doubt on America's determination to rigorously apply its immigration laws. In the late 1930s restrictionist elements in Congress and the public at large were claiming that America was being inundated by a flood of unassimilable and potentially subversive aliens. The result of such pressures, according to historians Richard Breitman and Alan Kraut, "was that, in cases of doubt, consuls invariably leaned toward refusal." Max's case would not seem to have been one in which there was much ground for reasonable doubt—Julius's financial weakness as a sponsor was outweighed by Max's teaching contract from Kanawha College—but the Stuttgart consulate, having already, as Consul Honaker reported in 1936, provided "one of the heaviest sources of immigrants into the United States over many years," may well have been looking for technicalities that would enable it to turn down applications in good (legal) conscience.

Max's failure to be admitted to America as a college teacher was by no means unique, or even unusual. According to one student of U.S. immigration policy, the American consuls abroad made it particularly difficult for Jewish professors to get non-quota visas, often using the "two-years' teaching prior to emigration" requirement as their justification for rejection. Victor Klemperer, a professor of literature who had been dismissed from his teaching post in 1935 despite having converted to Christianity, was denied a non-quota visa to America in 1938 because he had not been teaching for the previous two years. The consular files reveal many similar cases. Clearly, if the consuls had waived this requirement—whose injustice should have been obvious—many more German Jewish academics would have been eligible for entry into the United States. However, the State Department believed that allowing a large number of German Jews to enter American academia was contrary to the national interest. In September 1939 Assistant Secretary of State Messersmith sent out a circular instructing the consuls to "examine with unusual care" all applicants for non-quota visas to ensure that their admission did not pose a threat to American traditions and safety. This advice echoed a confidential report issued by Messersmith as Berlin Consul-General in 1933 warning against throwing open the portals of U.S. colleges to persecuted German Jewish professors. Messersmith objected to a wholesale admission of Jewish professors on grounds that these individuals would block or hamper the teaching careers of American natives. He also argued that foreign Jewish academics were "interested only in their own fields and thereby constituted a very different type of man from the professor in the United States in a similar position." But most important, the Jewish academics posed a *political* threat:

> If we open our doors widely to these men and if our universities and higher schools invited them out of sympathy . . . it is inevitable that a very considerable number of places in our universities will be held by professors of foreign background and training. . . . Among them . . . are a fair number who hold ideas which are totally out of accord with our own social and economic ideas prevailing in the United States. Not a few of them are men who hold ideas which while designated as "liberal", are in reality in direct opposition to our own social order.

Max Schohl, of course, was anything but a rabid leftist, but his actual political views were irrelevant to an immigration system that, like the American populace as a whole, trafficked in stereotypes about Jews, branding them in general as left-wing "subversives." Just as Max's intense German patriotism provided him no sanctuary from Nazi persecution, his obvious willingness to become a loyal and productive American had no impact on his effort to gain admission to the United States.

"Heavy and Dark Days"

Max Schohl was understandably devastated by the rejection of his application for Non-Quota Immigrant status. At least for the time being, he now gave up on America as a place of refuge for himself and his family, but of course he could not afford to give up on the effort to escape

Germany altogether. He therefore altered the destination of his envis-aged exodus to England, a country that he had always admired, and where he had some personal contacts he believed might help him gain visas and work.

England, however, presented its own challenges as a possible refuge for the likes of Max Schohl in the spring of 1939. Although overall Britain admitted a higher percentage of refugees per head of population than America, and, as we have seen, hosted the life-saving *Kindertrans-port*, the British government was not much more welcoming toward Jewish refugees than was that of the United States, especially in the late 1930s. Great Britain's immigration bureaucracy was sluggish and suspi-cious, certainly not inclined to throw open the nation's doors simply be-cause foreign folks in desperate straits were banging on them for dear life. After all, Britain, like the United States, was suffering from a severe depression in the late 1930s, and, as in America, there was considerable popular opposition to increased admittance of work-hungry aliens. Again as in the United States, the resistance to a more open refugee pol-icy derived in part from anti-Semitic prejudices in both the populace at large and some departments of the government, especially the Foreign Office. Finally, overshadowing all British policy toward German-Jewish refugees in the late 1930s was the "nightmare" scenario, as one author-ity has put it, "that an over-generous response to the plight of refugees from the Reich might create a precedent which could inspire the expul-sion of millions, not thousands, of totally destitute Jews from Eastern Europe, and thus confront the British and indeed other governments with a burden of unbearable dimensions."

British immigration restrictions, in fact, became considerably tighter following the Anschluss, which heightened London's fears of a mass mi-gration across the Channel on the part of Central European Jews. To stem such a tide, Whitehall now introduced a visa requirement for all people from the German Reich wishing to enter Britain. This allowed British consuls abroad to screen out those they deemed unsuitable *before* they showed up at British ports of entry. (The Home Office had discov-ered, as an official reported in June 1938, that many unacceptable candi-dates for admission were arriving at British ports of entry, and the consequent rejection of large numbers of refugees was causing "great hardship" and "serious public criticism.") Moreover, all refugees, including Jews, seeking a haven in Britain were obliged to show proof that they had guaranteed financial support for the time they planned to be in the country. Such proof could be established by posting a bond with the British Home Office. Finally, since Britain saw itself as temporary refuge rather than as "a country of immigration," most Jewish asylum applicants had to show that they had the capacity to re-emigrate to some other country after their residency permit for Britain had lapsed. Exceptions to these rules were made in two categories: internationally recognized scientists and artists (Britain hoped to capitalize on Germany's brain drain) and émigrés who had the desire and training to go into domestic service. (England's ruling elite feared that the country was about to suffer from a shortage of butlers, maids, cooks, and nannies.)

Max Schohl, alas, could not have convincingly presented himself to the British authorities as a potential butler even if he had had the inclination to do so. As a British passport officer explained in rejecting a German-Jewish doctor who had tried this tack: "Butlering requires a lifelong experience." Moreover, for all his accomplishments as a chemist, Max was not well known enough in the world chemical community to win exemption as a famous scientist. No, he would have to pay the going rate for sanctuary in England—a rate that was perhaps not exorbitant in itself but was certainly very dear to a man who had lost his entire fortune. Thus, in May 1939, Max found himself once again turning to his cousin Julius for help—this time not for assistance in breaking through the paper walls of American immigration policy but in raising the money to clear the steep financial walls encircling Britain.

May 9, 1939

My dear cousin Julius,

You will have received my last letter from April 6th, which I have sent as "registered." Today I must write at a very unfavourable matter. The American Consulate at Stuttgart has written me and it seems, we shall not have the fortune to come over. The consul's reply is the following: [Max quotes from a letter similar to that sent to McDaniel.] . . .

You see, there is no more any hope for us. You can think, in which position we now are, after we had surely believed, that your good plan would succeed.

We ask us, what shall we do now? It is completely impossible, to wait for several years; I cannot write over this matter; it is terrible for us and especially for my poor children.

But I will write you in this affair another too: A friend of mine in England, who knows our position, has written me some weeks ago, [that] it may be possible for us to come to England, but it takes much money. He means, a security of about 6 [to] 700 Engl. Pounds would be the base for a permit. My friend is not a rich man, but he wrote me, that he would give for me a security of about 300; he could not give more, because he had given the security for his parents and sisters, who are now in England. You can understand my dear cousin, I cannot demand of my relations in the States to give for me this great lot of money, although I do not need this money for me; its is only a security for the English State. Then I will work in England and I can make so much, that I can live with my family.

But when you believe that it will be possible that the American relations would help me, it would be an unexpected fortune for us; we have no more any hope.

When you could hear a favourable [response] by our relations in this affair, please write to my friend in London; I give you the address: Professor Dr. Emil Hene, 17 Holland Park, W. 11, London.

I cannot write more today; we all are very dreary; we see heavy and dark days before us.

Please write me soon as possible, my dear cousin,

Devotedly your cousin [Max]

The Dr. Hene referred to in Max's letter was a German-born chemist whom Max had known for years. They had worked together in Germany on various inventions, including a timed explosive device that Hene hoped to sell to the military. In 1934, before he could complete this project, Hene emigrated to England, where he continued to work on the bomb. Over the next two years he kept in regular contact with Max and once stayed with him in Flörsheim on a brief return visit to Germany. On that occasion the two chemists put the finishing touches on their incendiary project, which Hene promised to patent and sell in Britain, dividing the profits with Max. Alas, if Hene ever did manage to sell his bomb, Max never saw any of the proceeds.

In the first years after his own departure for England, Hene often urged Max to emigrate to that nation, assuring him that it would be no problem to be admitted. He was more or less correct about this, for until the introduction of the new visa requirements in 1938, aliens with some assets of their own and good prospects for work could generally obtain a residency permit in Britain. While disinclined to leave the Reich for good until 1938 (precisely, of course, when the British restrictions were tightened), Max did make a brief visit to England in 1936 to see his old friend and to explore possibilities for future collaboration. At that point the Nazi government gave Jews exit permits for specified stays abroad so long as they left the bulk of their fortunes and their families behind in the Reich. In fact, the Nazis assumed that most of the Jews who left on temporary exit permits would elect to stay abroad, and then hand over the rest of their fortunes to the regime to get their family members out. When Max crossed the German-Dutch border en route to England in 1936, an SS official sneered, "Another rat abandoning the ship!" To which Max replied, "I'll be back."

During his two-week stay in London Max visited with British chemists and engineers who pleaded with him not to return to Germany. Max, however, feared that if he remained in England he might not be able to get his family out of Germany, and in any event, he was not yet ready to flee the Reich for good. He crossed back into Germany on the day his German exit permit stipulated and, as chance would have it, encountered the same SS official who had bid him good riddance upon his departure. "See, I'm back," said Max to the astonished (and no doubt peeved) official.

While Max was shifting the focus of his emigration efforts from America to England, Julius Hess was uncharacteristically wallowing in despair. He was deeply ashamed of the way in which his own government had treated a man whom he revered and who was only looking for the opportunity to make himself useful on American soil, as countless immigrants before him had done. But in the end Julius blamed himself more than the American authorities for not getting Max to Charleston. Somehow he had not done enough, he thought, to bring his cousin to American shores. Depressed by this "failure," and bereft of alternative ideas for delivering the Schohls from their "heavy and dark" plight, Julius could not bring himself to write to Max for over three months.

During this period of silence from Julius, a now-famous saga transpired on the high seas that put the desperate plight of Jewish refugees from Nazism in a more vivid light than ever: the ill-fated voyage of the *St. Louis.* On May 13, 1939, this luxury liner of the Hamburg-America Line departed from Hamburg bound for Havana, Cuba, with 936 passengers on board, the vast majority of them German Jews. Many were women and children. All of them had passport visas (the Jewish ones stamped with a red letter "J") and "landing certificates" purchased for $262 per passage from the Cuban director general of immigration, one Colonel Manuel Gonzales. Seven hundred and thirty-four of the passengers also held American immigration quota numbers that would allow them to move on to the United States after stays of varying duration in Cuba. Only after the ship was well into its voyage across the Atlantic, and after the passengers had begun slowly to accustom themselves to being treated as human beings rather than as vermin, did they learn that their landing certificates for Cuba might not be valid. It seems that the official who had signed the documents, Señor Gonzalez, had been for some time selling such permits en masse to the shipping lines, which in turn passed them on (at a significant markup, of course) to needy Jews. For years this arrangement had seemed satisfactory enough to all concerned, but by 1939 anti-Semitism was sharply on the rise in Cuba, and there were loud demands to put an end to the influx of Jews into that country. (Havana itself already had a colony of some 2,500 Jews.) The government of Cuban President Laredo Bru therefore decided not to recognize the landing permits issued by its own immigration officials without an additional bond of 500 pesos and written approval from the Cuban secretaries of state and labor. Hamburg-America Line officials knew that the landing permits carried by the *St. Louis* passengers might not be recognized even before the ship sailed, but they hoped to finesse the matter with the Cuban authorities when the vessel reached Havana.

When telegrams from Cuba casting doubt on the validity of the permits reached the passengers en route, they understandably fell into deep gloom; suddenly the cruel uncertainty of the existence they had just fled returned with a vengeance. One man fell ill and died; others threatened suicide. Captain Gustav Schroeder, who himself had not been told about the permit problem, prevented mass panic only by assuring the passengers that he would do all in his power to get them ashore. Nonetheless, when the *St. Louis* reached Havana harbor the Cuban authorities refused to allow the ship to dock, and various efforts by officials of Jewish relief agencies in the United States, who hurried to Havana to negotiate disembarkation in exchange for payments to cover the passengers' upkeep in Cuba, failed to move the Cuban authorities. (It seems that the funds that were offered did not include sufficient bribes for the relevant officials, including President Bru.)

On June 2 the *St. Louis* was forced to vacate Havana harbor, but Captain Schroeder sailed out slowly, still hoping that the ship might be allowed to return to Cuba, or that perhaps he might disembark his miserable human cargo in Miami; after all, many of the passengers held American quota numbers. Washington, however, dashed this hope while the ship idled off the coast of Florida; Coast Guard vessels patrolled near the vessel, with orders to prevent any of the refugees from trying to boat or swim to shore. A telegram from the passengers to FDR pleading for his intervention went unanswered.

The ship thus sailed on in the direction of Hamburg, its passengers more distressed than ever. One slit his wrists and tried to jump overboard. Only at the last minute did the ongoing efforts of the Jewish relief agencies,

particularly the American Joint Distribution Committee, effect a saving solution whereby Belgium, Holland, England, and France each agreed to
take a portion of the passengers. In the end all the refugees found asylum,
but only for a time. Most of those who found sanctuary on the Continent
were later caught by the German invasion; of the 623 *St. Louis* passengers
given asylum on the Continent only about 40 survived the war.

The *St. Louis* affair was covered extensively in the American press, including the papers in Charleston. For Julius, this sad story, in which his
own government had come off so badly, plunged him further into despair. He had continued to hope that America might yet relax its immigration restrictions—allowing a renewed suit on Max's behalf—but this
hardly seemed probable in light of Washington's refusal to offer even
temporary refuge to the men, women, and children of the *St. Louis*. This
episode also carried another message for Julius: Be very cautious in
dealing with German shipping companies selling passages to freedom.

Julius's long silence in the spring of 1939 alarmed Max, who was of
course desperately hoping that his cousin could help him raise the
money necessary to get his family to Britain. On July 3 Max wrote to
Julius again, asking him not only for some response to his plea for financial help but also for reassurance that he, Julius, was all right. Some
injury to Julius, or perhaps a foul-up in the mail delivery, seemed to
Max the only possible explanations for the strange lack of communication from Charleston.

July 3rd, 1939

My dear Cousin,
    The last letter I have received of you is dated from March
23rd. I have answered with registered letter on April 6th and
once more on May 9th. But till today I have not received any
answer of you; may be, one of your letters could be lost. We
should not understand it, that you would no more give us an
answer. You have shown us as a very good friend in these
bad times and we have so great hope that you can help us.

I hope I shall get soon as possible any answer of you. Please write me, my dear cousin, if you are all right.

With our best wishes for you all, especially for my dear Aunt Lena, I am, awaiting your answer,

Devotedly, your cousin [Max]

Despite his suspension of letters to Flörsheim, Julius had not, for all his frustrations, been idle in the matter of Max's latest SOS. Ultimately it was not in his nature to abandon a rescue mission simply because one of the approaches had failed, especially when the stakes were so high. He took up the challenge of raising the money for the Schohls' emigration to England with the same energy that he had put into pursuing American visas, and in early July he thought he could report success:

Charleston, July 6, 1939

Dear Cousin Max and Family;

By this time you know without a doubt that I am doing all in my power to help you. I just sent you a cable stating that I am arranging "Guarantee Bond" to the English Government for you and the family. You of course do not realize how difficult it is for me who virtually has nothing to go out and raise the necessary amount of money to get you to England and have just about succeeded in doing same. Charlie and Ferdy Midelburg have agreed to put up $500.00 a piece providing I put up a like amount which will be a total of $1,500.00 or around 300 pounds in English money, which will be about the necessary amount to raise along with what your friend Dr. Hene is willing to put up for you. Before going any further dear cousin I hope you realize that if I personally had the money neither the Midelburg cousins or Dr. Hene would be privelleged [sic] to advance this money for you, it would be my own pleasure to do this and it would be done gladly, and I would be proud to know that I could help one of my own when the time came.

I do not know exactly how to go about this but as soon as I finish this letter to you I shall write to Dr. Hene for instructions as to what papers I have to file, the exact amount of money I have to raise, who and where to send it, and for whatever information or instructions he is willing to give me.

No doubt he will inform you immediately upon hearing from me. I hope when you receive my cable you will write him to the effect that we are going to raise the money for you and that no doubt he will hear direct from me asking for instructions.

Cousin Max I am ashamed that I did not write to you sooner but I just did not have any good news to write and did not feel like writing and telling you I had failed you. Thank God I can write you now and tell you we are succeeding in our efforts. I sincerely hope this letter makes you feel as good in receiving it as it does me in being able to send it.

Keep up your spirits now for just a little longer and everything will be alright [sic]. Must close now so I can get my letter off to Dr. Hene. With love to you all, from all of us, devotedly, your cousin, [Julius]

As he promised, Julius immediately wrote Hene asking for instructions on sending the money for the Schohls' emigration to England. But just as Max had been ashamed to ask his distant relatives in America for help, Julius clearly felt unease at having to turn to a perfect stranger for assistance in a project that he wished he could have handled all by himself.

July 6, 1939

Dear Dr. Hene;

Just so you will know immediately who you are receiving a letter from I would like to introduce myself by stating that I am a cousin of Dr. Max Schohl of Florsheim, Germany.

It must be a wonderful feeling to know that one has a friend who is willing to go as far as you have volunteered to go for my cousin Max. I have a feeling of pride myself that I am privelidged [sic] to write to one who has shown what friendship really means, to a friend in distress.

If it had been within my power to aid my cousin by myself gladly would I have done so, but unfortunately I was unable to do so. Upon receipt of Max's letter in which he told me of your most generous offer of half the amount required to get he and the family to England I started to work on my other cousins here in the states and between us have succeeded in raising just about the other half necessary.

Will you please, Dr. Hene, by return mail, let me know just how much we should send, how we should send it and give me all other information need as myself, and my mother are very much worried about Max and his family.

Awaiting a speedy reply and thanking you a million times for what you are doing for my cousin, I remain,

Sincerely yours, [Julius Hess]

Dr. Hene never replied to Julius, nor did he ever write again to Max. Like the envisaged profits from Hene's and Max's jointly developed explosive device, the offer of financial assistance remained a paper promise.

Upon finally hearing from Julius in July and learning that he had managed to put together funding to get the Schohls to England, Max allowed himself to believe once again that his family's ordeal might soon be over. Yet he was concerned that his friend Hene, having promised to provide about half the necessary security bond, had suddenly become uncommunicative. On the other hand, before lapsing into silence, Hene had passed on to Max the name of a friend of his in London, an engineer named E. K. Moessmer, who had offered to help the Schohls navigate their way through the British immigration bureaucracy. Moessmer had then personally taken up contact with Max and advised him that the cost of getting the Schohls to England would be somewhat higher than Max had been led to believe by Hene. Moessmer told Max that he would have to post a bond of 500 pounds for himself, with smaller amounts for the rest of his family. Max hoped that the Midelburgs would add another 100 pounds to the amount Julius had already raised, and that Hene would likewise offer another 100. He put all this information in a letter to Julius dated July 16, 1939:

My dear cousin Julius,

. . . You have done a very good work for us, my dear cousin, and now we can hope to come in sooner time to England. I cannot tell you in words how I would like to thank you for this great help and for all the troubles you have had in this affair. I am hoping in any time I can show you that I can never forget what you have done for us.

You write that you will come in communication with my friend, Dr. Emil Hene, London. I suppose you have written to him, declaring the matter because of the guarantee, which you and cousins Charlie and Ferdy will have given for us. Till now I have nothing heard from Dr. Hene; but I know he is for some weeks in Scotland and will return to London in some days.

Now I will give you another address of a very good man who makes all the heavy work to bring us to England. I do not know this man personally, but I had got his address by my friend Dr. Hene. This man has the best communications to the Officials in London and knows exactly all the ways for us to remove all stumpling [sic] blocks. The address is: Mr. E. K. Moessmer, 108 Leeside Crescent, London, N.W. 11. Mr. Moessmer must be a very good man for he has written a lot of letters to encourage us and not to forget that he will do what he can to help us. I have given him your address too. I think it will be good for us when you will write a letter to him declaring all the matter of facts because the guarantee.

Two days ago Mr. Moessmer has written me that the British Officials demand for me a irrevocable Banc-Guarantee of Engl. Pound 500. You can understand, my dear cousin, that it is very hard for me, to write that. You have done so much for me and now I must come and say, and I am sorry to say it, it is still a little too few. I cannot express in English, what I feel in the moment, but I think You understand me.

Therefore, I beg you to speak with our cousins, if they would not give £100 more as a guarantee for me; then I had by you £400, and the rest of £100 will be given [by] my friend Dr. Hene, so that I have the whole amount of £500. The Guarantee for my family will be given [by] Mr. Moessmer and Dr. Hene and I hear that is not difficult. Only for my person is demanded so a high guarantee.

I hope that you have understood all that I will tell you, my dear cousin, and I beg you to speak the matter with our cousins. Give me please in your next letter the address of our cousins, Charlie and Ferdy; I will write them and thank for their good and great help.

Perhaps it is important for you to know, that I have not necessary this guarantee-amount, for I have a position, when I come to England and I have a salary that I can make my life for me and my family. The guarantee is only for the English Government to give me permit. Now I will hope you will succeed in my affair and I can hear, that all will be good, so that we can soon come away.

I will repeat, that we all are full of thanks to you who has done for us so much and has took over all troubles to help us. With love to you all, especially my good aunt Lina,

Devotedly your cousin [Max]

Before hearing from Julius, Max wrote his cousin another letter regarding the English guarantee, apparently on the advice of Moessmer. By all appearances Max was full of admiration for Moessmer, despite never having met him. He accepted at face value Moessmer's claims to have useful ties to the British government and to have helped many other Jewish refugees. He also did not question Moessmer's assurance that entry permits would be forthcoming provided that he, Moessmer, received the guarantee money in timely fashion.

25 July 1939

My dear cousin,

I think you will have received my letter from 16th July. Yesterday I have received a letter from Mr. E. K. Moessmer, 108 Leeside Crescent, London, whose address I have given you in my last letter. Mr. Moessmer is a friend of Dr. Hene and a man with the best relations to the English officials. He has already done a great and good work to help many German refugees and is doing his best to help me and my family. I have written to you, that he has given a great guarantee for us to the English government and when I think he is a whole foreign man to me I can not thank enough for this good work.

Yesterday he has written, all the guarantees are all right and the permit will be given by the government when the bank-guarantee from America has arrived. Therefore I have sent you today a cable: 'Please send bank guarantee to Mr. Moessmer, 108 Leeside Crescnet [sic], London, N. W. 11; then permit will be given.'

I know you understand me and our need and I know further you will do your best to settle it.

Mr. Moessmer has written me from great difficulties in this affair because the English government will only allow in seldom falls [cases] the entering of foreign jewish people.

I have the good hope that we can come soon to England and then our great need is finished. I thank you ever and ever, my dear cousin for all you have done for us and I think in better days I will have the great favour once to see you personally. I hope with God's Help in not so longer time.

Please say my hearty thanks to our cousins Charlie and Ferdy; I have not their addresses, to write directly.

I must go to the post-office, to send this letter off. You can understand that every day for waiting is hard work for us.

Let me soon as possible hear from you and with much love to you all I am,

Devotedly your cousin [Max]

Max's unbounded trust in Moessmer is understandable. Like many other Jews in his predicament, he was so desperate to get out of Nazi Germany that he did not scrutinize any potential helpers. This particular self-proclaimed Good Samaritan may indeed have been what he said he was, but the files of the main Jewish assistance organizations in England show no evidence that Moessmer had helped other Jews get into the country. Nor, more important, do British immigration records contain any evidence that Moessmer ever contacted the Home Office on Max's behalf, let alone provide some sort of "guarantee."

On the other side of the Atlantic, Julius Hess, having received Max's letters and cable regarding the Moessmer connection, was encountering unexpected difficulty in raising the desired sum. The Midelburgs, it seems, had developed second thoughts about handing over their share of the guarantee bond:

August 5th, 1939

My Dear Cousin Max;

I received your letters of July 16th and 25th, but did not answer them at once as I was waiting to hear from Dr. Hene, so that I could give you some direct information. So far I have not had a word from him. After reading your last letter over very carefully I decided that instead of waiting to hear from Dr. Hene or Mr. Moessmer that I would write to Mr.

Moessmer right away and find out exactly how much we have to raise and to whom and how it should be sent.

I realize dear cousin that it is very hard for you and the family to be patient under the circumstances but it will not be for long I hope and then we can all breathe a sigh of relief.

I too am having my troubles, of course not like yours, but the task of raising the money has been a much harder job than you would think. You have asked me time and again to send you the Midelburgs' address which I have not done because you have nothing to thank them for as yet. Although both of the Midelburgs have more money than they could possibly spend they are very reluctant about turning loose of any of it. Both of them assured me they would do their part but when the time comes I will have to shame them into doing it or raise it all between my sister Norma and myself. You can rest assured though that I am doing all I can to help you and if the Midelburgs come across I will write you immediately so that you can thank them in person.

Please do not misunderstand or misinterpret this letter but I felt it my duty to write to you just how things stand. If I but had the money myself it would be both a pleasure and a privilege to do it all by myself for you and in return the feeling of doing something worthwhile for a relative in distress would be more than enough compensation for my efforts.

Again let me assure you that your wait will not be much longer and trusting this letter finds you and the family both in good health and spirits, I am,

Devotedly, [Julius]

Still hopeful that the Midelburgs would ultimately help in the Schohl rescue, Julius, as he had told Max he would, wrote Moessmer to inquire into the details of the money transfer. Like Max, he seems (at least initially) to have completely trusted both Moessmer and Hene, esteeming them all the higher in light of his difficulty in securing similar assistance from some of his own relatives.

August 5th, 1939

My Dear Mr. Moessmer;

You no doubt know by the name and address on this letter head just who I am and why you are receiving this letter.

Mere words cannot express my gratitude to you for the effort you are putting forth to help get my cousin Dr. Max Schohl and his family out of Germany and into England.

My cousin has written me just what you and Dr. Hene are doing on behalf of he and his family and just as I wrote Dr. Hene it gives me a feeling of pride to know that I am privileged to even write to two such men as yourself and Dr. Hene.

As I told my cousin it is very difficult for me personally to raise my portion of the guarantee but knowing the dire necessity of it I am willing to borrow the money from the bank in order to help him, and after hearing from him just what you two gentlemen are doing I feel that no matter how hard the strain is on me I am doing little enough.

I had arranged with my sister and one of my cousins to send approximately 300 pounds, but according to the letter I received from cousin Max this amount would not be enough so I am writing to you for the following information. Please let me know exactly just how much we are to raise, how it should be sent and to whom payable and if necessary what papers to fill out.

Due to the fact that I am very much worried about my cousin and the family would appreciate very much as quick a reply as possible to this letter.

Trusting I shall hear from you at a very early date, and again thanking you for your wonderful help, I am,

Very sincerely yours, [Julius Hess]

While Julius was working to "shame" the Midelburgs into helping Max, Moessmer was exerting more pressure on the German chemist to get the bond money to him as soon as possible. He told Max that he had persuaded a "prominent Englishman" to put up a guarantee for him, for which he, Moessmer, had offered all his patents as collateral. (If this were the case, why was the bond from Julius still necessary?) Like Julius, Max found the Midelburgs' behavior all the more damning given the apparent generosity of a total stranger like Moessmer. As he wrote Julius on August 13:

My Dear Cousin Julius,

In the moment I have received your letter of August 5th and I will answer at once. I have seen you have received my letter of July 25th and doubtless my cable of the same day. First I will thank you from all my heart for all your doing to help us; I know it and I feel it you understand all our troubles and cares which are not to describe.

I suppose you have written to Mr. Moessmer to London and I know surely this man will answer you at once. He is a man, so good and brave, how I had never believed that he can exist in the world! He is a whole unknown to me and I had only his address received by my friend Dr. Hene; but he is one of the best friends I have; he has done a guarantee for us by a prominent Englishman and in order to reach that he has given all his patents as a security to that English. That is a great deed of him and I hope I am able to attest him my thanks when I will be in England.

I have read your last letter with hot tears when I have seen that you and your sister Norma will do what you can to help us. I thank you both heartily and I feel it is the same blood which runs through our veins. Each word of your good letter is proof of that.

Therefore I cannot understand our cousins Middelburgs [sic]. When the things were opposite I know we could do all in our powers to help in such great need. There are yet four human lives of near relations which are in great danger! And they cannot feel with us? I cannot understand it and I will hope they will change their sense.

Please my dear cousin do what you can to help us; we are almost despairing; the long waiting has took away our powers; my dear wife the best and the bravest, is since three weeks so sick because she can no more believe on better times. But I myself cannot believe that we are condemned to perish in that country; we are innocence to our bad fate and we trust on our God and on you and all good men that they will help us.

I am waiting for good news of you and thank you and your sister Norma of all my heart.

I am devotedly, your cousin [Max]

Having received Julius Hess's flattering letter and inquiry regarding the details of the money transfer, Moessmer immediately cabled him: "Send £400 bank cheque payable to me, Moessmer." He followed this up with a letter explaining what he had done so far for Max in England (a slightly different version of the account he had given Max) and underscoring the urgency of the matter. He said nothing about any paperwork needing to be filled out. We should note that the "Evian Committee" (The Intergovernmental Committee on Refugees) to which he made reference did not submit applications for visas and that there was no such thing as an "S.O.S permit."

August 15, 1939

Dear Mr. Hess,

I have received your letter of the 5th and have cabled to you as follows:

SEND £400 BANK CHEQUE PAYABLE TO ME MOESSMER

The situation is as follows: My influential friends in the Evian Committee have applied for an S.O.S. permit for Dr. Schohl. The British Home Office have accepted this and I believe there is a possibility of it being granted shortly and that Dr. Schohl will be able to come here within the next 14 days. As the Home Office have asked me to give a life guarantee, it is most vital for me to find £500, of which I already have £100 and am very grateful for your offer to send, by bank cheque on a London bank, the balance of £400. As soon as I will be in possession of the £500, there will be no further difficulties put in the way of Dr. Schohl's arrival in this country.

Dr. Schohl's beautiful home is cut in pieces. The Nazis have confiscated 400,000 Goldmarks of his and he is to-day a very poor man. Dr. Schohl is one of the greatest German authorities in metallurgy and chemistry and when he arrives in London there will be no difficulty in my finding a position for him with the minimum of delay. I am working as Consulting Engineer to the British government and have influential friends in Dr. Schohl's special departments.

As the matter is most urgent, I should be most grateful if you would send the money as quickly as possible.

Yours sincerely.

[E. K. Moessmer]

Julius Hess was not suspicious by nature, but he seems to have been made somewhat uneasy by Moessmer's insistence that a check payable directly to him be sent forthwith, without any additional information on immigration procedures or requirements. Rather than do as Moessmer requested, he consulted his lawyer friend Philip Angel, to whom he gave a copy of Max's letter about Moessmer. Angel, in turn, contacted Cecilia Razovsky, the highly respected director of the National Refugee Service in New York City.

August 22, 1939

Dear Miss Razovsky:

I enclose herewith a copy of a letter written to Dr. Schohl's cousin. Mr. Moessmer, who is mentioned in the letter, cabled Mr. Hess to wire him the necessary number of English pounds so that Dr. Schohl and his wife may enter England.

We are not sure whether this should be sent direct to Mr. Moessmer or deposited with the proper officials in England. In other words, Mr. Hess would like to know what procedure should be followed in a case of this type. We felt there must be a legal procedure by which this must be done and would like to be advised.

Dr. Hene, mentioned in the letter, is a close friend of Dr. Schohl but Mr. Moessmer is not known to Dr. Schohl other than through Dr. Hene.

Very truly yours,
[Philip Angel]

The "legal procedure" about which Angel inquired was rather different than Moessmer had indicated. Aliens seeking refuge in Britain in 1939 were required to do more than put up a security bond; they had to submit an application for a visa and be interviewed by one of the British Passport Control officials abroad (in Max's case, at the British Consulate in Berlin). Since Britain saw itself as a temporary haven rather than as a country of immigration, the Home Office requested visa applicants to show some proof that they could move on after a specified stay (the maximum being two years, though this limit was rarely imposed on immigrants already in the country). Refugees hoping to go on to one of the British colonies had to have—as the Home Secretary assured the Colonial Office—"a definite assurance of admission to a Colony," a condition that could generally by met only by people "young enough to be able to start life afresh" and "engaged in a trade or profession which will be useful in a new country." If refugees indicated that they expected to go on to America, they had to provide a quota number indicating a wait time of less than two years. (By 1939 Britain was becoming wary of admitting Jews with American quota numbers because the American Consul-General in Berlin had warned Whitehall that "he did not think 50% of those people who hoped to come to the U.S. [via Britain] would ever be admitted to the USA.") Applicants also had to submit a birth certificate, medical report, and brief biographical essay with certificates of educational and professional achievements. German Jews applying for entry into England typically got assistance from the German Jewish Aid Committee, which would hold the necessary bond money pending the Home Office's decision. Bond money collected in America was generally deposited with the National Refugee Service in New York for later transfer to England.

Information regarding British admission procedures was kindly provided by Cecilia Razovsky to Philip Angel in a letter dated September 6, 1939. Unfortunately, by that time war had broken out in Europe, bringing an end to the efforts of rescue organizations like Razovsky's to get Jewish refugees into Britain.

September 6, 1939

Dear Mr. Angel:

Amplifying our wire of September 5 we regret to advise that the German Jewish Aid Committee, the committee with which we cooperate in England, is not at the present time in a position to accept admission of refugees because of the international situation. Conditions may change. . . .

As soon as immigration is resumed, we will be glad to do everything possible to help you in carrying out the plans. It will not be necessary to send the funds to England. If they are deposited in our office, we can so instruct the English committee and they can proceed with the application for a visa upon assurance that the money is deposited with us.

Will you please keep in touch with us and be assured that
we will take action as soon as possible.

Sincerely yours, [Cecilia Razovsky]

Of course, the "conditions" dictating a halt in Jewish immigration to
Britain did not change. Britain's declaration of war against Germany
on September 3, 1939, prompted Whitehall to close its Passport Control Offices in Berlin, Vienna, and Prague and to invalidate visas held
by "German nationals of the Jewish race" that had been "granted previous to the commencement of war." The suspension of immigration
lasted for the duration of the war. To the extent that Britain had been
an "island refuge" for German Jews, it was a refuge no more.

The outbreak of what became World War II naturally brought an end to
Max Schohl's effort to emigrate to England. It is quite possible, however,
that he would not have been able to get into England even if the war
had not come along. Apart from the possible unreliability of his English
"sponsors," who, had they actually received funds from Julius, may not
have used them on Max's behalf as promised, Max was in a weak position owing to his age and lack of prospects for timely re-emigration.
Moreover, because British passport offices in Central Europe were overrun with Jewish asylum seekers in mid-1939, there was a huge backlog
in the processing of visa applications. At the same time, in Britain itself
so few Jewish refugees were moving on to other destinations that the
Home Office feared that "a pool of refugees might be formed in England." In response, the Home Office began doing what it could to tighten
the admissions procedure even further in the weeks before the war.

For the Schohl family, the only silver lining in this very black cloud
was the fact that Cousin Julius had not sent any of the money he had
collected in America on to Mr. Moessmer in London. This money, as it
turned out, would be much needed in the next phase of the Schohls'
campaign to find sanctuary somewhere outside Hitler's Reich.

CHAPTER SIX

The Last Trial

The Chilean Option

The outbreak of World War II inspired a much different response among the German public than did the opening of hostilities in 1914. There were no joyous celebrations in the streets, no happy soldiers shouting "On to Paris" as they boarded trains for the front. In a diary entry dated September 1, 1939, the CBS correspondent in Berlin, William Shirer, observed: "The people in the street were apathetic when I drove to the *Rundfunk* for my first broadcast at eight fifteen A.M. Across from the Adlon the morning shift of workers was busy on the new I.G. Farben building just as if nothing had happened. None of them bought the extras which the newsboys were shouting."

The approximately 170,000 Jews still remaining in Germany when the war broke out had less reason than anyone to be enthusiastic about this development. War made finding a safe refuge from Hitler's Germany considerably more difficult than it had been before, and of course the territory under Nazi control soon expanded as a result of German conquests. France and Britain, now at war with the Reich, were closed off to refugees from Germany. Anticipating a new wave of asylum-seekers from Europe, the United States tightened its visa-granting procedures. American consuls in Europe now insisted that all would-be immigrants, even those whose visas had already been approved, show steamship tickets before their visas would be handed over. The last boat to carry refugees from Germany directly to America had sailed in April 1939.

Max Schohl, of course, was among the thousands of German Jews who, in September 1939, had literally missed the boat. And yet, amazing as this may seem, his first reaction upon learning of the outbreak of war was not to bewail his fate but to try to enlist in the German army, so that he might fight once again for his country. The day after Britain and France declared war on Germany he went to the regional Wehrmacht command and offered his services, citing his previous distinguished record as an officer in World War I. Clearly, in his eyes the "call of duty" in time of war outweighed all the persecution and humiliation that had been heaped upon him by his countrymen since 1933. As quixotic as it was poignant, Max's gesture occasioned incomprehension, though fortunately not ridicule, at the Wehrmacht command: the would-be enlistee was gently told that in light of his age and racial status his services would not be needed.

Having had his offer to fight for his fatherland spurned, Max resumed his quest to get himself and his family to a safe haven before yet more options were closed to him. Now he could not afford to be picky at all, and when he heard that Chile was accepting German-Jewish immigrants he set his sights on that distant nation as a possible refuge. The trouble was, getting to Chile was expensive, and Max had little money left and no chance of earning more. Convinced that the chances of escaping Germany were growing dimmer by the day, Max turned once again to his American cousin for help. Along with this latest SOS to Julius, he had to provide the Nazi censors with a German translation, a new requirement brought on by the war. Revealingly, Max softened some of the phrases in the German version; for example, instead of saying that his family would "die" if they did not escape Germany, as he did in the English version, he used the locution *zu Grunde gehen* ("to go under"). Still, his message was dire enough, and he risked having his letter turned back by the censors to convey the seriousness of his plight.

Flörsheim, 23 October 1939

My dear cousin

About two months ago I have written the last time to you. Meanwhile great and heavy things have happened. These things have changed our position and our hopes in a very bad manner. It will be clear for you all that it is completely impossible for us to come to England. To emigrate in U.S.A. is impossible too, as you know. But we cannot remain here because we have no more money to make our life. It is impossible for me to get any position here to [earn] money for our life. And what shall we do now? Perhaps we can live about two months; for a longer time it is impossible. The cares for our children let us no rest by day and night. We are in a despairing situation. You cannot think how despaired our life is, my dear cousin; we all have often desired that we could die to have our rest. Today I make the last trial to save us, when it is possible. Last week I have heard that it is possible to emigrate to Chile (South America). I was told that I could get a position as a chemist; I have some friends in that country and I am sure they will help me. At any rate I could work and we could make our life. This affair is in the hands of a great shipping society in Germany: "Palestine and Orient Lloyd Berlin." I have been coming in touch with this society and I was told the following: It is doubtless possible for us to emigrate in Chile; permit for working will be given with the permit for entering. And now comes the stumbling block: It takes a lot of money and not that in German money but in a foreign standard. The permit to enter with the permit to work makes costs of $165 for each person. When these amounts are paid on a foreign bank, then the permits will be given. But the ships-tickets will be paid in dollars too and that for each person about $269 (3rd class). That is more than $400 for each. You have done so much for us my dear cousin to bring us to England and therefore I come to you to beg you from all my heart to help us to come to Chile. I have no other person in the whole world who could help us in this situation. Naturally I accept that you have not yet sent any money to England for us. . . . I know you will do what you can do. I know too it is a lot of money we need. When however all relations will help together in U.S.A. then I think it will be possible. Charley and Ferdy Middelbourg [sic] cannot tell you 'no' when they know that four persons of their own family must die because they have not this money to save their life. We four, my family, we have no [responsibility for] our bad fate. But in our adders [veins] runs the same blood as in theirs; they cannot answer for our God when they do nothing and let the things go how they must go. But when you have not full success to get the amount for four then I beg you to try to get the amount for two of us. In this case I myself and my elder daughter Helene Marianne, we could go first for Chile. There I hope to serve so much that I can send the money for my wife and my younger daughter that they can come as soon as possible. My wife must go meanwhile to a sister of hers and my younger daughter can perhaps come to friends of us. My good old mother must go to a hospital for common costs; how bad for this good old woman who has done all her life what is good and right! I have told you my dear cousin exactly our situation how it is. I am sure you will do what you can do and I hope on you, how I have ever hoped on you. Today the shipping society has written that the amount of $165 for each person shall be paid as soon as possible to "Incasso-Bank, Amsterdam/Holland for Palestine and Orient Lloyd Berlin and that for entering Chile for Dr. Max Schohl and Family (or daughter)." The costs for the ships-tickets can be paid later on. When these amounts to Amsterdam will be paid, we can travel on February next. I send you this letter with the hottest wishes, my dear cousin, that you might have whole success to get the money we need. It is the last possibility to save our life. Please write me as soon as possible. You cannot think with which hopes we are awaiting your answer; it is deciding for life and death. We hope you [are] all well and with our best regards for all relations, I am

Devotedly your cousin, Max

The Palestine and Orient Lloyd firm to which Max referred was not actually a shipping line but a travel agency, one of several based in Germany that made enormous profits from the exodus of German Jews. This company, along with other Berlin-based agencies such as the Französische Reisebüro on Unter den Linden, dispatched agents throughout Europe in search of foreign consuls who would trade visas for hard currency. Like the Cuban immigration official who peddled invalid landing permits to the *St. Louis* passengers, some foreign consuls, especially those from South American countries, did a land office business in the sale of visas without first clearing these transactions with their home governments. The Uruguayan consul-general in Hamburg was recalled after having made a fortune in visas that his country had no intention of honoring. Such shady practices on the part of the consuls did not overly worry the travel agencies; their clients paid in advance, and the victims had no legal recourse if swindled.

This is not to say, of course, that Max was likely to have been swindled by the Palestine and Orient Lloyd, only that a modicum of caution was called for in dealing with these firms, as well as with the shipping companies and consular offices involved in the immigration arrangements. Most Jewish refugees, however, were too desperate and vulnerable to exercise much prudence.

Understanding Max's desperation, Julius Hess took it upon himself to be cautious on his cousin's behalf. As he had done in the case of Moessmer's request for instant cash, before sending any money to Holland he asked his friend Philip Angel to inquire into the viability of

Chile as an emigration destination, and to check up on the Palestine and Orient Lloyd as a travel broker. Angel turned once again to Cecilia Razovsky of the National Refugee Service for the information. Two weeks later, she responded as follows:

November 21, 1939
Mr. Philip Angel
Charleston, West Virginia

Dear Mr. Angel:

We regret very much that your letter has remained unanswered to this date.

Apropos your specific question, we can only answer this way. We know that Chile does admit émigrés and that it is necessary for the United States relatives to provide funds for show money—required amounts vary—and also the steamship tickets, which cost in the vicinity of $250.00 per person via the Italian or Holland America Lines.

As for the Palestine-Lloyd, this is a private agency and as you can understand we cannot commit ourselves definitely one way or another. Any arrangements entered into by relatives must be on their own responsibility. The important point to determine is the validity of the permits issued. Perhaps the United States relatives could deposit the money with the specification that it will be refunded to them if the family is not admitted to Chile.

The arrangements for the steamship tickets can be best made by purchasing them from one of your local agents. He will cable to his office abroad and they in turn will communicate with Dr. Schohl when reservations are available.

We hope the above information will prove helpful, and if we can serve you in any other way please write to us again.

Sincerely yours,
Cecilia Razovsky

Having been reassured that, at least in principle, the Schohls could immigrate to Chile, Julius launched an investigation into the precise modalities of the process. He had Philip Angel inquire of Cecilia Razovsky how much "show money" would be required by the Chilean government. Through emissaries in Washington, D.C., he also inquired at the Chilean embassy to ascertain the specific requirements for immigration to that country. An embassy representative informed Julius's emissary that immigration to Chile was restricted for one year as of April 1939, but that some Spanish and German refugees were still being allowed to enter the country. The embassy could provide no specific details on immigration requirements, insisting that such information had to be obtained from the Chilean consul-general in Berlin, "the only Chilean Consulate able to pass upon and issue visas for entry into Chile."

The immigration situation in Chile, as it applied to Jewish refugees from Germany in the late 1930s, was in fact quite confused—and capricious. Like many other Latin American countries, Chile harbored various nationalist and anti-Semitic elements opposed to Jewish immigration. The influential German colony in Chile, partly infected with Nazism, did what it could to foment anti-Jewish sentiment. The Chilean government, again like many of its neighbors, focused its immigration efforts on the recruitment of hearty young agricultural workers and entrepreneurs with capital to generate jobs—categories hardly favorable to Jewish refugees, most of whom were urbanites and virtually all of whom were without significant financial resources. This reality was well known to officials in the United States, who, until the outbreak of war, hoped to encourage Latin American countries to take as many Jewish refugees as possible, thereby relieving pressure on North America. As George Warren, secretary of the PACPR, wrote Secretary of State Hull in November 1938: "Very few [Latin American] governments are willing to accept members of the urban professions which predominate among the involuntary emigrants from Germany." Acceding to pressure from economic nationalists and racist groups, the authoritarian government of President Arturo Alessandri, an admirer of Benito Mussolini, had advised Chilean consuls abroad in 1936 not to issue visas to "Jews and anarchists." However, a few of the consuls had continued to dispense visas to Jews who could pay the requisite bribes, with the result that some Jewish refugees still managed to get into Chile, often after paying additional brides to the local immigration authorities. A new government under President Pedro Aguirre Cerda took power in 1938 with the promise to clean up corruption in the immigration system and to liberalize the admission policies for Jewish refugees. Cerda, however, was promptly subjected to impeachment proceedings for condoning the sale of visas to Jews. It was for this reason that his government ordered the one-year restriction on immigration alluded to by the Chilean embassy in its communication with Julius's representative.

Of course, neither Julius nor Max could have known much about the internal wrangling over immigration policy in Chile, although, as in the cases of America and England, the fate of their joint efforts to effect the Schohls' escape from Nazi Germany hung on the outcome of such distant disputes.

Julius, in any event, was tied up with a wrangle closer to home in his ongoing effort to convince the Midelburgs to help the Schohls find refuge outside Hitler's Reich. At this stage in his efforts, he was able to convince Charles Midelburg to pitch in, but not the wealthier Ferdy. Once again, he was overcome by a sense of shame on behalf of his rich American relative, as well as a feeling of guilt over not being able to handle the entire matter on his own. In a letter to Max dated November 28 he tried to be as upbeat as he could, but his frustration and anger showed through:

November 28th, 1939

Dear Cousin Max;

I can realize how anxiously and hopefully you await this answer to your letter, and I also realize how you must have felt during the past two months not hearing a single word from me. But please believe me that you and your family have never been out of my thoughts. Just at the time we thought we might get you to England the trouble started and

I could not tell if you had received my letters or if you and your family were all well and still together; due to this fact I have spent many sleepless nights.

I shall not write more of the above matter but get right into the details of your last letter. Just as soon as I received it I got in touch with your Refugee Committee to find out if there was a possible chance to get you to Chile. Today I heard from them and was informed that there is a chance to go there, not a very concise one but a chance. Today letters were sent to the Chilean Embassy in Washington to find out just how much money each one would have to have to be permitted to enter Chile. As you have already surmised I have had great difficulty in raising the money necessary to getting you out. Today I saw Charles Midelburg again and he is willing to put up $500.00 if my sister Norma and myself put up the same amount. I am sorry to say but I shall not ask Ferdy Midelburg again to help out. This means that we will be able to raise $1,500.00 which according to your figures will not be quite enough to get you all out, but as you stated if just two of you could come you yourself could help get the other two out. It hurts me very much to have to write about just two of you coming instead of all of you. If you should write to thank Charles Midelburg I would suggest that you do not even mention Ferdy's name or refer to his not being willing to help.

It surely seems like all my letters have been holding vain promises but I know you must realize I am doing all in my power for you. I promise you this that if this plan can possibly be worked out you are as good as on your way to Chile.

Please do not give up as sure as there is a God above you will receive help.

Love to you all, [Julius]

Fortunately, Julius's sister Norma Kaufman also took up Max's case with Ferdy Midelburg. Norma was a considerably more forceful and charismatic personality than her brother. Strikingly beautiful, she turned every man's head in town. "That dame sure is a looker," said a visiting salesman once to Grover Kaufman upon seeing Norma enter the Kaufman Brothers store, not realizing that she was Grover's wife. "Yes, she is," replied Grover, "and I slept with her last night." To which Norma added, winking salaciously at her husband, "And we're on again for tonight, baby!" Now, Norma went confidently to work on Ferd Midelburg with the same combination of wit and resolve that she applied to all challenges, especially those involving men. The Kaufmans and the Ferdy Midelburgs happened to be vacationing near each other on Miami Beach in December 1939, so Norma took this opportunity to apply personal pressure on Ferdy. As she related to Julius in the first of three letters from Miami Beach, a check of her own was forthcoming for Max, but Ferdy was proving hard to crack:

Friday Night

Dear Julius and All,

Your letter received this morning, enclosing the one from Max. It is one of the most pathetic letters I ever read, and you can rest assured that Grover and I will do our share. Let us know when you want the money.

I called Ferd this morning to see if he was home but he was out and the maid said he would be in around 4 o'clock. I went over there at 4:30 but he had been in and out again. I left Max's letter and wrote one to Ferd, telling him we were all going to help get Max and family over. I left my phone number, but he never called me, so I called him a few minutes ago. He said at first that none of us are helping with Julius Goldberg and family in New York, and that he has been helping Aunt Lanehe for 18 years—that if we could help with them, he would go in with us on this. I told him that whether he helped or not we were going to go ahead and bring Max and his family over, if possible. He seemed to think that it depended on him—that if he would put up then we would. I told him that he was all money [and] that it didn't depend on him. He cooled down and said to let him think it over, and he would call me tomorrow. I told him that even if he is helping the others, that he is plenty able to do so, and that if I were able I would be happy to do more. I also told him that you would probably have to borrow the money, but that you were glad you could help. Then I told him that if for no other reason, he should join with us as we were the only ones Max could call on, and that he certainly didn't want to be the one to stand back. I believe I have convinced him—but you never can tell. I will let you know as soon as I hear from him. . . .

The promise of a check from Norma cheered Julius, for, with Charles Midelburg's help, he would now have enough money to pay the passages for at least two of the Schohls to Chile, and if Ferdy came in he could cover the costs for the entire family. However, having followed the saga of the ill-fated *St. Louis* in the Charleston papers, Julius worried that the Schohls might make it to Chile only to be turned back because their visas were not valid. Still, considering the alternatives to not acting quickly, he believed the "gamble" was worth it. As he wrote Norma in early December:

December 4, 1939

Dear Norma,

I received your letter and was certainly thrilled in your reply. We are going to have to act very quickly on this matter, because Lord knows if Holland will be next or not.

Please send me your check immediately, because I want to start this thing moving at once. The first thing I am going to do is have the Bank here send the money to the Bank of Holland, for the purpose of obtaining Visas, but here's where the hitch comes in. If Ferdy does not come in with us, I can only obtain Visas for two of them, and of course, it will not take quite as much money for the two, but I am in hopes that Ferdy will break down and join us.

At first I felt there was an element of gamble in bringing them out this way, but the gamble is so one-sided that I cannot but feel it is bound to work. The purchase of the steamship tickets, of course, is no gamble. The only thing that worries me will be the validity of the Visas issued by the Chilean Council [sic] in Germany, and if they get there, whether the Country of Chile will recognize them. If you remember, that is what happened in the Cubian [sic] affair. According to the Refugee Committee, this has never happened in Chile, and Chile is accepting refugees of a selected class, approved by their Council abroad.

I shall wire Max Schohl just as soon as I hear from you, to make application to the Chilean Council for his Visas, advising him money has been posted in the Incasso Bank, as per the instructions in his letter; that as soon as he obtains his Visas to wire me so that I can purchase his steamship tickets from this side, so that there will be no question of his passage. The reason I am writing you all of these details is that I feel that you are as greatly interested in what we are doing, and how it is being done as I am, and feel that you have a perfect right to know. If there is anything that I have left unexplained, please write and ask me for it. The biggest Christmas present I will be able to get this year will be a letter from you stating that Ferdy Midelburg is going to enable us to bring up the entire family. I shall send this airmail, and would love an immediate reply. . . .

With love to you both, [Julius]

A few days later Norma wrote Julius with (qualified) good news: Ferdy would do his part after all. However, fearing a swindle by the

Palestine and Orient Lloyd, Ferdy intended to withhold his contribution until it was certain that it would be used for the designated purpose.

Sunday Night, Miami Beach

Dear Julius and All,

Ferd was over this morning and promised to give $500 for Max, but only when he arrives in Chile. He said he has had two experiences of sending money over, and the people had never got out, and he has never seen anything of the money. He suggested that you investigate thoroughly the organization that Max requests to get him out. I think you could find out . . . through the Coordinating Committee if there is such a society as the "Palestine and Orient Lloyd, Berlin."

I hope you have written Max that help will be forthcoming. I only hope that this time we will be successful in getting them out of Germany. . . .

Ferdy Midelburg's promise of $500 *after* Max arrived in Chile was not much use, since emigrants were required to put up the entirety of their visa and ship-passage costs in advance before being allowed to leave for their ports of embarkation. Apparently Norma made this clear to Ferdy, for he finally relented and gave her a check—along with a grudging compliment regarding her persuasive abilities. Norma immediately sent the check to Julius, along with an explanatory note:

Miami Beach, Thursday Night

Dear Julius and All,

As you can see from the enclosed, I got Ferd's check. I just came back from there, and he said I could talk the "balls [bugs?] off a dead man's eye." Anyway, here it is and I know

you'll be happy that he came across. I assured him that you
would take every precaution that we would not be sending
our money on a "fool's errand." I trust that you have investi-
gated the organization, which Max is so confidant can help
him. I do hope that this time we will be successful in getting
them out. . . .

Julius was in fact doing what he could to ensure that the money he
collected would be used to get the Schohls out of Germany. His various
efforts on this score bear relating in some detail as they point up how
confusing and risk-laden this business was, not just for the potential
emigrants but also for their sponsors in the United States. Anxious as
they were to get their German relatives out, the American sponsors understandably did not want to get bilked in the process.

At Julius's request, Philip Angel wrote again to Cecilia Razovsky,
asking if the National Refugee Committee would handle the arrangements for the Schohls' emigration to Chile, acting on Max's behalf either vis-à-vis the Palestine and Orient or some other agency. Angel
assured Razovsky that Julius Hess did not expect the committee to assume legal responsibility for the Schohls, but he, Julius, "would feel a
whole lot safer if your committee would handle the money as he feels
that in such case it would be handled at minimum risk."

Julius also had his bank in Charleston send an inquiry to the Chase
National Bank in New York, which had considerable experience in han-
dling international money transfers in immigration cases, asking for
their advice regarding the dispatch of funds to Europe for Max. Referring to Max's instruction that $165 per family member be deposited in a
Dutch bank, Julius's banker asked "if this amount . . . represents a fee
for securing the visas or is it in the nature of an amount which must be
shown as belonging to Dr. Schohl and his family before they can gain
entrance to Chile?" Noting that the Schohls intended to use the services
of the Palestine and Orient Lloyd to travel from Germany to Chile, the
Charleston bank also wanted to know if it could make a remittance
through Chase to Holland "with the assurance that the money so sent

would be used by the Palestine and Orient Lloyd for the purpose intended?" Chase's reply was not very helpful:

December 11, 1939

Gentlemen:

This will acknowledge receipt of your letter of December 7,
1939. While we have been asked from time to time by customers to make financial arrangements for emigrants from
Germany, we have no direct knowledge of regulations for the
various countries. We are under the impression that these
regulations vary in different cases and are changing constantly. Consequently we are not in a position to tell what the
$165 deposit represents. We wonder however whether Dr.
Schohl checked with the Chilean Consul in Germany.

While we could effect a transfer at your request to the Incasso Bank with instructions to the effect that the funds are
"for Palestine and Orient Lloyds G.m.b.h. Berlin for entering
Chile for Dr. Schohl and family (or daughter)," we could give
no assurance that the funds would be used by the Palestine
and Orient Lloyds for the purpose designated.

Yours very truly,
[Charles J. Spies]

Although Julius did not send any money to Holland until December
14, 1939, upon learning from Norma that the Midelburg contributions
were forthcoming he had written Max that the funds he requested
would be posted forthwith to the Incasso Bank in Amsterdam. Max in
turn had alerted Incasso to expect the transfer. On December 9 the
Palestine and Orient Lloyd wired Julius that the Incasso Bank had "not
yet received the $1,000 amount" promised by Dr. School [sic]," and
that the funds must come immediately to ensure the Schohls' timely
emigration. Julius was understandably confused by the $1,000 figure.

As he understood the situation, Max needed $165 per person for entry permits—or $660—to start the emigration process; the money for steamship tickets could be sent once the entry permits were secured. He immediately cabled the Palestine and Orient asking for an explanation, but he did not receive an answer until December 19, when the travel agency cabled him that the $1,000 represented entry permits and passage costs for two persons.

In the meantime, not being sure exactly how to proceed, but worried that if he did not act immediately all would be lost, Julius had the Chase Bank wire $660 to the Incasso Bank in Holland on December 14. He also cabled Max informing him of the transfer and requesting further instructions regarding the handling of the passage money.

Two weeks later, having heard nothing from Incasso or Max, a worried Julius dispatched a plaintive letter to Incasso asking for their assurance that the funds he had sent were being used for their intended purpose. "I realize," he conceded, "that it is not your duty to impart such information but I feel sure that whoever receives this letter and reads it will surely realize the anxiety suffered by one part of a family over on this side of the ocean and wondering if his efforts are all in vain trying to help relatives interred in Germany."

On the same day, December 28, Julius sent an anxiety-filled letter to Max, reminding him of his request, cabled two weeks earlier, to wire back further information on the money transfers. Clearly Julius did not know that since the outbreak of war Jews in Germany were no longer allowed to send cables, only letters. Mail service, moreover, was now considerably slower because of the war. Julius explained to Max what he had done so far and pleaded for some sign of life from Flörsheim.

December 28th, 1939

Dear Cousin Max;

Day by day I have been waiting your reply to the Cablegram I sent you on December 14 advising you I had sent by Cable the necessary amount according to your letter for the cost of four Visas, $165 per person. Four permits total $660.

My Cable read as follows: Money Cabled Amsterdam for four permits wire further instructions. This money was cabled by the Chase National Bank of New York City to the Incasso Bank N. V. Amsterdam, Holland, for Palestine and Orient Lloyds G. M. B. H. for entering Chile for Dr. Schohl and family.

On December 9th I received a cable from Palestine Lloyd as follows: "Amount according letter Doctor Schohl $1000 not yet arrived Amsterdam urgent otherwise departure impossible. Answer cable. PalestLloyd Berlin." I did not know what to do because the amount varied from what you told me in your letter. I cabled them back the same day paying in advance for their return answer and I did not receive this answer until December 19th which was as follows: "Thousand dollars represents permit and passage for two persons." It took so long to get their answer that like I told you above I went ahead and cabled the permit money for four persons and cabled you the same day to that affect [sic] asking you to wire me further instructions. I have been waiting and waiting for your answer because thank God I have been able to raise the money to get you all out.

Now I am greatly worried because I have not heard from you, not on account of the money sent but as to your welfare so please let me hear just as quickly as possible if you are alright [sic]. In regards to raising the money I got Charlie Midelburg to put up $500, and my sister Norma got Ferdy Midelburg to put up the same amount and Norma and myself are putting up like amounts ourselves, so all I am waiting for is the cable from you for your passage money.

With love and hope to you and all your family and may God speed your wire to me advising me you are ready to depart, I am,

Devotedly, [Julius]

Max had in fact written to Julius on December 14, before he received Julius's cable of the same day, but his letter did not arrive in Charleston until after the turn of the year. Max had also written a thank you letter to

Charles Midelburg. Max's letter to Julius was full of optimism regarding his prospects in Chile, but it also contained a note of urgency: the money for the permits and ship tickets had to be deposited in Amsterdam immediately if the Schohls were to be able to sail in February as they hoped.

December 14, 1939

My dear Cousin Julius,

To day I received your airmail letter from November 28th and at once I will answer, because my heart is so full of thanks for you. Your very good news have let us forget all troubles of the last months and now, we are sure we can come out with your great help. Believe me, my dear cousin, I have no words to express, what I and my family are feeling in these hours. We can only say, our God shall pay your good doing, to you and to your sister Norma and Cousin Charley. And you have the satisfaction having saved me and my family and I think this great deed will not remain unpaid by our God. Meanwhile I have heard that I can get a position in Chile; a friend of mine has a friend in Santiago, who is Professor in chemistry at the university and this man is ready to help me for a position in chemical industry. Naturally it is important to speak Spanish; we all speak a few and believe, when we are in the country about three months, we can [speak] so much as we need for working. Out of your letter I could not learn, which amount you will send for us. With a thousand dollars I could go myself with my daughter Helen; with fifteen hundred I would take both my daughters with me and my dear wife could come later on. I am sure when I can work in Chile, I can send the money for my wife in some months. Certainly, my dear cousin, you have had so great troubles for arising this amount, that we must be very content, when we can go out in two parties.

And now the most important thing. The Palestine and Orient Lloyd Berlin has let me know, when the dollar-amount has arrived in Amsterdam, at once the permit in

Chile will be demanded per cable and it was possible for us to come out with the February boat. Therefore the Palestine Lloyd has cabled you; I myself cannot cable abroad; only the shipping societies. . . .

Now we hope from day to day to hear that the dollar-amount has arrived in Amsterdam and we can begin our preparations for the emigration. And when this happy day is come, we all know that only you, my dear cousin, has finished this saving work. I beg you tell your sister Norma how we all are full of thanks for her and for her help and tell her please that I am sure I can give back the money in one or two years, when I have worked in Chile. I have heard the salary for Chemists with experiences are quite good; therefore I can hope that I can give back all the money on you and all who will help me in my great need. Certainly I cannot say at which time I can do it; but I know surely that day will come and I can give back the money to you all, which I need now for saving us. Please give the enclosed letter to cousin Charley; I have not his address. Because cousin Ferdy I cannot understand why he will not help us, I will write you another time to this fact. I know my dear cousin our fate is in your, the best, hands.

In love to you all, [Max]

On December 22 Max wrote again to Julius to inform him that the Palestine and Orient Lloyd had received Julius's $660 payment and to thank him once again for his help. But he also reminded Julius that additional funds for the steamship tickets would have to arrive before any of the Schohls could sail. Not knowing yet that Ferdy Midelburg had agreed to put up $500, and that Julius therefore had the full $2,000 at his disposal, Max assumed that he would have to leave his wife in Germany for the time being. What may seem in our eyes to have been a cruel calculation regarding his spouse made sense given the higher level of danger to Max and his daughters than to Liesel Schohl, who as an "Aryan"—albeit a "corrupted" one—could expect to endure somewhat less persecution than her daughters while awaiting her turn to emigrate. Liesel was fully in agreement with this arrangement. Much more concerned about getting her husband and daughters out of Germany than about escaping herself, she urged Max to go to America without her. She was confident that she would be able to join them in their new home eventually, but if she could not she was ready to sacrifice herself for her family.

December 22, 1939

My dear cousin Julius,

Hoping you have received my air-mail letter of December 14th, I thank you very much for your cable, [which] I received a week ago. Yesterday the Palestine and Orient Lloyd wrote me that $660 arrived for my emigration in Amsterdam. I cannot describe the happy feeling of us all; this day was the happiest one since a long time; this money is for us a silver-stripe in the darkest clouds. I believe you can understand my dear cousin what I will tell you, but I have no words enough to express it.

You have cabled me to cable further instructions. I have written to you that I cannot cable because it is not allowed in war-time. Only the shipping societies can cable in important affairs. I know the Palestine and Orient Lloyd has cabled you [about] the money which is necessary to emigrate for Chile. I have written, that each person needs $165 for permit to enter and about $270 for the ticket; it is a long voyage and very dear and must be paid in dollars and cannot be paid in marks. I have understood your last letter that you can send for us $1500—and that of yourself and your sister Norma and cousin Charley each $500. When I am right with this, the amount of $1500 was enough for me and my two children and for the permit of my dear wife; the charges for the boat ticket for her, I would hope I could send, when I have my position in Chile, so my wife must wait some months longer before emigrating. Certainly it was finer, when she could go with us together but that is not to change and we must be content that we can go in such manner. Hoping that have all understood, my dear cousin, let me please know as soon as possible when I can await the other money for the tickets. With that money in Amsterdam we can buy the permits for us all and I have ordered them. Perhaps it is possible for us to catch the February boat for Chile, when you can send the other money the next days. What shall I tell you with my poor words how I have to thank you? We all feel we have no better friend than you my dear cousin. We cannot make many words but our hearts are full of thanks to you for all times.

In love your cousin [Max]

While Julius was waiting anxiously to hear from Max—hopefully to learn that the Schohls were on their way to Holland to board a ship for Chile—the Chilean government closed its doors indefinitely to refugees from Europe. Fighting for his political life against conservatives who bewailed the recent influx of Jews to their country, President Cerda could not afford to be seen as pro-Jewish.

Moreover, Cerda's government, along with other Latin American regimes, was now under pressure from Washington to be vigilant in their immigration policies lest Nazi agents disguised as Jewish refugees infiltrate their countries. Convinced that the United States would soon be at war with Germany, the Roosevelt administration did not want Latin America to become a haven for Nazi activities and a possible jumping off point for attacks against the United States. Certain influential members of Congress struck an even more alarming note regarding the "threat" to America from European refugees south of the border. Senator Robert Reynolds of North Carolina insisted that "alien enemies" had already worked their way north from Latin America: "They are coming north across the Rio Grande, and other[s] . . . are already here by the hundreds of thousands. . . . The 'fifth column' is here and the Trojan horses in great herds are grazing upon the green, tender grasses of the pastures of America."

Unaware that Chile was no longer an option for Max, Julius Hess went ahead and wired an additional $1,100 for the Schohls' ship tickets

to the Incasso Bank on January 24, 1940. As he explained in a letter to
Norma, he now hoped that Max and company would make the February boat to Chile.

January 31, 1940

Dear Norma,

I promised you that I would give you all the details of
what has happened regarding Max Schohl, so here goes.

In one of my letters I informed you that I had written
Max, that I was sending money for four permits, and also cabled him on the day the money was sent to that effect. That
cable was sent on December 14th. I did not hear from him
until January 6th, but the letter I received [then] was written
before he received my cable. About a week later I received
another letter from him in which he stated that he had received my cable, and had also received word from the Palestine Orient that the money had arrived for his permits, and
that application was being made immediately to get them.

On December 28th, I had written him again that I had
not heard from him, or from the Palestine Orient, and was
very much worried from not having heard. I explained in
detail in that letter that I had raised all the money necessary
to bring all the family out; for you see, at the time I wrote
him in November and December, I was only assured of raising $1500, and poor Max was under the impression that
only three of them would be able to get out.

Last week, I cablebed [sic] $1100 more which represented
money for their steamship tickets, I was afraid to wait any
longer for fear my delay might spoil the chances of them getting out, in February. The day after I cabled the money I received a Cablegram from the Palestine Orient, advising me,
as per my letter of the 28th, to forward the passage money
for Max Schohl and family immediately. Their cable was evidently an answer to the letter I wrote Max on the 28th of

December, in which I advised him that I had the money on hand, and was only waiting word from him to forward passage money on. Evidently, when he received my letter, he immediately got in touch with the Palestine Orient and asked them to cable me, because as you know, he is not allowed to send cables any more. I do not expect to hear from him again for quite some time, as it takes a good month now for letters to come from there, or to get to him. My hopes are, that he will be able to leave Germany the early part of February, and if that is the case, I might possibly get a wire from him when he reaches Amsterdam before sailing. He can only go to Amsterdam three days ahead of sailing time, and only if he has his steamship tickets and his permit in his possession. From all indications, the Palestine Orient have made arrangements for his Permits and reservations on the February boat, just what date the February boat leaves, I don't know, but believe me, I sure will get a thrill out of hearing from them, that they were about to sail. . . .

[Julius]

Shortly after writing this letter to Norma, Julius learned, via an air letter from the Palestine Orient dated January 25, that there would be no emigration to Chile for Max Schohl and his family; they would have to search out some other Latin American refuge:

Berlin, January 25, 1940

Dear Sir:

Your esteemed letter to the Incasso Bank in emigration matter family Schohl was submitted to us for reply.

We want to inform you, that the submitted $660 are received at our account in Amsterdam.

In the Immigration matter Schohl we are sorry to tell you, that nothing is done until now. Chile, where the family intended to immigrate has closed entirely in the meantime for an indefinite time.

For that reason we submitted family Schohl some new propositions for Immigration to Paraguay and Brazil and we should get their decision in the next few days. After this will be done, we will use your money for the proper purpose.

Very truly yours,
Palestine and Orient Lloyd

FLIGHT

The closing of Chile came as a shock to Max, who had been confident that he had finally lined up a safe haven for his family, and one in which he could productively work. Like Julius, he blamed himself for turns of fate that were in fact beyond his influence. So depressed was he over his "failure" that he hinted at suicide. Liesel took pains to assure him that his family would *not* be better off without him, as he seemed to believe, but needed him now more than ever. Whether or not he was fully convinced of this, Max pulled himself out of his immobilizing gloom and turned his mind once again to the challenge of escaping Germany.

As noted above, the Palestine and Orient Lloyd had suggested Paraguay or Brazil as alternatives to Chile, and Max now decided to focus his efforts on Brazil. (He never seems to have considered Paraguay as an option; it lacked much of an urban culture and its jungles were known to be inhospitable in the extreme.) Max had some contacts in Brazil because his former company had maintained a sales office in São Paulo. This vast country, moreover, had a sizable population of Jews; some 96,844 Eastern European Jews had migrated there between 1913 and 1932, and between 12,000 and 15,000 German Jews had settled there following Hitler's seizure of power. This latest influx, however, had generated an anti-Semitic backlash that was finding expression in the country's immigration policies. The authoritarian regime of President Getulio Vargas, which had close ties to Nazi Germany, began imposing sharp restrictions on Jewish immigration in the mid-1930s, and in 1937 even ordered its consuls abroad to deny visas to Jews. As in the case of

Chile, the main consequence of this step was to drive up the cost of visas and to make their purchase a risky gamble. In 1937 a number of would-be emigrants to Brazil who had purchased what they thought were valid visas were denied entry upon reaching the country; eighty Jews who had managed to get in were arrested and deported. Reflecting on the prospects for Jewish refugees in Brazil, one of the country's immigration officials told George Rublee of the Intergovernmental Committee on Refugees that "the way to get Jews into Brazil and other South American countries is to call them non-Aryan Catholics," since "what every country wants is the non-Jewish element among the refugees."

In early March Max learned from the Brazilian consulate in Berlin that his visa applications, for which he had paid $450 apiece, had been approved and would soon be sent to him. However, before the documents arrived he was ordered to appear at the Gestapo office in Frankfurt, with which he was obliged to keep in regular contact. The Gestapo now informed him that he had to be out of Germany by March 31, 1940, or face arrest. Officials in the *Gau* (Nazi administrative region) of Hesse, it seems, were anxious to make their district one of the first to be *Judenrein*; they didn't care where the Jews went, only that they left forthwith. (As it happened, Flörsheim itself would eventually be cleared of its last Jews by deportation, not emigration. Following deportations in 1942 and 1943 to Theresienstadt and other concentration camps, Mayor Stamm could finally declare his town "Jew-free" on April 1, 1943.)

For Max and other Jews fleeing Germany in the early spring of 1940, the exit options were limited. Switzerland would have been an attractive refuge, but that country had started turning Jews away as early as October 1938. (It was the Swiss, as a matter of fact, who had convinced the German government to include the letter "J" on Jews' passports to facilitate the process of excluding them.) France was out of the question because it was at war with the Reich. Neutral Belgium and Holland had not yet been invaded by Germany—that would come in May 1940—but German refugees could enter those countries only if they had valid visas for other nations and steamship tickets in hand. Since Max was not yet in possession of his Brazilian papers and travel documents, he decided to head southeast into Yugoslavia, where he and his family could remain until they had everything they needed to depart for Brazil. (Their envisaged port of embarkation was Genoa, Italy, but the Schohls could not enter that country until they were ready to sail.)

In preparation for their anticipated emigration to Brazil via Yugoslavia and Genoa, the Schohls filled large wooden crates with whatever items of household goods and clothing the government would allow them to remove from the country. The crates would be shipped to Genoa and stored there until the family arrived to embark for Brazil. To ensure that no contraband items went into the boxes—removing valuables like jewels, silverware, coins, stamps, and works of art was strictly *verboten*—police officials closely monitored the packing process. Nonetheless, knowing that a few easily traded valuables could critically ease the entry into exile, the ever-resourceful Liesel Schohl stuffed some of her best jewels into a small leather pouch and managed to sneak this pouch into one of the crates when the policeman wasn't looking.

Liesel's jewels would indeed come in handy later on, but they were the only truly precious items that the Schohls were able to take with them. Before departing, Liesel secretly sold or gave away other family treasures to prevent them from falling into the hands of the Nazis. She consigned the family's Rubens painting to an "Aryan" acquaintance in town, while the Franz Hals went to her favorite brother, Heini. The grocer and butcher who had slipped illegal food supplies to her family received small amounts of cash. She turned over her Meissen china to Dr. Hamel for safekeeping, asking that he return it "if any of us ever comes back." (In fact, Dr. Hamel did return the porcelain to Liesel Schohl after the war, and it now features proudly in Käthe Wells's china cabinet in Charleston.)

More painfully, Max also had to leave his aged mother behind in Germany because she was too old and sick to travel, much less join the family in exile. Max entrusted her to an old folks' home in Frankfurt just before he left. She did not stay there long. She was deported in 1942 to Theresienstadt, where she died on August 23, 1942.

On March 30, 1940, the eve of the deadline imposed by the Gestapo, Max handed over his home and all its remaining contents to the Nazi authorities. The house became the property of the city, which soon began using it as a refuge for Germans from nearby towns who had been bombed out of their own houses. As soon as the property transfer was complete, the Schohls took a taxi to Frankfurt to board their train to

Yugoslavia. Each had ten marks, the maximum amount of money the government now allowed refugees to remove from the country. Young Käthe found the taxi trip exciting, but Max was so choked up that he could hardly speak.

The Schohls possessed second-class tickets on the Orient Express to Zagreb, but when they arrived at the station they found that their seats had been reassigned to four junior-level SS men. Since there were no other second-class seats to be had, and the Schohls lacked the money to purchase first-class berths, it appeared that they would be stranded in Frankfurt, missing their deadline to depart Germany. Sympathizing with their predicament, the conductor asked a middle-aged gentleman who was sitting alone behind a newspaper in one of the first-class compartments if he would mind having some company; if he was willing to share his compartment, the conductor would give the Schohls an informal upgrade. Dropping his paper for a moment to inspect Max and his family, the gentleman assented. Max clicked his heels and ushered his women into the compartment. Just before departure, police officers came through the train to check travel documents. In displaying his family's passports to the officials, Max tried to be discreet so that their fellow passenger would not notice the red "J" stamped on them.

Once the trip was underway the Schohls' traveling companion frequently dropped his newspaper to glance at his compartment mates. Soon the travelers began to make idle conversation, and it turned out that the accommodating gentleman was a Greek diplomat who shuttled frequently between the Balkans and Germany. Relieved that their benefactor was a foreigner and not a German official, Max confided to him the nature of his family's journey, whereupon the gentleman replied that he had guessed from the outset that they were Jewish refugees. Sotto voce, he expressed his disgust with the Nazis' racial policies and his sympathy for the Schohls' plight.

By the time the train had reached the Salzkammergut in the Austrian Alps, the Greek diplomat had totally abandoned his newspaper and was devoting his full attention to young Käthe, who was sitting demurely across from him and answering his many questions as best she could. Apparently satisfied with her answers, the diplomat suddenly signaled for Max's attention and, with a stiff bow, asked him for his daughter's hand in marriage. He then discretely left the compartment to await a decision that, given the Schohls' predicament, he assumed could only be favorable.

Max may have been reduced in circumstances, but he was not about to hand over his daughter to a total stranger without first discussing the proposition with Käthe and the rest of the family. Before Käthe could offer her view on the matter, Liesel cautioned her not to reject the offer out of hand. "We might need this man," she admonished. Hela too saw merit in the proposition: "You could marry the guy and then poison him," she advised. But Käthe herself, when she was finally allowed to speak, insisted that she would sooner die than marry the old man, and that settled the matter. Upon the diplomat's return Max gently informed him that he and his wife considered their daughter too young for marriage, though they were much flattered by his proposal. Surprisingly, the fellow showed no ill will, and as the train approached the German-Yugoslav border he offered to take charge of the Schohls' passports, noting that Nazi border officials sometimes confiscated travel documents presented by Jews. Although understandably reluctant to part with their precious passports, the Schohls turned them over to the diplomat. During the stop at the border he disappeared into the station, returning after an agonizing half-hour absence with freshly stamped documents and the words, "Welcome to Yugoslavia." As soon as the train passed safely over the border, Max visibly relaxed and, for the first time, told his family the full story of what had happened to him in Buchenwald in 1938.

The Schohls paused briefly in Zagreb (Croatia) en route to Belgrade, where they planned to pick up their Brazilian visas. Belgrade in the spring of 1940 seemed magical after all the horrors of Germany. Here the family could sit at sidewalk cafes and walk the streets without fear of being hounded. Max had contacts in the city through a fellow Flörsheimer, Jakob Altmaier, who had lived there for a time after fleeing Germany in 1933. Altmaier had arranged for the visitors' visas that allowed the Schohls to travel to Yugoslavia. Among Altmaier's friends in Belgrade was the owner of the International Hotel, where the Schohls found comfortable rooms. Max also met the head of the local chapter of B'nai B'rith, who provided access to Belgrade's substantial Jewish community. Max, however, was impatient to move on to a place where he could work, and he made daily inquiries at the Brazilian Embassy about the visas. After a week or so, he learned that Brazil, like Chile, had suddenly closed its doors to Jewish refugees from Europe. There would be no emigrating to that country.

What to do now? The Schohls had come to Yugoslavia on three-week visitors' visas, and Max was terrified that they might be sent back to Germany. They had no national standing in Yugoslavia because the German government had deprived them of their citizenship. Like the thousands of other German-Jewish refugees kicking around Europe at this time, they were adrift in a legal limbo, vulnerable to the whims of officials who in general were no more anxious to harbor such folks than were the leaders of their former homeland. In desperation Max turned to the B'nai B'rith for help.

The Belgrade B'nai B'rith, it turned out, had contacts with Serbian farmers and businessmen in the rural interior who, for a fee, would provide room and board to refugee Jews. The refugees were expected to make what contributions they could to the local economy. As long as they made such contributions, and stayed clear of the major cities, the Yugoslav government would extend their visitors' visas. Thus it was that in May 1940 Max and his family found themselves departing Belgrade not for Genoa and Brazil, but for a place they had never heard of: the small agricultural town of Ruma, about fifty miles northwest of the capital.

After cosmopolitan Belgrade, Ruma came as a shock. Its streets were hot and dusty, its buildings ramshackle. The women all wore long skirts and kerchiefs over their hair. There were approximately twenty native Jewish families in town, but most of them lived in the manner of Polish shtetl Jews and wanted nothing to do with the exotic refugees from Germany.

An exception to this rule was Bela Hauser, a Serbian-Jewish businessman who owned an animal feed and seed store. He spoke fluent German and had a son studying at Oxford. As the B'nai B'rith's contact man in Ruma, he arranged lodging for the Schohls with a family of Serbian farmers who had a spare room to let. This room turned out to be a far cry from the comfortable suite at Belgrade's International Hotel. To the horror of Liesel Schohl, it was thoroughly infested with bugs. As they settled in, Max firmly instructed his wife not to complain: "Would you rather live with bugs or die with the Nazis?" he asked. The Schohl girls, for their part, turned up their noses at the straw pallets that served as beds. "We're expected to sleep on *those*?" they cried. "Yes," replied papa, "and you'll like it. Or would you prefer to sleep on satin and die?"

As it happened, the Schohls did not have to remain long in this primitive habitation. After a few weeks Bela Hauser found them much more pleasant accommodations in an uninhabited manor house, complete with a working kitchen and even a ballroom. Knowing that his women would be much happier there, Max agreed to the landlord's stiff terms, withdrawing money from his Incasso account in Amsterdam to pay the rent. As it now looked like they would be in Yugoslavia for a while, Max also arranged to have the crates containing the family's bedding and household goods shipped from Genoa to Ruma.

With time the family began to adjust to life in their new home. The girls picked up some Serbo-Croatian from the Serbian boys who mooned around the Schohl house, trying to attract the attention of these beautiful foreigners. Hela fell deeply in love with one of her language instructors, a young man named Bogdan, whom she subsequently married—or, at any rate, *claimed* to have married after discovering that she was pregnant. Blond and buxom young Käthe, now as much a siren as her raven-haired sister, also had her pick of beaux, though she refrained from settling her affections on any one of them. She liked nothing better than getting herself smartly *verputzt* (made up) and going out dancing with a whole pack of love-struck Serbian studs. To earn a little pocket money, Hela worked as a seamstress, while Käthe taught German to a young Hungarian-Jewish refugee. Both the girls learned to appreciate the spicy Balkan food. Max, ever the chemist, experimented with the production of a fungicide, copper vitriol, whose main ingredient he derived from the copper-rich soil of the region. In addition to selling the copper sulfite to local farmers, he found part-time work making dye in a leather tannery. His expertise as a chemist soon reached officials of the Yugoslav army, who hired him to do consulting work at an explosives factory near Ruma. Lack of a work permit, however, prevented him from seeking full-time or reasonably well-paying employment. Liesel managed to run the household and do most of the shopping in Ruma without learning more than a few words of Serbo-Croatian. "Maxl, just teach me the money," she said to her husband upon arriving. When she noticed that there was a band of impoverished Gypsies camped nearby, she broke a local taboo by making friendly contact with them. To the Gypsies' astonishment (and gratitude), she brought them clothes from the family supplies. Thereafter one of the Gypsies, an accomplished violist, repaid the Schohls with occasional evening serenades.

Because upon fleeing Germany the Schohls had assumed that they would soon be embarking for Brazil, they had not notified Julius Hess of their departure; they planned to write him from Italy just before sailing. Thinking that Max and family were still in Flörsheim, and learning from the Palestine and Orient agency that Chile was eliminated as a possible emigration destination, Julius wrote Max to ascertain what he intended to do now. He hoped his cousin would decide to go to Brazil:

Charleston, April 3, 1940

Dear Cousin Max and All;

It has been so terribly long since I last heard from you that I am again becoming worried about you all. I thought surely by this time you would be well on your way but according to the letter I received from the Palestine Orient Lloyd of which I am enclosing a copy something else has come up to delay your departure.

I kept putting off from day to day to write either of you or the Palestine Orient thinking that each day would bring me a letter telling me where you are going. I just could not wait any longer so today I sent a cable to Palestine Orient asking them to cable me where you were emigrating to because as you know the permit money and passage money is already waiting for you. I also sent you a cable asking you to instruct Palestine Orient to answer my cable by cable.

You will notice in the letter I am enclosing that they suggest Paraguay and Brazil. If at all possible go to Brazil instead of the other country as I believe your chances of employment would be much better. Above all things Dear Cousin please let me hear from you no matter what happens because I cannot rest in peace when I am so uncertain as to what is happening to you all and as it has been so terribly long since I last heard from you I again must state I am very worried about you.

Have courage my Dear Cousins and all will be alright [sic] in the near future. With love to all from all of us,

Devotedly, [Julius]

On April 3, just after sending the above letter, Julius received a cable from Western Union saying that the telegram he had dispatched to Max the day before was undeliverable because "addressee has left [and] his present address is unknown." On April 4, Julius learned via a cable from the Palestine and Orient that the Schohls had left for Yugoslavia, with the intention of emigrating to Brazil, but he heard nothing from Max himself until April 20, when he received a card postmarked Zagreb and dated April 2:

My dear cousin,

After terrible troubles we have arrived yesterday night this town [and] are so happy to have escaped the German hell. We are well and we cannot see what we can do further to coming in a country where we can work and serve. Today we are very happy having saved our lives. And you my dear cousin have made this great thing [possible]. We are full of thanks to you. Next days more. Your cousin Max and family.

Relieved to have heard at last from his cousin, Julius wrote him back immediately, enclosing a gift of $5. Julius's suggestion that Max expressly thank Ferdy Midelburg for his belated contribution to the rescue effort was another indication of just how difficult it had been to bring Ferdy around.

Charleston, April 21, 1940

Dear Cousin Max;

I received your postcard yesterday and you will never know how happy I was to hear from you. I have been terribly worried about you all for the past two months. Although you are not aware of it I sent you a cable last month which was returned to me with the notation that you had left the country. I then cabled Palestine-Orient and they cabled back that you and family had gone to Jugo-Slavia temporarily and from there would attempt to go on to Brazil.

Please write me all details and what ever your plans might be. Let me know if the money we sent to Holland will be available for your use and if you are in need of anything at the present time. I am so happy to know that for the time being at least you are safe and well. To help celebrate this joyous feeling I am enclosing a little gift for you all, an Express Money Order, in the amount of Five Dollars which is sent with much love from my wife and myself.

I had not told Mother a thing about you for quite some months as every time I spoke of you it upset her terribly and as I did not have good news to tell I kept quiet, but when I heard you all had gotten out I immediately told her all that had taken place, poor old soul cried from joy. As she is very near 82 years old and cannot see so good anymore please do not feel bad because you have not received any letters from her, but she thinks of you all continuously.

When your mind is at rest and you have the time I would suggest that you write to Ferdy Midelburg, Logan, W.Va. and thank him for putting up his share of the money we sent to Holland for you, of course I keep them all posted on what is happening and whenever I hear from you but I think it would be very nice for him to hear from you personally.

Before I close I might tell you that now that you do not have a typewriter, at least I do not think you have, if it will be easier for you, you can write to me in German as I have lots of people who can translate it for me, and please write me as often as you can.

With love to you all and may God keep you well and happy, I am,

Devotedly your cousin [Julius]

"Jews Can No Longer Live in Europe"

Although the Schohls had found a measure of safety in Yugoslavia and had made the best of their circumstances there, they knew that they were not truly secure in the Balkans. Europe was fiercely at war, and Nazi Germany, having overrun the Low Countries and France in spring 1940, could be expected to turn its sights eastward at any moment, despite Hitler's "Non-Aggression Pact" with Stalin. Therefore, in summer 1940 Max revived his quest to emigrate to the United States, which he heard might soon be admitting refugees from war-torn Europe on an emergency basis. The American consul in Belgrade apparently told him that if he could secure four affidavits, each one put up by a different sponsoring relative, plus steamship tickets, the possibility still existed of reaching American shores. Believing the United States to be his last best hope, Max dispatched a new round of SOS letters to both Julius Hess and Ferdy Midelburg in August 1940. The one to Ferdy was conciliatory and plaintive, reflecting Max's sense of degradation over his mendicant status. In it he thanked Ferdy for "all you have done," discreetly overlooking the difficulty in securing his cooperation. Max added that with more help from America he hoped soon to be able to reach the United States and "prove to you, dear Ferdy, that I am worthy of your help." Max's letter of the same date to Julius, which he wrote in German (following Julius's suggestion), pointed out that although the Schohls were relatively safe for the moment, that situation could change any day, since "Jews can no longer live in Europe." Max also confessed that he was having to use some of the funds from Amsterdam to live on because the Yugoslav government would not let him take a well-paying job, despite high demand for his services.

Ruma, Yugoslavia 3.8.40

My dear Cousin Julius,

After wandering around here for months, we've finally found a place where we can have a little peace and security. The government of this country has allowed us to stay here until we can move on. That's a small consolation, but better than traveling around on the roads, not knowing what tomorrow will bring.

I check daily at the post office for letters from you, but so far have heard nothing. I have written you three letters and two postcards. . . . I know that the mails function poorly in these unquiet times but I assumed that at least one of my communications might have reached you. I'm sure that you've answered me, but, with the exception of your letter of 21 April, I haven't received anything you might have sent. I thank you for that letter and the enclosed check for $5. I think [the lack of communication] derives from the fact that we've had to move so often and could provide no stable address.

Now we are fairly well accommodated and can remain here in peace until we manage to move on. But of course conditions can change any day, and [on a long-term basis] Jews can't live any more in Europe. There seem to be changes in the wind here too. Nevertheless, I hardly need tell you how relieved we are that we no longer have to live in Germany; you can't imagine what that means to us.

. . . In my last letter, Cousin Julius, I asked for your advice regarding our emigration. You are aware that we tried in vain to go to Chile and Brazil; South America is closed to Jews from Europe. Therefore, our only hope is to get to the USA. I know that this is not possible right now, but perhaps the time will come when it will again be an option. I inquired at the American consulate if we might come to the US with our current wait-list numbers and the necessary affidavits.

He told me that it could be possible, provided we had all the paperwork in hand plus of course the steamship tickets.

My dear cousin Julius! Through your help we were able to escape Germany. Now I ask you from the bottom of my heart to help us get to the USA! We need four separate affidavits. If you and your sister Norma, as well as cousins Charley and Ferdy each contributed, then the thing should come off without a hitch. You've already helped us with a lot of money, which has allowed us to avoid going under, but the affidavits won't cost anything and I imagine that for Cousins Charley and Ferdy it would be a source of satisfaction to be part of this. I certainly know that you and Norma will help however you can. Though you've never met us, you know and feel that we are of the same blood. Your letters have exuded so much love that I know I can count on you the way I count on my God.

. . . I don't think you can offer me any other advice but to emigrate to the USA. I've tried to find work here and managed immediately to pick up a few things. I could have earned a decent wage because a large chemical firm wanted to employ me, but the government won't allow that. My lodge brothers in the B'nai B'rith tried to get me a work permit, but that's impossible and I just have to be satisfied to be able to stay here for a little while until we can move on. . . .

Healthwise we are doing well. Life is not expensive here, though I've had to use some of the money from Holland so that we wouldn't starve.

I heartily hope that you are all doing well and that this letter finds you in good health. We speak often of you and try to imagine the hour when we can embrace. I fondly hope to see your dear mother, Aunt Lina, once more in my life. I send greetings to you all, especially to your wife and sister Norma. I've enclosed a list of our personal data [for the affidavits]. And now once again, I thank you Cousin Julius for all that you have done; I hope that one day I can prove that we are worthy of your generosity.

With love [Max]

The Schohls' financial situation soon became much worse. Just before Max wrote the above letter, the American government placed a freeze on dollar accounts held by Dutch banks working in partnership with U.S. financial institutions. The money sent by Julius for Max's steamship tickets to the Palestine and Orient Lloyd account at the Incasso Bank of Amsterdam was affected by this ruling because Incasso's dollar holdings were managed by the National City Bank of New York. On August 8, 1940, the Palestine and Orient informed Max that they could no longer wire him money from the Incasso account. Indignant, Max replied to the travel company that the American government surely did not mean its funds freeze to damage people like him, and he asked them to instruct the Incasso Bank to appeal to the National City Bank and the American government for special dispensation. He also wrote to the American bank himself explaining his problem. National City responded that it would be willing to apply for the necessary government approvals to transfer funds from the Palestine Orient's Incasso account to Yugoslavia if Max succeeded "in inducing the Palestine and Orient Lloyd to instruct us to hold these funds at your disposal." Alas, Max was not able to induce the travel agency to take this step, with the result that the Palestine and Orient company simply sat on the money that Julius had entrusted to it to get the Schohls out of Europe.

Unaware that the remainder of the money he had sent to Amsterdam was now essentially lost, at least to Max, Julius wrote to the Palestine and Orient on August 23 to ask about the status and disposition of the funds. "I am wondering if the balance of this money is being held for [Max] for further transportation passage when the time comes for him to emigrate or if he will be able to use the money to some other purpose, such as living expenses." Julius added that he was on that day sending Max new affidavits "to be presented again to the American Consul to see if I can possibly get them into this country and the reason for my letter is to find out if his passage money which was sent to you is still available to him." The Palestine and Orient never replied.

Deprived of access to their Amsterdam money, the Schohls had to get by on the tiny amounts they could pick up through their various odd jobs in Ruma, and on occasional gifts sent by American relatives. In fall 1940 Aunt Lina sent a few dollars, as did Norma Kaufman. In a thank you letter to

Lina dated September 9 (written in German), Max emphasized once again his frustration at being dependent on handouts. "You know the nature of the Schohl family; they would rather give than receive. I have acted on that principle for my whole life and never dreamed that I would one day be in the position where I had to be supported. It's a sad situation, but I did not bring it on myself and now I must adjust to it as thousands of others are doing. Therefore, dear Aunt, you can well understand with what impatience I await more ordered circumstances in which I can again work."

Max's eagerness to escape Yugoslavia was well founded. Ruma lay close to Serbia's border with Croatia, whose most influential political figure, the Ustaše leader Ante Pavelić, was agitating for the creation of an independent Croatia and its expansion eastward to the gates of Belgrade. Were Pavelić to realize his goals, Ruma would fall under his control. The fascistic and brutally anti-Semitic Ustaše movement was a very potent force, enjoying backing from both Mussolini and Hitler. While not at this point pushing for the breakup of Yugoslavia, the German government was covetously eyeing the mineral and agricultural resources of that Balkan state and demanding full political and economic cooperation from Belgrade. Hoping to pacify Hitler, the Yugoslav government offered trade concessions and even introduced some anti-Jewish measures of its own.

As a refugee from Nazi Germany's racial persecution, Max feared what such measures might portend, and he dispatched a new appeal to Julius in October 1940. Written in blunt German, this letter was Max's most embittered communication to date. The chemist had not received the affidavits that Julius, via a letter from his sister Norma, had promised to send immediately. Hearing that other Jewish refugees in the Balkans had been able to sail for the United States from Athens via Lisbon, Max could not understand why *his* American relatives were not making it possible for the Schohls to join the exodus.

Ruma, Yugoslavia, 14 October 1940

My dear cousin Julius

    After receiving the most recent letter from your dear sister Norma, in which she informed us that you were securing us affidavits, we felt new hope that we would finally be delivered from the European hell. I can imagine that it's no easy thing to help us, but I also believe that with a little good will my proposition [regarding the four affidavits] could be carried out. It is after all no risk to any of you, since we are all employable people who will be happy to be working again. In the meantime, the situation in this country has gotten much worse. You will have read in the press that here too anti-Jewish laws have been introduced. What that means can be fully appreciated only by someone who has experienced the German scene. Moreover, the danger exists that Hitler might appear here with his troops any day now; if this happens, all the work to save our lives will have been in vain. After all, it's well known what Hitler did to the émigrés that he found in Holland and Belgium; these people experienced a terrible fate.

You can imagine, dear Julius, in what constant fear we now live. We know no peace and anxiously await the news that would spell our delivery. I know for certain that it's not your fault that you have not yet been able to send the affidavits. But the other cousins cannot be so inhuman as to let a whole family, a family of their own blood, simply go under. In more normal times we, for our part, have always been willing to make sacrifices to help others in the family. And now our very lives are at stake—yet nobody is willing to vouch for us so that we might be saved. That is such a sad situation that I really can't believe it exists. You might think about our poor innocent children, who will surely go under if we are not helped. You can't be responsible for that—not before God or before your own conscience.

Please dear cousin send me news about how things stand; though deeply frustrated, I still have hope that we might be helped.

Practically every month a ship leaves from Athens for New York via Lisbon. Many of the Jewish refugees from here have already left, through help from their relatives in America.

Why should we be left here to go to ruin? We have done nothing that merits such a fate.

I plea with you once more, Cousin Julius, send me good news. I know that you will do your best, and I just hope the others will follow your example.

May the good Lord allow that we can soon see each other, and that I find my old Aunt Lina still alive, the last of the old generation. Greet all the relatives for us, especially your dear wife, your sister Norma and Grover, and also your dear old mother. Be aware yourself that you have our innermost thanks for all that you've done for us—and for that which I am sure you will still do.

Awaiting anxiously your reply, I am,

With heart-felt greetings and kisses, Your cousin [Max]

Julius had in fact sent the affidavits to Ruma, but as the mails were in chaos, the packet never arrived in Yugoslavia. Yet even if the documents had made it to Ruma, the Schohls would probably not have gotten to America at this late date. In light of the widening war, Washington was further tightening its immigration restrictions, reasoning that some of the refugees from fascism might be Communists or even Nazi secret agents trying to operate as a subversive "Fifth Column" inside the United States. American consuls in Latin America and across Europe were instructed to exercise extreme prudence in issuing visas, so that "undesirables" could not exploit the world crisis to gain access to the United States. (George Messersmith, Washington's former consul-general in Berlin, could write from his new post in Cuba in November 1940 that he was very glad that the refugees in that land who wanted to move on to America were being carefully screened, since "all too many of them are quite out of sympathy with our institutions." He added that his "humanitarian impulses" did not lead him "towards extending any succor towards such refugees.") The difficulty of obtaining an American visa was further compounded by the fact that, as a State Department memo lamented, U.S. consulates in Europe, especially in Southern France, Spain, and the Balkans, were "besieged" by refugees seeking entry to America. Responding to anguished appeals from Jewish groups to streamline the visa-granting process and to loosen the requirements, Assistant Secretary of State for Special Problems Breckinridge Long insisted that Washington could do no more than it was already doing. He also advised against the American government's making any public comment on Germany's latest actions against the Jews, stating that such comments would not be effective and might open Washington to accusations "of interfering in the internal affairs of another government." (Long's rigid stance in the Jewish refugee crisis earned him the enmity of many Jewish officials in the Roosevelt administration, including Treasury Secretary Morgenthau, who unsuccessfully tried to get him stripped of his responsibility for refugee affairs.)

To make matters even more difficult for refugees hoping to reach America from the Balkans, on October 28, 1940, Italy invaded Greece, drawing that nation into the war and thus closing its ports to passenger shipping. A few months later Yugoslavia itself was overrun by German troops sent by Hitler to assist his Italian ally's floundering Balkan campaign.

On the eve of the German invasion of Yugoslavia one more letter reached Charleston from Ruma. It was written not by Max, who was now so embittered and depressed that he had essentially given up on his American relatives, but by Liesel:

Ruma, Feb. 1, 1941

Dear Ones,

Since last September we didn't hear anything from you, dear Aunt, or from you, dear Norma, or from you, dear Julius. I hope everybody of you is well, especially you, dear Aunt. This letter I write without knowledge of my husband. In his letter he asked you dear Cousin for an affidavit. This letter was sent by airmail October 10th, 1940. I don't know if you got it. I understand my husband very well. So today I imagine [feel] like a beggar. We all are very sorry about this begging. We thought at that time, when you was so kind to pay for us the tickets to Brazil, the begging is finished now. But you know,

Brazil was closed a short time after we arrived in Jugoslavia. Because we had no way to arrange our living, we had to take for that your pounds [from Amsterdam]. . . . Max always ordered some pounds from Amsterdam and we changed them to Dinar. Since the war came to Holland, the USA closed up the accounts of pounds. Now we don't know when we will get the money. Maybe we have to wait till the war is over. That would mean a lot of trouble for us. We didn't intend to leave Jugoslavia because this country is "little Amerika" especially for chemists. For the last six months Max got a lot of offers of nice jobs in big factories. They all promised him to look for the permission to work, because foreign people is not allowed to work. Now I don't believe that he will get it and so I ask you for affidavits for us. The reason is that we are very anxious [fearful] that the war will come to the Balkans too. Please do that for my children. Maybe you have friends who would like to give the affidavits for the girls. Both of the children are smart and know how to work. Please don't let my children perish. I am sure that if my husband were in America, he would have paid up a part of the loan.

I suppose it takes a couple of weeks till you will get this letter. Will you be so kind and send us a cable if we can get the affidavits? Next week friends of us start to America via Russia. So it is possible. But if it should be impossible—I don't believe so—please help us with stockings size 9[fr 1/2]; shoes, size 38[fr 1/2]—39, clothes (dresses) and coats for summertime, size 44–46. All can be used so we have not to pay duty. . . . If we didn't have so good friends here in Ruma—they are not rich people—we would have had to freeze this winter. Stockings are very expensive here. We can live three days for the price of one pair. If we can get the affidavits don't send anything because I don't know how long a parcel to here takes. Please excuse this letter but the threats to the children trouble me.

Health for you and many regards, especially for you, dear Aunt.

Yours, [Liesel]

Arrest, Deportation, and Death in Auschwitz

The German/Italian invasion and occupation of Yugoslavia brought the rapid dismemberment of that fragile state. Italy grabbed the southern part of Slovenia, coastal Dalmatia, Istria, and the Adriatic islands, while establishing a protectorate over Montenegro; Hungary, Germany's and Italy's ally, annexed the territory it had lost to Yugoslavia after World War I; Germany itself absorbed northern Slovenia and countenanced the establishment of an "independent" Croatian puppet state under Ante Pavelić, which was expanded to include Bosnia, Herzegovina, and the region (including Ruma) just west of Belgrade. The new Croatian state was divided into Italian and German military zones, with the Germans installed in the eastern part. The remaining part of Serbia fell under direct German military rule.

Citing a need to purge their state of anti-Croatian elements, Pavelić and his minions unleashed a reign of terror against the resident Serbian population, decimating villages and creating thousands of instant recruits for resistance movements like the Communist-backed partisans and the royalist Chetniks. Pavelić's Ustaše state also targeted Gypsies and Jews. Echoing the Nazis' Nuremberg Laws, the Croat government, which defined itself as "Aryan" (though this was news to the Nazis), unveiled a "Decree on the Protection of Aryan Blood and the Honor of the Croat Nation," which banned marriages between Aryans and non-Aryans and sexual relations between male Jews and female Croats (male Croats were free to rape female Jews). As of May 22, all Jews in Croatia had to wear the Yellow Star. Again in emulation of the Germans, Croatia established a number of brutal concentration camps, the most notorious being the one at Jasenovac, where, according to the official propaganda, Jews would be "afforded the opportunity to work for the benefit of Croats and Croatdom for the first time ever," and Gypsies could "at last work for the good of society." Serving Croatdom in Jasenovac generally meant being worked or tortured to death. Some 200,000 people (the majority of them Serbs) are estimated to have died in this hellhole, about 40,000 in one four-month period in 1942 when a Franciscan monk known as "Brother Satan" ran the camp. Among the roughly 40,000 native Jews living in the new Greater Croatia, between 20,000 and 30,000 were murdered.

Julius Hess received no more communications from Ruma but in July 1941 he got a letter from a former teacher of Käthe Schohl's to whom she had just written, describing the family's situation as "desperate." The teacher, who had emigrated to the United States and joined the American army, relayed Käthe's plea for help in his letter to Julius, adding censoriously: "I should remind you that you had promised to help. . . . I am sure that *I* can't do anything, I am in the army, and my own parents are in occupied France trying to come over to the USA."

The Schohls' situation in Croatia following the German invasion was indeed desperate. As the Wehrmacht approached Ruma, the Schohl family, following the example of the Hausers, fled into the nearby Black Mountains, where Bela Hauser knew a farmer who could shelter them. Initially, Max had not wanted to go—he said he was tired of running— but Liesel and the girls persuaded him to accompany his family on this flight into the unknown. After an approximately three-day walk into the mountains, the Schohls found lodgings in a tumble-down barn belonging to a poor Serbian family who had barely enough food to sustain themselves. Yet the Serbs gave what they could, their largesse including one precious egg a day to be split among the newcomers. There were no toilets, not even an outhouse, but Max, the old soldier, brought his womenfolk up to speed regarding which leaves to use—and which leaves *not* to use—for latrine duty. As soon as they arrived in this mountain haven the Schohls knew that they could not stay long, and after about three weeks they decided to return to Ruma and take their chances with the region's new rulers. As they said their good-byes to their impoverished hosts, Max broke his rule regarding the honoring of ladies other than his mother, and kissed the old farmwoman's gnarled hand.

Upon returning to Ruma the Schohls discovered that their rented manor house, whose address was now listed as "Adolf Hitler Strasse 41," had not been touched by the invading Germans. However, within a few days a young Wehrmacht lieutenant appeared at their door and requested that some of his men be quartered on the premises. Explaining that he himself was a retired German officer and World War I veteran, Max announced that he would be "honored" to have the soldiers stay in his house. He offered them the ballroom. According to Käthe Schohl's recollections, the soldiers settled in as unobtrusively as possible, and when one of them politely asked Liesel if he might heat up his mess-kit food on the kitchen stove, Frau Schohl invited the whole group to dinner. Thereafter, for the duration of the soldiers' month-long encampment at the Schohls', they ate dinner every night with the family. As if he were back in the officers' casino, Max regaled the men with stories from the First World War. Although they knew Max was Jewish—he admitted this right away—the soldiers listened raptly to his war stories and treated him with the respect due a retired officer. There was nary a "Heil Hitler" uttered, and upon leaving the men left presents of tobacco and sausage. "They were correct in every way," insists Käthe Schohl to this day.

No doubt the soldiers were "correct," but one must not assume from this example that the Wehrmacht was always, or even usually, correct in its dealings with the civilian population of the Balkans, especially the native and refugee Jews. Other contemporary accounts, buttressed by a wealth of recent scholarship, reveal a picture of widespread criminality on the part of the Wehrmacht units operating in southeastern Europe. The commander of the German forces in Serbia, General Franz Böhme, needed no prompting from Berlin to order wholesale killing of Serbian Jews and Gypsies. Between September 1941 and February 1942 his command orchestrated reprisal killings of some 28,000 people: 7,756 "rebels" and 20,149 "expiratory individuals" (all male Jews). Böhme's idea of "correctness" was to desist from the execution of women and children in Belgrade after ordering the gunning-down of some 10,000 Jewish men in cold blood. While in parts of Croatia the Ustaše militias may have been the chief tormentors of "alien" noncombatants, in Yugoslavia as a whole, and especially in Serbia, the Wehrmacht was the main agent of butchery.

That being said, for the Schohl family conditions certainly deteriorated following the arrival in the region of a Croatian militia group, along with an SS unit composed primarily of *Volksdeutsche*, Croatians of ethnic German descent. To prove their dubious "Germanness," the *Volksdeutsche* made a point of persecuting any Jews they encountered. In July 1941 a group of *Volksdeutsche* showed up at the Schohls' house and arrested Max on the authority of the Croatian state. They took him away without saying where they were headed or what they intended to do with him. As soon as they had left, Liesel Schohl rushed to the local Wehrmacht post and demanded that the army intervene on her husband's behalf. She showed the commander Max's war medals and explained that she herself was an Aryan with four brothers fighting for the Reich. Impressed by her gumption and her credentials, the commander prevailed on the *Volksdeutsche* leader to release Max.

In addition to arresting Max, the SS and various Croatian militia groups made life miserable for the Schohls by forcing them to perform manual labor, much of it humiliating and pointless. Max was put to work in the fields, while the girls were made to clean pigsties and wash windows. For a time the girls also had to move heavy stones from a destroyed synagogue from one corner of a vacant lot to another. Despite their haggard looks and filthy clothes, they lived in constant fear of being raped.

Determined to relieve himself and his family of this degradation, Max accepted the proposition of an ethnic German pig farmer and vintner named Franz Wagner, who asked the chemist to build a laboratory to produce copper sulfite fungicide for his grapes. In exchange for Max's assistance, Wagner, who had a son in the SS, promised to see to it that no harm came to the Schohl family. Before accepting Wagner's offer, Max insisted that the German military command sign off on this agreement, in hopes of having protection against his protector. Shortly after having gone to work for Wagner, Max was obliged to move his family into a boarding house in town. The order to move came from the Gestapo, which had just established an office in the area. The Gestapo office, alas, was directly across the street from the Schohls' new residence.

Wagner's "protection" notwithstanding, in September 1942 Max found himself taken away yet again to perform forced labor for the Croatian militias. Once again, Liesel went to the local Wehrmacht post, now under the command of a Major Rank, to plead Max's case. In addition to Max's medals, she took along a testament ("Uredovna Potvrada") from the Croatian War Ministry stating that Dr. Schohl was doing valuable work for the Croatian cause at Wagner's farm. On Rank's advice, Liesel forwarded these materials to the Croatian Army Command, asking that (as she put it in her letter) "my husband be permitted in the future to carry out undisturbed his important work in the interest of the Croatian state." Max was quickly released.

However, the chemist was not left "undisturbed" for long. In early 1943 Max was arrested by the Ustaše militia on charges of having aided the partisans (which, as a matter of fact, he had done). He was taken away along with ten Serbians, and the rumor was that all were to be executed on orders of a much-feared regional Ustaše chief named Tomić.

After consulting Major Rank, a terrified Liesel Schohl, accompanied by a Wehrmacht driver, drove to Tomić's base at Mitrovica where Max was being held. When Tomić appeared on the scene, presumably to preside over the executions, Liesel threw herself at his feet, pleading for her husband's life. Seeing that she was German, Tomić granted her request. She quickly pulled Max out of the group being led to the killing field and sped with him back to Ruma.

On August 15, 1943, Max was arrested yet again, this time by the Gestapo. Under orders from Himmler, Gestapo agents throughout German-occupied Europe were rounding up Jews who had not yet been shot, worked to death, or murdered in mobile gassing vans, for deportation to the industrial death camps in Poland. In Croatia the deportations had begun in early 1942, with the Croatian government informing Berlin that it "would appreciate the deportation of its Jews to the East." Croatia's Jews included *all* Jews living in the state. Most were to be sent to Auschwitz, via Austria. Max would be among them.

Of course, Max did not know his fate when a local policeman came by to pick him up on that hot summer day in August 1943. He assumed that the Wehrmacht would soon spring him, as they had in the past. He was therefore surprised when the policeman advised him to take along a warm coat, and he refused to do so. He also declined to take along his war medals, which Liesel urged him to do.

As she had always done when Max was taken away, Liesel went to Major Rank to secure his intervention. This time, however, Rank said that there was nothing he could do for Max. Local Wehrmacht commanders were under strict orders not to interfere with Gestapo operations. Rank advised Liesel to go herself to the Wehrmacht headquarters in Zagreb and talk to the commanding general there, Edmund von Glaise-Horstenau. He gave her a letter to take with her that described Max as a patriotic German and a valuable asset to the local economy.

As instructed, Liesel hastened to Zagreb and managed to see Glaise-Horstenau. She showed him Rank's letter. The general seemed sympathetic, but insisted he could do nothing for Max. In all probability, he added, Max was being sent to the concentration camp at Auschwitz. When she asked Glaise-Horstenau what Max might expect to encounter in Auschwitz, he asked her how old Max was. "Sixty," she replied. "Then he's lucky," said the general, but he did not elaborate.

What Glaise-Horstenau meant by "lucky" was the probability that Max, like most of the older deportees who were sent to Auschwitz, would be gassed immediately rather than subjected to a torturous forced-labor routine before being sent to the execution chambers. In Max's case, however, we do not know whether this rule applied because data exist only for the date of his death, not for the date of his arrival in the camp. Four months after his arrest, in November 1943, a Serbian woman in Ruma showed Liesel a postcard she had received from her son, who had been arrested about the same time as Max, saying that he was interned at a camp in the Tyrol with Dr. Schohl. They were awaiting transport east, he added. In August 1944, as they themselves were being deported back to the Reich, the Schohl women were told by a Gestapo officer that Max Schohl had died in Auschwitz on December 9, 1943.

Max had indeed died in Auschwitz in 1943, but not on December 9. His death certificate, which now resides in the camp archive, states that he expired on December 1, 1943, in the camp hospital as a result of "heart muscle weakness compounded by bronchial pneumonia." The death certificate was signed by a Dr. von Helmersen.

Is this description of Max's death accurate, or was it simply a cover for murder by gassing or some other direct means? (His wife and daughters, who never received a copy of the death certificate, naturally came to assume that he had died in the gas chamber.) Like the exact duration of Max's stay in Auschwitz, the precise circumstances of his death will have to remain a mystery. Strange as it may seem, however, there is a good possibility that Max indeed died of heart failure. Fake death certificates were regularly sent to family members following the executions of mentally or physically handicapped persons in the infamous T4 (euthanasia) program, but this was not the case with the mass gassings that took place in the death camps during World War II. The gassing victims generally disappeared into *Nacht und Nebel* ("Night and Fog"), as the Nazi phrase had it. With specific respect to Max, it is possible that despite his relatively advanced age, he was considered potentially useful by the camp authorities because of his chemical expertise. One of the units in the Auschwitz complex, Auschwitz III Monowitz, was established on the grounds of an I.G. Farben chemical plant for the production of synthetic rubber (Buna). As of November 1942, according to British Intelligence, some 1,568 inmates were working at the Buna factory. (Among the Monowitz inmates, later on, was the Italian chemist Primo Levi, who wrote movingly about the brutal conditions under which even "privileged" prisoners lived and worked. The life expectancy for Jews at Auschwitz III, which actually never exported a single gram of Buna, was three to four months.) It may well have been that Max was being conscripted to serve his fatherland one last time when the deprivation and degradation of camp life broke his health and put him in the infirmary. If this indeed were the case, it would not have amounted to much of a reprieve; due to unsanitary conditions and a lack of drugs, the hospital was considered "an anteroom to the crematorium." Nor was there any real chance, by the way, that Max might have been "saved" by an Allied bombing raid on Auschwitz. This option was not even proposed until mid-1944, when it was rejected for several reasons, including the belief that it would have killed a lot more prisoners than guards. But however we reconstruct Max's final days, as far as the culpability for his death goes, it hardly matters whether his demise occurred in the camp hospital or in the gas chamber: Max was killed by the state that he had loyally served and loved for virtually his entire life.

Epilogue

ON AUGUST 14, 1944, a year after Max Schohl's arrest and deportation to Auschwitz via the Austrian Tyrol, the Schohl women were themselves arrested and deported. Their ultimate destination, however, was not one of the death camps in the east, but a forced-labor facility in the Reich. They owed their relative good fortune to the quirks of Nazi racial policy. Liesel Schohl, as we have noted, was not of Jewish "blood," and her daughters were *Mischlinge*. Having conscripted prisoners of war and enemy civilians into their workforce since the early months of the war, the Nazi government was now, in mid-1944, combing occupied Europe for additional workers who could be forced into service to keep the Reich's factories and farms operating. Being for the most part healthy—Liesel suffered from a variety of ailments, but could still work, while Hela was carrying the child she had conceived with her Serbian "husband," Bogdan, who had gone off to fight with the partisans—the Schohl women were prime candidates for the slave-labor mills that played an increasingly crucial role in the Nazi economy in the last phase of World War II.

The first leg of the Schohls' journey back to the Reich took them from Belgrade to Vienna. While waiting for their train at the Belgrade station they witnessed the arrival and hasty departure of one of the cattle-train transports carrying Serbian Jews to the death camps in Poland. During the transport's brief stop, some of the "passengers" thrust tin cups through slats in the boxcars, calling out for water. The Schohls' first reaction upon seeing this appalling spectacle was fear—fear that this might be *their* train. "They'll never get me on that train," vowed Hela. "I'll kill myself first." Liesel, ever the good Samaritan, started to give water to an old woman leaning out of one of the cars, but changed her mind when a Gestapo man on the platform informed her that if she did so she would end up on that train herself. As the train pulled out the Schohls were overcome with relief—and with guilt for feeling relief.

Their own exit from occupied Yugoslavia was not terribly harrowing—they traveled on a normal train, albeit accompanied by a Gestapo guard—but their brief stay in Vienna reminded them that there was nothing "normal" about their situation or status. Each of the Schohl women was interrogated separately by a Gestapo official in Vienna, who had the authority to decide whether the refugees in his charge should be sent on to work stations in the Reich or to the extermination camps in the east. Before their interrogations, Liesel admonished her daughters to insist that they had not been raised in the Jewish faith and were completely secular. Käthe and Hela dutifully claimed that they did not see themselves as Jews, while Liesel herself stressed her full "Aryan" origins. Whether these protestations were instrumental in securing the Schohl women tickets to the west rather than to the east is difficult to know; in any event, they were given passes to travel to Wiesbaden and instructed to report to that city's Gestapo headquarters in the Paulinenstrasse upon their arrival.

Wiesbaden, of course, was familiar territory to the Schohls, being only about fifteen kilometers from Flörsheim. The parent Electro chemical firm at which Max had initially worked after the war was located in the Wiesbaden suburb of Biebrich. It was to this suburb, in fact, that the Wiesbaden authorities now sent the Schohl women. Käthe and Hela were assigned to work in a cardboard packaging factory called Kartonen-fabrik Becker, while Liesel was assigned to a different factory. The women were reunited at night in a prisonlike rooming house, where they lived under guard with other forced laborers, most of whom were *Mischlinge*.

The Schohls had no sooner arrived in Wiesbaden than a loud siren went off, signaling an attack by Allied aircraft. In late 1944 and early 1945 the Wiesbaden-Frankfurt area was repeatedly bombed, sending inhabitants scurrying to public and private air-raid shelters. During working hours, however, forced laborers like the Schohls were not allowed to stop work to take shelter, and at night their only haven from the bombs was the shallow basement of the rooming house. The sound of sirens and approaching aircraft brought mixed emotions among their company: joy that the war might soon be over; fear that they might not live to see this happy day.

While the fear of death by bombs was intermittent, pain from hunger was constant. At this point food was strictly rationed for all Germans, but forced laborers like the Schohls got far less than ordinary citizens. Indeed, the daily allotments were so meager that the only way to survive was to steal food or to prostitute oneself for extra rations. In the Schohls' case, Käthe took upon herself the dangerous task of stealing potatoes from the rooming house supplies during nightly air raids. On one occasion she managed to bag three whole spuds, enough for a family feast.

In mid-March 1945 the Schohls could hear the sound of artillery fire on the other side of the Rhine River. They also heard the whistle of trains, and one of their guards informed them that they would soon find themselves on one of those trains heading to a camp somewhere to the east. But instead of a trip east came liberation. The American Third Army crossed the Rhine at Oppenheim on March 21. From there it was a quick jump to Wiesbaden, which the American 274th Infantry Regiment ("The Trailblazers") overran in the next few days.

As the American troops poured into Wiesbaden, local Nazi leaders did their best to make themselves scarce or inconspicuous. The warden of the Schohls' work prison threw his golden swastika pin on the floor as he prepared to vacate the premises, prompting Käthe Schohl to return it to him with the words, "Haven't you forgotten something?" Yet she claims to have been too numb with hunger and fatigue to do much celebrating at the moment of her liberation; that would come only when the reality of her deliverance had set in and she had had time to eat a few square meals and clean herself up. She was able, however, to try out her English on the first American soldier she met, who turned out to be a Jewish boy from the Bronx. "We're Jewish," she told the soldier. "That's funny," he replied, "so far every German we've encountered has either been a 'Jew' or a 'resistance fighter'; we've yet to meet our first Nazi."

In the ensuing months the Schohls, and especially Käthe, found a benevolent protector in the form of another Jewish-American soldier, Sergeant Walter Berliner. He arranged for Käthe to get a job as an interpreter at the Enlisted Men's Club, where she made good money. Later that year he helped the Schohl women regain access to their old home in Flörsheim, which had stood abandoned and semi-derelict for some time. All the furniture had been smashed or stolen. Berliner secured furniture for the house from the extensive stock that the American occupiers had "liberated" from Nazi-owned residences and offices. How empty the house must have seemed, however, without the presence of its former patron.

Several months before taking possession of the house, while still living in Biebrich, Käthe Schohl resumed the family's contact with Julius Hess in America. Of course she had much to report: the tragic news regarding Max's fate and the Schohl women's own harrowing odyssey. There was also the happier news about Hela's new baby, a daughter, although the child's father was in all likelihood another casualty of the war. As for the family's current state, Käthe pointed out that though all were safe, Liesel was quite ill, and the food situation left much to be desired, since many staples were strictly rationed. Could Julius help?

Wiesbaden-Biebrich June 1, 1945

Dear Uncle Julius!

You will be astonished to get a letter from me. I am the daughter of your cousin, Dr. Max Schohl. In short sentences I will tell you what happened in the last years. Excuse, I don't know perfectly English, but I hope you will understand me.

You remember, we emigrated to Jugoslavia in March 1940, father, mother, my sister and I, because we could no longer live in Germany under the Nazi regime. We thought we could get the visa for Brasilia, but it was not possible, and so we lived in Jugoslavia. There our father was employed by the War Ministry as a chemist. When the Germans came to Jugoslavia in 1941, we again lived under a regime of force. Now the following years were very hard for us. In August 1943 our father was sent to the concentration camp at Auschwitz, Poland, where the German secret police killed him after three months. In August 1944, our mother, my sister and I were ordered by the secret police to return to Germany, and to work under police inspection in a factory. Now we lost for the second time our home. It was only allowed to take a small trunk with us, and not more. We returned by accompaniment of the SS. They brought us here to Biebrich, and now we worked and always were under inspection. Hard labor.

Let me quickly pass over the last ten months. The loss of our father, and everyday the death in our neck—I have no words to tell you, what I feel. My sister married in Jugoslavia a Serbian, and four months ago she got a child. Her husband was in the war, we saw him a short time before we got the order to return to Germany. Never again we heard something about him. I think he is dead. After our deliverance by the U.S. army, I went to the Military Government in our town, and they promised me to help us, that we get a compensation for all that the Germans took from us. But that will not be for a long time. Our mother is very sick. Now she has time to think about all the pain which we have had in the last 12 years, and from time to time she becomes more ill. My sister is a tailor, and I give English lessons, because all people now wish to learn English, and I have much to do, so we can quite good earn our living.

But most terrible it is with the food. For our little baby we have hardly anything, and our mother wants more food, that she becomes healthy. But it is impossible. I am afraid for the future. It will be more worse than yet. The war in Germany annihilated the fields, so that we can not hope for the new harvest. We get in one week: 50 gr. Butter, 50 gr. Beef, and one [loaf of] bread. Dear Uncle Julius, is it possible that you can send us a packet of food? You can send it at this address: Sgt. Frank Sidlo, Co. A, 3137 Signal SV. GN., A.P.O. 655, NY. NY. . . .

Our grandmother, the mother of our father, Johanna Schohl, widow, lived in Germany in a Jewish hospital. She could not emigrate with us because of her sickness. In 1942 she was sent to a concentration camp, where she died. You remember dear Uncle Julius, the Dollars which you sent us for our emigration were in Amsterdam, Holland, and as the war came to Holland, the USA confiscated the remainder of the $500. I know, Uncle Julius, we have to thank you for so much, and I don't know whether I can give you one day repayment for it all. But I know nobody but you . . . which I could write, and the need drives me to do that. I hope to hear from you soon. Many kindly regards from mother and sister. I thank you from all my heart.

> Yours truly, [Käthe Schohl]

It took some time for Julius to receive Käthe's letter, which a returning soldier brought with him to America and mailed in the United States. Not surprisingly, as soon as Julius got this SOS call he dispatched a generous care package, along with a letter expressing sorrow over the deaths of Max and his mother, joy at the rest of the family's survival, and a query regarding what else the Schohls might need.

On September 14, 1945, Käthe replied:

Dear Cousin Julius,

Yesterday I got your very welcome letter and your package. I can not tell you how happy we were to hear from you.

A long time ago I sent you my letter and I thought you never received it.

Now let me thank you with all my heart, mother and sister too, for your package. You can not imagine how glad we were about it. You asked me what we need. We need just about everything. Mostly what we miss is fat and sugar, and if you can send it, wool for us and the baby, so that we have something for the winter. If you will be so kind and send us from time to time a little parcel, we would be very thankful. I am not ashamed for asking you about anything, because it is important for our living. I am only sorry that I can do nothing for you. Now dear cousin Julius, I thank you very much for your question about money. But we don't need money. I am young, 22 years old, and I can work. I am proud that I can tell you, I earn our living. Since our father is not more with us, I have taken his place. With money you can buy nothing here.

We are glad to hear that aunt Lena is in good health. For her next birthday we wish her all our love the best. Our mother is feeling better now, and our baby is the sweetest girl and our sunshine. She is now seven months old, and is starting to learn to speak.

From cousin Norma I got a letter the same day when your letter came. It is really nice, that she thinks of us too.

We got back our house in Flörsheim/Main, and I think in two or three months we can move to it. Still we have no furniture for the house (it was broken in November 1938 by SA men), I am looking for some and it is very difficult. I must say, the Americans help us whenever they can. At present we are acting to get back one part of our former factory. I shall be then in the factory and continue the work of our father.

A very nice thing happened a few weeks ago. One year before we left Germany, a very good friend of mine went to San Francisco. I haven't heard from him for many years. And here in Biebrich we found each other again, after such a long time. He is now Master Sergeant Jack Hauser. He was the only son, and it is so terrible his parents couldn't go with him to Frisco, so they were sent to a concentration camp and died. We were so happy to see each other. Jack has 95 points, and he went back to the States a few days ago. But he will come back as soon as possible, and then we shall try to marry. He wants me to go with him to the States, but I can not leave my mother and sister, so he will try to stay here for the next three years. But today it is so that you can not say what you want to do tomorrow. Every day something else happens. I gave Jack your address and asked him to write to you, because I thought you have never gotten my letter.

Another thing, a Jewish family from Flörsheim (they and we are the only ones from Flörsheim who came back), who came back from the camp Theresienstadt, were together with our grandmother Johanna Schohl, and they were with her when she died. Don't ask me about that. We can never forget what happened and what we saw. That is what makes our mother so sick: the thoughts of my father.

I am always happy to get a letter from you. Mother and sister send many regards to you and your family, and many thanks once more for your kindness.

My best wishes to you all.

With greetings, [Käthe]

As Käthe's letter makes clear, she had taken over Max's role as the family's primary breadwinner, and she was even hoping to restart her father's factory. She was so conscious of her family responsibilities that she turned down an offer to go to San Francisco with Sergeant Jack Hauser, an old friend who had become a new flame. Yet, again to cite her letter, in the chaos of postwar Germany one could never know what the next day might bring.

As it turned out, Käthe did go to the United States within the coming year, but not in the company of Jack Hauser, who never returned to Germany. The crucial catalyst here was Liesel Schohl, who had been urging Käthe to go to America ever since the liberation. Although she did not say as much, Liesel had come to believe that young Käthe could achieve the success in America that Max had foreseen for himself in that country; she could in effect take Max's place on the other side of the Atlantic. (Hela, who had earlier seen herself becoming a Max-like success in America, decided that she wished to remain in Germany after all.) Dismissing Käthe's protestations that her family duties required her to remain where she was, Liesel made her see—as she had once made Max see—that it was high time to move on.

Once she had made up her mind to emigrate to America, Käthe had no trouble securing the necessary U.S. entry permits. In one of the uglier ironies of this whole story, visas became much more readily available to European Jews *after* the Holocaust than they had been during it. Within two weeks of submitting her application to the U.S. consulate in Stuttgart she received her visa. For help in organizing her move to the States she turned to the Hebrew Sheltering and Immigrant Aid Society (HIAS), which handled the immigration of thousands of Jews. As for the costs of getting to America, Käthe was ready to apply for financial assistance from HIAS, but this turned out to be unnecessary because Cousin Julius, with whom she hoped to stay until she could get on her feet in the States, insisted upon paying her passage himself.

Julius, in fact, was overjoyed at the prospect of Käthe's coming to America, which he had not expected. He was to quick to inform her that she would be more than welcome to stay with him:

May 29, 1946

Dear Kate;

I received your most exciting letter of May the 15th and it just about knocked me out. I was so excited I had to read it two or three times before I could make myself realize what you were saying. You see this was all such a surprise to me I just did not know what it make of it as I had no idea you had even thought about coming over here for quite some time. You stated you had written me twice since last February but I did not receive either one of your letters and what you wrote in those might have been information about your future plans. For instance, what have you done with the plant and what and how will your Mother, Sister and Baby do when you leave? You see, I am in the dark in regards to all those things.

In regards to your coming over here and living with us, you can rest assured that you will be welcome. We will do our utmost to help you along, you need have no fear about coming or how you will get along, everything will work out just fine. I have not yet heard from UNRRA or HIAS but no doubt, it is too soon to hear from them yet. If possible, cable me the date you expect to arrive in New York, and I will try to be there to meet you at the boat . . .

Your cousin, [Julius]

In June 1946, in response to a letter from HIAS advising him that Käthe had received her visa and was ready to sail, Julius sent the organization a check for $225 to cover the costs. A week later he received the kind of news for which he had waited so fervently—and futilely—from 1938 to 1943; it must have brought joy and sadness at the same time:

Mr. Julius Hess June 13, 1946
905 Highland Road
Charleston, W. Va.
Re: Schohl, Kaethe
Germany

Dear Friend:

We are pleased to advise you that the above who sailed on the SS 'Marine Flasher' is/are expected to arrive in New York on or about Monday, June 17, 1946.

Kindly advise us whether someone will come to New York to meet the immigrant(s). If not, please immediately send us the necessary funds for the transportation from New York to the final destination.

Pier Service
HIAS

Julius Hess was waiting at the pier in New York when the *Marine Flasher* docked. He looked dapper in a white suit and Panama hat from the Kaufman Brothers store. Käthe, too, was all dolled up, though she had no idea how young ladies dressed in America. After a brief stay in New York, Julius took Käthe home to Charleston, introducing her to everyone in town as "my daughter from Germany."

The first days in Charleston were not easy for Käthe. To her, the town "seemed like another planet," what with its humid summer heat and strange ways. Her acclimatization was not necessarily aided by well-meaning friends of the Hesses, who assumed that she needed to be taught how to use a flush toilet and handle her silverware. Considerably more painful was her first encounter with Charlie Midelburg, whom Julius insisted she meet. Apologizing for not being quicker to help her father, Charlie gave her a $100 pass to his movie theater in town.

Sensing her loneliness and homesickness for Germany, Julius did his best to get Käthe out into society—the Jewish society of Charleston. He took her regularly to the Southmoor Country Club, which in addition to the usual constituency of geriatric golfers boasted a few eligible young bachelors among its membership. The man who quickly caught Käthe's eye was certainly eligible though not quite so young: thirty-six-year-old Herman Wells, an auto parts dealer. Seizing the initiative, Käthe prodded the shy Mr. Wells to ask her out on a date, which he happily did. Following a six-month courtship they were married in Julius's house, the wedding reception being held (where else?) at the Southmoor Country Club. The marriage, which produced two children, lasted until Herman Wells's death forty-seven years later.

Although Herman Wells became the male mainstay in Käthe's life she remained extremely close to Julius, who was indeed a father to her in her new life in America. During long summer evenings on Julius's front porch she filled him in on all the grim events that lay behind Max's letters. Julius remained Käthe's confidant until his own death in 1967, at age sixty-nine. Yet it was only nineteen years later, upon the death of Bea Hess in 1986, that Käthe discovered just how powerfully committed Julius had been to her family's salvation during the Holocaust. Sorting through Julius's files in the basement of his home, she stumbled across a box containing all the letters written by Max and other members of her German family to their relatives in America, along with copies of their replies. Julius may not have known all the stories behind the Schohl letters, but he had known enough to save everything.

Back in battered Germany, Käthe's mother and sister Hela were making their own adjustments to radically altered circumstances. Shortly after the war Hela wrote to the Red Cross and learned that her Serbian lover, Bogdan, had in all likelihood been killed in the partisan assault on occupied Belgrade. (She was able to confirm this during a trip to Yugoslavia in 1953.) In 1949 she married the man who had been her first serious boyfriend way back in the early thirties, Josef Braumann. Just as her mother had once converted to Judaism to marry Max, Liesel now converted to Catholicism to marry Braumann. The conversion was not particularly painful for her because she had retained a secret fascination with Catholicism since her childhood. Although Hela had twin boys with her new husband, the marriage was rocky from the start—perhaps a lesson in the perils of trying to rekindle old flames. Three years before marrying Braumann, Hela had moved back into the Albanusstrasse house with her mother. The women promptly opened a small clothing and textile shop called "Schogi" (combining the family names Schohl and Gims) on the premises. Schogi was postwar Flörsheim's first—and for some time its only—clothing store. After her remarriage, Hela and Braumann turned to a different market opportunity and opened a bar in a small adjoining shack that was said to serve also as an informal *Bumslokal* (brothel). The Albanusstrasse house remained in the family's possession until the mid-1950s; today it serves as an old folks' home. None of the current residents has any knowledge of, or interest in, the structure's tangled past.

Unlike Käthe, Liesel and Hela had no ambitions regarding Max's former chemical factory. In the months immediately following the war the facility became a *"Polenlager,"* a camp for German-ethnic expellees from the former eastern German regions recently annexed by Poland. In 1947 an expellee named Ewald Persicke, who had owned a shoe factory in his former home, bought the building and set up a new shoe-manufacturing enterprise, which by 1953 was employing 125 people, 40 percent of them expellees. The shoe factory gave way in 1957 to a company that built water systems for large commercial developments. This operation prospered for many years thereafter in the building boom accompanying West Germany's "economic miracle" of the late 1950s, 1960s, and early 1970s. When that boom ebbed in the mid-1970s the water system plant closed, leaving the town of Flörsheim with a derelict industrial site on its hands. In the early 1980s the site was cleared for the construction of a housing complex, which stands there today.

While the Schohl family made no effort to resurrect Max's chemical plant, Liesel Schohl and her daughters applied through the postwar German courts for compensation for the loss of the Electro plant in 1935, as well as for the racial persecution they suffered at the hands of the Nazis and their minions in Germany and Yugoslavia. Their claims, beginning in 1948 and spreading over several years, constitute a small part of the enormously complicated saga of restitution for the victims of Nazi crimes in the postwar era. (This story played itself out mainly in West Germany, not in East Germany, because the government of the Federal Republic, unlike that of the GDR, passed legislation to compensate the new state of Israel and individual German-Jewish victims for sufferings and losses endured by Jews under the National Socialist regime.) The intent of the West German restitution legislation was certainly laudable, but the legal efforts by victims to obtain compensation, which understandably required extensive oral and written documentation, proved often to be painful as well as laborious.

Along with personal statements chronicling the details of their family's persecution—the vandalism of their home during Kristallnacht, Max's internment in Buchenwald, their Gestapo-ordered flight from Germany, their trials and tribulations in German-occupied Yugoslavia,

Max's deportation to and death in Auschwitz, and their months of forced labor in Biebrich—the Schohls submitted letters from eyewitnesses who supported their claims. For example, to back their contention that they had been subjected to *"Ghettohaft"* (ghetto-internment) in Ruma and made to work for the German occupiers and their allies, they submitted a letter from a former Wehrmacht soldier who wrote that the Schohls had been "under control of the Gestapo" in Ruma and forced to perform humiliating labor for the *Volksdeutsche* SS. In a ruling dated November 2, 1950, the Hessian state court denied the Schohls' claim for *"Haftentschädigung"* (compensation for arrest) on grounds that Ruma had not been a Nazi detention camp; nor, in the eyes of the court, had the family's movements been sufficiently limited to constitute "arrest" according to German law. The court also stated, however, that this judgment had no bearing on the other compensation claims the Schohl family was making.

In September 1954 Liesel Schohl and Hela Braumann appealed the verdict denying them compensation for arrest and forced labor in Ruma, submitting additional written testimony from a former employee of Franz Wagner (the *Volksdeutsche* pig farmer for whom Max had worked), who stated that all Jews in Ruma were subjected to *Ghettohaft* in that they were not allowed to leave the town. He further stated that the Schohls, like other Jews in the area, had been forced to wear the Yellow Star and perform various kinds of labor for the German occupiers and their Croatian allies. In a letter to the court dated September 27, 1954, Liesel Schohl reiterated the details of her family's persecution, stating in particular that the chemical factory belonging to her husband had been "driven into bankruptcy by the Nazis"; that her home had been ransacked by the SA in November 1938; that her husband had been interned in Buchenwald following Kristallnacht; that the Schohls had been "ordered to leave Germany by the Gestapo" in March 1940; and that during their three-and-one-half-year "internment" in Yugoslavia her husband had been arrested five times, placed in various work camps, and eventually sent to Auschwitz, "where he was gassed." "On these grounds I claim arrest-compensation in the appropriate amount," she concluded. Hela Braumann's compensation application, in addition to advancing similar claims, mentioned "inhuman treatment" by the SS during forced labor, including denial of proper nutrition, periodic beatings, and verbal abuse. She stated that as a result of this treatment she had suffered injuries to her spine and hip joints requiring ongoing medical attention. In a later claim Liesel also listed injuries resulting from physical abuse in Ruma and Biebrich, as well as heart troubles stemming from the "emotional shock generated by the deportation and murder of my husband."

On September 7, 1956, the Hessian court awarded Liesel Schohl financial compensation in the amount of 6,750 marks (about $1,690). The award was based on a calculation of 150 marks for each month of persecution during the period from May 31, 1941, to March 28, 1945— that is, from the time of the German occupation of Ruma to the American liberation of Wiesbaden. The government paid no restitution for Max's death or for the loss of his factory, but in a separate settlement Liesel Schohl managed to gain a modest compensation package from the two former employees of Max's who had forced him out of the directorship in 1935 and briefly run the business before its final closure.

Neither Liesel Schohl nor Hela Braumann remained in Flörsheim for the remainder of their days. In the late 1960s Liesel moved to Karlsruhe, where she died in 1975 at seventy-eight years of age. Hela, who divorced Braumann and married a businessman named Weiss, moved to the Lake Constance region; she died on March 10, 2000. During her final illness she discovered a desire to return to her roots and to die as a Jew. She drafted a will stating that, her Catholic conversion notwithstanding, she wished to be buried with her mother in the Jewish cemetery outside Flörsheim. After much complicated negotiating between her sons and the chief rabbi of Frankfurt, Hela got her wish. In a ceremony presided over by the chief rabbi himself, her remains were interred next to an urn containing her mother's ashes in Flörsheim's old Jewish cemetery at Wickerbach, under a headstone that also memorializes Max Schohl and his mother Johanna.

Having been rendered "Jew-free" by the Nazis in 1943, Flörsheim remains essentially Jew-free today, and there are few physical reminders of the Jewish community that was once a vital part of the local scene. There is of course the cemetery outside town, which in addition to a few scattered headstones contains a memorial plaque dedicated to the Jews of Flörsheim and the surrounding villages. In the words of the plaque, these "last remaining men, women, and children were persecuted and expelled on account of their faith and race." Having been extensively vandalized in the Nazi period, the cemetery was desecrated again shortly after a memorial ceremony there in 1989. Unidentified vandals painted swastikas on the headstones; sprayed the slogans, "Dead Jew equals Good Jew," "Put Jews in Camps," "Death to Judaism," and "Heil Hitler" on the wall encircling the cemetery; and, for good measure, threw some of the grave markers into a nearby creek, just as the Nazis had once done. In the town itself the only reminders of the vanished Jewish community are a lovingly restored ritual bath (*Mikva*), dating to the thirteenth century, and one wall of the synagogue that was wrecked by the Nazis during Kristallnacht and then torn down in 1939. In 1960 the Jewish Restitution Successor Organization submitted a claim for 268,000 marks for the loss of the synagogue structure and all its contents. Liesel Schohl supported the claim with a letter to the court. Two years later, in connection with a ceremony marking the 250th anniversary of the synagogue's construction and the thirtieth anniversary of its desecration, the town council dedicated a plaque affixed to the surviving wall.

In addition to Synagogengasse (the pre-Nazi street designation was reinstated in 1968), present-day Flörsheim boasts an Altmaierstrasse and a Dr.-Max-Schohl-Strasse. Like the street honoring the Altmaier family, the lane named for Max Schohl, which runs from the Hauptstrasse down to the Main River through the housing development where the chemist's factory once stood, must be seen as a well-meaning, though hardly adequate, attempt on the part of the town of Flörsheim to atone for its treatment of one of its most illustrious Jewish citizens.

Of course this gesture should also be seen as part of a much broader picture: in this instance the belated and often awkward attempts by postwar German officials to atone for the crimes of the Nazis by memorializing the victims. In Max's case, the commemorative gesture did not occur until 1984, following a proposal submitted by the local CDU faction in the town assembly calling for such a step. The proposal made particular note of Max's charitable contributions and claimed that his "social conscience is still fondly remembered by older residents." The proposition was duly accepted by the town council, and on December 8, 1984, Mayor Dieter Wolf presided over a ceremony during which the little street was officially christened. The Schohl family was represented at the ceremony by Hela Schohl-Weiss, who had traveled up from Lake Constance for the occasion. The mayor read a statement saying, inter alia: "By naming a street after [Max Schohl], we honor and remember a citizen of Flörsheim who, without reservation, helped his fellow man whenever he could."

Käthe Schohl-Wells had been invited to the street-christening ceremony but had to decline the invitation to attend to her ailing husband in Charleston. "It killed me that I couldn't be there," she told the *Charleston Daily Mail*, which devoted an article to the occasion. Today she professes no bitterness toward her former hometown, but one wonders. In any event, one might argue that she is closer to Max in her American apartment on the banks of Charleston's Kanawha River than she would have been at a belated atonement ritual on the banks of the River Main. The mementos and photographs of her father that surround her in her home serve to remind her, she says, of the importance of "not letting the world forget."

Notes

INTRODUCTION

PAGE

xviii **of his co-religionists:** On the German Jews' fatal unwillingness to make a timely exit from Nazi Germany, see John V. H. Dippel, *Bound Upon a Wheel of Fire: Why So Many German Jews Made the Tragic Decision to Remain in Nazi Germany* (New York, 1996).

xviii **directly from the Nazi Reich:** Bat-Ami Zucker, *In Search of Refuge: Jews and United States Consuls in Nazi Germany* (London and Portland, OR, 2001), 46.

xviii **time in 1939:** David S. Wyman, *Paper Walls: America and the Refugee Crisis 1938–1941* (Amherst, MA, 1968), 221.

xviii **German-Austrian quota:** Wyman, *Paper Walls*, 168–169; Herbert A. Strauss, "Jewish Emigration from Germany. Nazi Policies and Jewish Responses (II)," *Leo Baeck Institute Year Book* 26 (1981): 359.

xix **only 15,284 a year:** Zucker, *In Search of Refuge*, 47.

xix **during the Holocaust:** See, in addition to the above citations, Maurice R. Davie, *Refugees in America: The Report of the Committee for the Study of Recent Immigration from Europe* (New York, 1947); Arthur D. Morse, *While Six Million Died: A Chronicle of American Apathy* (New York, 1967); Henry L. Feingold, *The Politics of Rescue: The Roosevelt Administration and the Holocaust, 1938–1945* (New Brunswick, NJ, 1970); Saul S. Friedman, *No Haven for the Oppressed: United States Policy Toward Jewish Refugees, 1938–1945* (Detroit, 1973); Monty Penkower, *The Jews Were Expendable* (Urbana, IL, 1983); David S. Wyman, *The Abandonment of the Jews: America and the Holocaust* (New York, 1984); Richard Breitman and Alan M. Kraut, *American Refugee Policy and European Jewry, 1933–1945* (Bloomington, 1987); A. J. Sherman, *Island Refuge: Britain and Refugees from the Third Reich, 1933–1939* (London, 1973); Bernard Wasserstein, *Britain and the Jews of Europe, 1939–1945* (London, 1979); and Louise London, *Whitehall and the Jews, 1933–1948* (Cambridge, England, 2000).

xx **had to work:** See Peter Novick, *The Holocaust in American Life* (Boston, 1999), 48. For critical assessments of Wyman's "abandonment of the Jews" perspective, see Frank W. Brecher, "David Wyman and the Historiography of America's Response to the Holocaust: Counter-Considerations," *Holocaust and Genocide Studies* 5, No. 4 (1990): 423–446; and Henry L. Feingold, "Review of David Wyman's *The Abandonment of the Jews: America and the Holocaust, 1941–1945*," in *FDR and the Holocaust*, ed. Verne W. Newton (New York, 1996), 145–158. For an account that argues that the West could not have done *anything* of consequence to save more Jews, see William D. Rubinstein, *The Myth of Rescue: Why the Democracies Could Not Have Saved More Jews from the Nazis* (London and New York, 1997). Rubinstein's contention that the democracies' refugee policies in the 1930s were "remarkably generous" (p. x) strikes me as perverse in light of the policy makers' own insistence that the immigration regulations had to be restrictive because of popular pressure against a more "generous" policy. Rubinstein's assertion that "72 percent of German Jewry escaped from Nazi Germany before emigration became impossible" (p. 16) fails to note that thousands of those who "escaped" managed only to flee to other European countries, where they were eventually interned—and killed—by the Nazis.

CHAPTER 1

1 **"cult of *Kultur"*:** Paul Mendes-Flohr, *German Jews: A Dual Identity* (New Haven, CT, 1999), 27.

2 **"are our misfortune":** Heinrich von Treitschke, "Unsere Aussichten" (1879), in *Der Berliner Antisemitismusstreit*, ed. Walter Boehlich (Frankfurt/M., 1965), 13.

2 **"and nothing else":** Quoted in Ruth Gay, *The Jews of Germany: A Historical Portrait* (New Haven, CT, 1992), 165.

3 **their entrance examinations:** Mendes-Flohr, *German Jews*, 130.

3 **age of thirty-seven:** On Haber, see Fritz Stern, *Dreams and Delusions: The Drama of German History* (New York, 1987), 51–76.

4 **"friend of the Jews":** Interview with Käthe Schohl Wells (KSW), January 14, 2001, Charleston, WV.

4 **strength of 61,432:** Wolfgang Schmidt, "Die Juden in der bayerischen Armee," in *Deutsche Judische Soldaten*, ed. Militärgeschichtliches Forschungsamt (Hamburg and Bonn, 1996), 67.

4 **"privileged class position":** Martin Kitchen, *The German Officer Corps, 1890–1914* (Oxford, 1968), 37.

5 **and bad eyes:** Ibid., 38.

5 **"downright ruinous":** Schmidt, "Die Juden," 78.

6 **"*Mit Hurra in den Tod"*:** For a wartime memoir set in Max's regiment, see Hermann Kohl, *Kriegserlebnisse eines Frontsoldaten der 17. bayer. Infanterie-Regiment "Orff"* (Stuttgart, 1932). Max kept a personal copy of this memoir, its pages interspersed with his own drawings and observations.

6 **"flow for the fatherland":** Quoted in W. Michael Blumenthal, *The Invisible Wall: Germans and Jews—A Personal Exploration* (Washington, DC, 1998), 293.

6 **"Thank God for that":** Quoted in Schmidt, "Die Juden," 79

7 **"has awakened again":** Quoted in Mendes-Flohr, *Germans and Jews*, 20.

8   **"on enemy soil":** Max Schohl, "Voice in the Night," Schohl Family Papers.

9   **"of former soldiers":** Alfred Westphal, "Die Kriegervereine," in *Deutschland als Weltmacht: Vierzig Jahre Deutsches Reich,* ed. Kaiser-Wilhelm-Dank (Berlin, 1912), 762.

11   **"back to health":** "A Soldier's Story," Schohl Family Papers.

11   **"not bad":** Interview with KSW, January 14, 2001.

11   **Flörsheim's larger employers:** Peter Becker, *Anmerkungen zu Mirjam. Flörsheim Geschichte und Geschichten 1900–1950* (Flörsheim, 2001), 991.

13   **predations of international finance:** Martin Sabrow, "Märtyrer der Republik. Zu den Hintergründen des Mordanschlags vom 24. Juni 1922," in *Die Extremen berühren sich: Walter Rathenau 1867–1922,* ed. Hans Wilderotter (Berlin, 1993), 221–236.

13   **usurious rates later on:** See David Clay Large, "Out with the Ostjuden: The Scheunenviertel Riots in Berlin, November 1923," in *Exclusionary Violence: Antisemitic Riots in Modern German History,* ed. Christhard Hoffmann, Werner Bergmann, and Helmut Walser Smith (Ann Arbor, MI, 2002), 123–140.

14   **4,210,500,000,000 marks:** The best study of the devastating German inflation is Gerald D. Feldman, *The Great Disorder. Politics, Economics, and Society in the German Inflation 1914–1924* (New York, 1993).

14   **"rule the hour"***: Deutsche Allgemeine Zeitung,* July 29, 1923.

15   **were acted out:** On separatism in Flörsheim, see Bernd Blisch, "Die 'Separatistenzeit' in Flörsheim am Main—September bis Dezember 1923," *Rad und Sparen: Zeitschrift des Historischen Verein Rhein-Main-Taunus e. V.* 25 (1994): 32–52.

15   **loss of the war:** Werner Schiele, *Auf Roten Spuren: Die Geschichte der Sozialdemokratie in Flörsheim am Main* (Flörsheim, 1988), 66.

16   **to the destitute:** Ibid., 60.

17   **drive up rents:** Ibid., 69.

17   **4.50 marks per day:** Ibid.

17   **20 marks per unit:** Ibid., 70.

18   **"little Lenin from Flörsheim":** Ibid., 68.

18 **two tiny bells:** Blisch, "Die Separatistenzeit," 40.

19 **towns of the region:** On Flörsheim's emergency currency, see Albert Ciesulski, "Das Flörsheimer Notgeld von 1923," *Flörsheimer Geschichtshefte* No. 2 (September 2000): 13–18.

19 **"entire district of Wiesbaden":** Ibid.

20 **know no bounds:** Interview with Irmgard Radczuk, September 20, 2001, Flörsheim.

21 **throughout the Weimar era:** See Werner Schiele, *Juden in Flörsheim am Main* (Flörsheim, 1999), 365, 378.

21 **to the municipal council:** Ibid., 362–365, 360.

22 **"German-Christian spirit"; "garden of poetry":** Ibid., 367–369.

22 **"God lasts forever":** Ibid., 352.

23 **moderate Socialist SPD:** Ibid., 372.

23 **following in town:** Ibid., 384.

CHAPTER 2

27 **out of work:** Schiele, *Auf Roten Spuren*, 109–111.

27 **"the general misery":** Schohl to Bürgermeister, Sept. 4, 1931, SAF, Abt. V, Fach 17, Nr. 15.

28 **"nothing but scum":** Schiele, *Auf Roten Spuren*, 116.

28 **"Arm Yourself for Rebellion":** SAF, Abt. VII, Fach 23, Nr. 2.

28 **the Brown plague:** Schiele, *Auf Roten Spuren*, 110.

29 **"Flörsheim for National Socialism":** Quoted in Schiele, *Juden in Flörsheim*, 391.

29 **"in their direction":** *Flörsheimer Nachrichten*, September 21, 1929.

30 **good for the family fortunes:** Becker, *Anmerkungen*, 273.

30 **"No Entry to Jews":** *Flörsheimer Zeitung*, July 16, 1932.

31 **"in this town":** Ibid., July 20, 1932.

31 **"wait calmly":** Quoted in Saul Friedländer, *Nazi Germany and the Jews. Volume I: The Years of Persecution, 1933–1939* (New York, 1998), 15.

31 **"keep him fenced in":** Gordon Craig, *Germany 1866–1945* (New York, 1978), 568.

31 **in October 1932:** Schiele, *Juden in Flörsheim*, 394.

31 **of the total vote:** Ibid.

32   **Jewish Social Democratic activist:** On Altmaier, see Werner
     Schiele, *An der Front der Freiheit. Jakob Altmaiers Leben für die
     Demokratie* (Flörsheim, 1991).

32   **"longer than Adolf Hitler":** Quoted in Schiele, *Juden in Flör-
     sheim*, 396.

33   **"or lay assessor":** Quoted in Schiele, *Auf Roten Spuren*, 127.

33   **"service of the new Germany":** Quoted in Becker, *Anmerkungen*,
     277.

33   **"have some deeds":** *Flörsheimer Nachrichten*, April 5, 1933.

33   **businesses and services:** Friedländer, *Nazi Germany*, 17–19.

34   **"of Jewish-owned businesses":** Quoted in Schiele, *Juden in
     Flörsheim*, 395.

35   **died in the war:** Friedländer, *Nazi Germany*, 15.

35   **to own farms:** Ibid., 26–34; Schiele, *Juden in Flörsheim*, 397–398.
     See also Josef Walk, ed., *Das Sonderrecht für die Juden im NS-Staat*. 2.
     Auflage (Heidelberg, 1996), I: 225, 243.

35   **Hermann Altmaier's bakery:** Schiele, *Juden in Flörsheim*, 401.

36   **"drama of municipal cleansing":** Quoted in ibid., 399–400.

38   **"obedient servant":** Schohl to V. Horn, November 6, 1933,
     Schohl Family Papers.

39   **of the negatives:** Heeresarchiv München to Schohl, May 26,
     1939, Schohl Family Papers.

39   **"within the Gemeinde":** Kahn to Landrat, May 27, 1933, SAF,
     Abt. V, Fach 17, Nr. 15.

39   **"prevailing regulations":** Kultusgemeinde Flörsheim, August
     26, 1933, HSAW, Abt. 425, Nr. 884.

39   **"and their mothers":** Polizeipräsident Frankfurt to Herren Bürg-
     ermeister, Nov. 14, 1933, SAF, Abt. V, Fach 17, Nr. 15.

40   **still residing in Flörsheim:** Stamm to Polizeipräsident, ibid.

40   **"bread from a Yid":** Quoted in Becker, *Anmerkungen*, 993.

40   **relations with them:** Friedländer, *Nazi Germany*, 142; Walk, *Son-
     derrecht*, I: 127. On the Nuremberg Laws, see also David Bankier,
     The Germans and the Final Solution: Public Opinion under Nazism (Ox-
     ford, 1992), 142–144.

40   **red, white, and black:** On April 27 Mayor Stamm explicitly forbade Max Schohl from flying the Reich colors. See Flaggenverbot,
SAF, Abt. V, Fach 17, Nr. 15.

41   **Jewish religious community:** Friedländer, *Nazi Germany*,
148–149.

41   **at a later date:** Ibid., 149.

41   **legal solution to the Jewish question:** Ian Kershaw, *The Hitler
Myth: Image and Reality in the Third Reich* (New York, 1989), 235–236.

42   **"moral and economic existence":** Buchhandler Vereinigung,
ed., *Die jüdische Emigration aus Deutschland 1933–1941: Die Geschichte
einer Austreibung. Ausstellung der Deutschen Bibliothek* (Frankfurt/M.,
1985), 79.

42   **handicrafts, and Hebrew:** Ibid.

43   **"stroke of a pen":** Quoted in Marion A. Kaplan, *Between Dignity
and Despair: Jewish Life in Nazi Germany* (New York, 1998), 88.

43   **"rejoin the racial community":** Ibid., 89.

43   **to stay on:** Walk, *Sonderrecht*, 139.

44   **"as soon as possible":** Quoted in Becker, *Anmerkungen*, 998.

44   **"by him is approved":** Quoted in ibid.

45   **"relief from the law":** Ibid., 998–999.

46   **survived in July 1938:** Kaplan, *Between Dignity and Despair*, 24.

46   **"in Christian hands":** Bürgermeister to Städtische Krankenhaus
Kaiserslautern, August 16, 1933, SAF, Abt. IX, Fach 34, Nr. 3.

46   **its racial status:** Chemische Fabrik Flörsheim to Bürgermeister,
June 28, 1935, ibid.

46   **"non-Aryan ownership":** See letters in ibid.

47   **bankruptcy protection:** Becker, *Anmerkungen*, 999; *Flörsheimer
Zeitung*, July 4, 1935.

47   **78,000 marks in debt:** *Flörsheimer Zeitung*, August 4, 1936.

47   **of the bankruptcy settlement:** Becker, *Anmerkungen*, 1001.

48   **"in the neighborhood":** Quoted in ibid., 999–1001.

48   **market himself:** Interview with KSW, January 14, 2001.

49   **left unmolested:** Schiele, *Juden in Flörsheim*, 102; Becker, *Anmerkungen*, 717.

49 **"Jews unwelcome":** Quoted in Schiele, *Juden in Flörsheim*, 408.

49 **died of his injuries:** Ibid., 409.

49 **going on in town:** Interview with KSW, January 15, 2002.

50 **on the family table:** Ibid.

50 **"to flee Germany":** Kaplan, *Between Dignity and Despair*, 63.

51 **"start in on the Jews":** Interview with KSW, January 14, 2001.

CHAPTER 3

53 **"asylum for mankind":** Quoted in Friedman, *No Haven for the Oppressed*, 17.

54 **"inferior elements":** Ibid., 24. See also Robert A. Divine, *American Immigration Policy, 1924–1952* (New Haven, CT, 1957), 1–2.

54 **"wherever they enter":** Edward A. Ross, *The Old World in the New: The Significance of Past Immigration to the American People* (New York, 1914), 146–157. On later connections between the eugenics movement and Nazism, see Stefan Kühl, *The Nazi Connection: Eugenics, American Racism, and German National Socialism* (New York, 1994).

54 **"stream of our population":** Quoted in Friedman, *No Haven for the Oppressed*, 21.

54 **"Kikes, and Hunkies":** Ibid.

55 **"pretty good club":** See Martin Weil, *A Pretty Good Club: The Founding Fathers of the United States Foreign Service* (New York, 1978).

55 **men from Groton:** Ibid., 48. On the U.S. Foreign Service, see also Robert D. Schulzinger, *The Making of the Diplomatic Mind: The Training, Outlook, and Style of United States Foreign Service Officers, 1908–1931* (Middletown, CT, 1975).

55 **"keep out the undesirables":** Quoted in Breitman and Kraut, *Refugee Policy*, 32.

56 **"will be refused":** Quoted in Morse, *While Six Million Died*, 135. For a brief examination of the position of refugees under U.S. immigration law in the 1930s, see Read Lewis and Martin Schibsby, "Status of the Refugee under American Immigration Laws," *Annals of the American Academy of Political and Social Science* 203 (May 1939): 74–82.

56 **"citizen of the United States"**: Harold Field, "Unemployment and the Alien," *South Atlantic Quarterly* 30 (1931): 61.

57 **35,576 in 1932**: Morse, *While Six Million Died*, 136.

57 **1,320 in 1932**: Breitman and Kraut, *Refugee Policy*, 33.

57 **"because of conscience"**: Quoted in Friedman, *No Haven for the Oppressed*, 22.

57 **weaken potential enemies**: Breitman and Kraut, *Refugee Policy*, 54.

58 **opportunities to its Jews**: Breitman and Kraut, *Refugee Policy*, 45. The Stuttgart Consulate also reported "a marked increase in the number of persons of the Jewish faith making applications at the office for immigration visas, both quota and non-quota, and for passport visas or temporary visas." See Dominian to Secretary of State, April 11, 1933, NA 811.111, Quota 62/404.

58 **"humane application of Immigration Law"**: Lehman to Hull, September 7, 1933, NA, 150.626, J/37.

58 **Jewish visa applicants**: Breitman and Kraut, *Refugee Policy*, 12; see also George Martin, *Madam Secretary: Frances Perkins* (Boston, 1976).

58 **remained unfilled**: Breitman and Kraut, *Refugee Policy*, 14.

59 **"to FD's administration"**: Quoted in ibid., 8.

59 **"activity against them"**: Carr Memo, May 31, 1933, LC, Carr Papers, Box 10.

59 **"governmental and social systems"**: Phillips to Dodd, November 27, 1933, LC, Dodd Papers, Box 42.

59 **"dangerous Jewish persecutions"**: Dodd to FDR, July 30, 1933, ibid.

60 **"shrewdly and successfully"**: Howard M. Sachar, *A History of the Jews in America* (New York, 1992), 476.

60 **"residents of the United States"**: "Current Immigration to the United States from the Consulate District of Berlin, Germany," October 27, 1934, NA, 811.111, Quota 62/468.

60 **"unsympathetic way"**: Razovsky report, July 1935, AJA, Felix Warburg Papers, Box 316, Folder 2.

61 **"considered at all"**: [unidentified] to Max Kohler, August 1, 1933, Yivo, Exo–29, RG 347.1.29, Box 16, Folder 297.

61 **"between the two countries":** Kohler to Hull, August 23, 1933, Yivo, Eric Waldman Papers, Box 14, Folder 266.

61 **"to us at home":** Messersmith to Billikopf, January 3, 1935, AJA, Jacob Billikopf Papers, Box 19, Folder 10.

61 **"in the same way":** Committee on German Jewish Immigration Policy, October 4, 1935, AJA, Waldman Papers, Box 316, Folder 2.

61 **back in the building:** Breitman and Kraut, *Refugee Policy*, 47.

62 **income of over $50,000:** Warburg to American Consulate, Stuttgart, March 12, 1936, AJA, Warburg Papers, Box 329, Folder 4.

62 **"make him a public charge":** Quoted in Friedman, *No Haven for the Oppressed*, 23.

62 **"could save us":** Quoted in Frederic Grunfeld, *Prophets Without Honor: A Background to Freud, Kafka, Einstein, and Their World* (New York, 1979), 287.

62 **"provoking painful discussion":** Breitman and Kraut, *Refugee Policy*, 44.

63 **might do so:** Ibid., 49; Zucker, *In Search of Refuge*, 90.

63 **increased to 20,301:** Breitman and Kraut, *Refugee Policy*, 50. For slightly different figures, apparently not based on fiscal years, see Herbert A. Strauss, "Jewish Emigration from Germany. Nazi Policies and Jewish Responses, II," *Leo Baeck Institute Yearbook* 26 (1981): 359.

63 **fired for this action:** Ibid., 361.

63 **helping the German Jews:** On this see Joseph W. Bendarsky, *The "Jewish Threat." Anti-Semitic Politics of the U.S. Army* (New York, 2000), passim.

64 **"put in concentration camps"** : Quoted in ibid., 230.

64 **"control":** Quoted in ibid., 237.

64 **in the 1930s:** On the impact of American anti-Semitism on immigration, see, inter alia, Thomas J. Curran, *Xenophobia and Immigration, 1820–1930* (Boston, 1975); Leonard Dinnerstein, *Antisemitism in America* (New York, 1994); John Higham, *Strangers in the Land: Patterns of American Nativism, 1860–1925* (New Brunswick, NJ, 1955); Donald S. Strong, *Organized Anti-Semitism in America: The Rise of Group Prejudice During the Decade 1930–1940* (Washington, DC, 1941).

64   **"Jewish Communists":** Friedman, *No Haven for the Oppressed*, 27.

64   **"Jewish in origin":** Quoted in ibid., 29.

65   **"by cursory examination":** Paul Reveres to FDR, April 8, 1933, NA, 150.626 (Jews).

65   **"in a spiritual Creator":** Weaver to Hull, April 5, 1933, ibid.

65   **"Jewed to death":** Nevel to Carr, March 31, 1933, ibid.

65   **"swindlers, thieves and murderers":** Smith to FDR, January 24, 1934, ibid.

66   **"friendship with Germany":** Jackson to Hull, January 24, 1934, ibid.

66   **greed, and clannishness:** Wyman, *Paper Walls*, 22.

66   **"too much power":** Quoted in ibid.

66   **sides knew it:** Henry L. Feingold, "Courage First and Intelligence Second: The American Jewish Secular Elite, Roosevelt, and the Failure to Rescue," in *FDR and the Holocaust*, ed. Verne W. Newton, 52.

66   **exacerbating anti-Semitic sentiments:** A cautious policy was especially favored by the American Jewish Committee. See Frederick A. Lazin, "The Response of the American Jewish Committee to the Crisis of German Jewry, 1933–1939," *American Jewish History* 68 (March 1939): 283–304. For a full account of American Jewry's response to the Holocaust, see Henry L. Feingold, *Bearing Witness. How America and Its Jews Responded to the Holocaust* (Syracuse, NY, 1993). See also Feingold, "Was There a Communal Failure? Some Thoughts on the American Jewish Response to the Holocaust," in *FDR and the Holocaust*, ed. Verne W. Newton, 89–108.

66   **would have been successful:** For a good discussion of the American Jews' limited options, see Breitman and Kraut, *Refugee Policy*, 80–111.

67   **fasts, and demonstrations:** Ibid., 82–85.

68   **"whatever way possible":** Quoted in ibid., 89.

68   **"travel on German boats":** Quoted in ibid., 91.

68   **under the circumstances:** Ibid., 92.

69   **"thank our Führer":** Quoted in Evan Burr Buckey, *Hitler's Austria: Popular Sentiment in the Nazi Era, 1938–1945* (Chapel Hill, NC, 2000), 31.

69   **brothers in Germany:** On the wave of anti-Semitism accompanying the Anschluss, see ibid., 22–24.

69   **95 percent Jewish:** Friedman, *No Haven for the Oppressed*, 39.

69   **"ever did in Germany":** Quoted in Kenneth S. Davis, *FDR: Into the Storm 1937–1940* (New York, 1993), 195.

70   **"in the law's vestments":** Quoted in Deborah Lipstadt, *Beyond Belief: The American Press and the Holocaust* (New York, 1986), 88.

70   **"refuge at this time":** Quoted in Friedman, *No Haven for the Oppressed*, 42–43.

70   **"keep them all out":** Ibid., 43. See also Breitman and Kraut, *Refugee Policy*, 87–88.

70   **rigid exclusionist policy:** Friedman, *No Haven for the Oppressed*, 44.

70   **for Jewish financiers:** Davis, *Into the Storm*, 196.

71   **opportunities for all Americans:** Friedman, *No Haven for the Oppressed*, 48.

71   **such a public gesture:** Wyman, *Paper Walls*, 44–45.

71   **"philanthropy as such":** Quoted in Feingold, *Politics of Rescue*, 26.

72   **"relieving the situation":** Minutes of the First Meeting of the PACPR, May 16, 1938, Yivo, Joseph Chamberlain Papers, Box 3, Folder 58.

72   **"fully available":** Wyman, *Paper Walls*, 43.

73   **"local conditions"; "importing one":** Quoted in ibid., 49–50.

73   **"for permanent settlement":** Quoted in ibid., 50.

73   **propaganda at Evian:** Breitman and Kraut, *Refugee Policy*, 60.

73   **"against Jewish refugees":** Quoted in Wyman, *Paper Walls*, 50.

79   **inclined to do so:** On Senator Holt, see *Biographical Dictionary of the American Congress 1774–1996* (Alexandria, VA, 1996), 1232.

79   **"under Jane Addams"; "in the CCC":** Quoted in Weil, *Pretty Good Club*, 60.

79   **"real cause for war":** Quoted in ibid.

80   **life insurance agent:** On Julius Hess, see "Ex-Banker Hess Is Now Buyer," *Charleston Gazette*, October 2, 1955; "Clothing Store Veteran Goes Into Insurance," ibid., September 29, 1957.

82   **"Queen Bee of Zionism":** Interview with KSW.

83   **"can your daughter do?":** Ibid.

83 **$4,500 from all sources:** Affidavit in Schohl Family Papers

83 **"of a close relative":** Quoted in Zucker, *In Search of Refuge*, 93.

Chapter 4

91 **achieving this aim:** Friedländer, *Nazi Germany*, 270.

92 **"not to be hampered":** Ibid., 271.

92 **"people will act":** See Goebbels's diary entries in "50, dann 75 Synagogen brennen: Tagebuchschreiber Goebbels über die Reichskristallnacht," *Der Spiegel*, July 13, 1992, 126.

92 **"Get yours early":** Quoted in *Time*, November 21, 1938, 19

93 **"treatment of the Jews":** Ibid.

93 **town's Jewish community:** Friedländer, *Nazi Germany*, 274–275.

93 **"to Jewish property"; "of the business day":** Quoted in Schiele, *Juden in Flörsheim*, 411.

94 **nothing much, so far:** Vertraulicher Bericht über die Judenaktion in Flörsheim, HSAW, Abt. 501, Nr. 1987.

94 **hardly a word:** Gerson Vernehmung, July 17, 1946, ibid.

94 **tapestries, and rugs:** For a list of items stolen, see Kristallnacht November 1938 enstandende Schaden, HSAW, Abt. 518, Nr. 1209.

94 **"a complete end":** Willewohl Vernehmung, HSAW, Abt. 501, Nr. 1987.

95 **tossed them in:** Schiele, *Juden in Flörsheim*, 412.

95 **hunting wild stag:** Vernehmung Else Stamm, January 14, 1948, HSAW, Abt. 501, Nr. 1987. See also Schiele, *Juden in Flörsheim*, 413.

96 **known to the authorities:** Vertraulicher Bericht, HSAW, Abt. 501, Nr. 1987.

96 **do the same:** Interview with KSW, January 15, 2002, Charleston, WV.

97 **"you dirty sow":** Vertraulicher Berlicht, HSAW, Abt. 501, Nr. 1987.

97 **"die of shock":** Vernehmung Hela Schohl, July 17, 1946, ibid.

97–98 **complete devastation; "so ashamed":** Interview with KSW, January 15, 2002.

98 **"completely in shock"; "too terrible":** Quoted in Schiele, *Juden in Flörsheim*, 416, 417.

99 **his hand in Germany:** *Maingau Zeitung*, November 12, 1938.

99 **only outsiders:** Hofmann Vernehmung, January 14, 1948, HSAW, Abt. 501, Nr. 1987.

99 **Flörsheimer who had:** Kohl Vernehmung, January 14, 1948, ibid.

99 **with Max's wife:** Duchmann Vernehmung, July 17, 1946, ibid.

99 **"could not move":** Kraft Vernehmung, ibid.

100 **to the Herzheimer family:** Rogalla Vernehmung, March 17, 1948, ibid.

100 **in the affair:** Ludwig Stamm Vernehmung, January 13, 1948, ibid.

100 **seven and twelve months:** Schiele, *Juden in Flörsheim*, 418. These lenient sentences were not unusual. For an account of Kristallnacht trials in postwar Germany, see Dieter Obst, "Die 'Reichskristallnacht' im Spiegel westdeutscher Nachkriegsprozessakten und als Gegenstand der Strafverfolgung," *Geschichte in Wissenschaft und Unterricht* 44, no. 4 (1993).

100 **"not my Germany any more":** Interview with KSW, January 13, 2001, Charleston, WV.

101 **government-appointed experts:** See Walk, *Das Sonderrecht*, 245–255.

101 **"and take action":** Interview with KSW, January 13, 2001.

101 **"last few days":** *Time*, November 21, 1938, 18.

101 **"centuries to come":** Ibid.

102 **"Bolshevist revolution":** *New York Times*, November 11, 1938.

102 **primitive fury:** *Washington Post*, November 11, 1938.

102 **"throwback to barbarity":** *St Louis Dispatch*, November 12, 1938.

102 **"council of nations":** Quoted in Friedländer, *Nazi Germany*, 299.

102 **"sinking of the *Lusitania*":** *Time*, November 28, 1938, 10.

103 **"whole thing to them":** Joseph Goebbels, *Die Tagebücher von Joseph Goebbels. Sämtliche Fragmente, Part I, 1921–1941, Vol. 3*, ed. Elke Fröhlich (Munich, 1987), 352.

103 **Reich at all:** See Lipstadt, *Beyond Belief*, 106–109.

103 **and his advisors:** See Alfred Gottschalk, "The German Pogrom of November 1938 and the Reaction of American Jewry," *Leo Baeck Memorial Lecture* (32), 4.

103 **with the Nazi leader:** London, *Whitehall*, 32–33.

104 **"to frighten Germany":** Quoted in ibid., 99.

104 **"undesirable immigrants"; "expensive business":** Quoted in ibid., 109, 100.

104 **"into foreign policy":** *Time*, November 28, 1938: 10.

105 **"report and consultation":** Quoted in Lipstadt, *Beyond Belief*, 105.

105 **"have the quota system":** Quoted in Davis, *Into the Storm*, 367.

105 **"for American citizenship":** Quoted in ibid., 368.

106 **"to war with Germany":** *New York Herald Tribune* quoted in Lipstadt, *Beyond Belief*, 106.

106 **"has previously performed":** *New York Times*, November 16, 1938.

106 **"especially the well-off":** Kropat, *Reichskristallnacht*, 138–139.

107 **"won't need them":** Interview with KSW, January 14, 2002, Charleston, WV.

107 **"great and free":** David Hackett, *The Buchenwald Report* (Boulder, CO, 1995), 32. See also Blumenthal, *Invisible Wall*, 364.

109 **"feel the cold":** Hans Berger, "Erinnerungen an die Kristallnacht und meine Erlebnisse in KZ Buchenwald," in *Bürger auf Widerruf: Lebenszeugnisse deutscher Juden 1780–1945*, ed. Monika Richarz (Munich, 1989), 484. Schiele, *Juden in Flörsheim*, 421.

109 **"exposed heads":** Berger, "Erinnerungen an die Kristallnacht," 486. Schiele, *Juden in Flörsheim*, 421–422.

110 **"thought he was dead":** Wolf-Arno Kropat, *Kristallnacht in Hessen—Eine Dokumentation* (Wiesbaden, 1988), 225–228.

110 **"closing hour":** Berger, "Erinnerungen an die Kristallnacht," 488.

111 **"welcome" they received:** Blumenthal, *Invisible Wall*, 367–368.

111 **"rich Jews":** Ibid., 369.

112 **"connection to Göring":** Interview with KSW.

112 **"still not back":** Quoted in Schiele, *Juden in Flörsheim*, 423.

113 **"exercise of handicrafts":** Walk, *Sonderrecht*, 254.

113 **"to Aryan ownership":** Landrat to Bürgermeister, December 3, 1938, HSAW, Abt. 425, Nr. 430; Schiele, *Juden in Flörsheim*, 425.

113 **drivers' licenses:** Friedländer, *Nazi Germany*, 285.

114 **changed to Mälzergasse:** Schiele, *Juden in Flörsheim*, 356–357.

114 **"criminal activities":** Quoted in Friedländer, *Nazi Germany*, 283.

114 **preparing to emigrate:** Auswanderung von Juden, January 21, 1939, HSAW, Abt. 418, Nr. 1564.

114 **radio ban:** Einziehung der Rundfunkapparate von Juden, September 21, 1939, HSAW, Abt. 425, Nr. 430.

115 **"with Jewish children":** Quoted in Friedländer, *Nazi Germany*, 284–85.

115 **"Jew in Germany":** Quoted in ibid., 283.

115 **Jews in the streets:** Ibid., 288.

116 **"worst place of all":** Blumenthal, *Invisible Wall*, 360. For a colorful memoir of exile in Shanghai, see Ernst G. Heppner, *Fluchtort Shanghai: Erinnerungen 1938–1948* (Berlin, 2001).

CHAPTER 5

120 **"fifteen years of age":** Friedman, *No Haven for the Oppressed*, 172–73.

135 **"race in Europe":** Adolf Hitler, *Reden und Proklamationen, 1932–1945: Kommantiert von einem deutschen Zeitgenossen*, Part I, Vol. 2, ed. Max Domarus (Munich, 1965), 1058.

135 **temporary visa expired:** Zucker, *In Search of Refuge*, 128–29.

137 **state's educational system:** On Governor Holt, see John G. Morgan, *West Virginia Governers 1863–1980* (Charleston, 1980), 149–161.

137 **letters to Hull:** Schohl, Max: NA, 811.111.

139 **"present circumstances"; "position on that":** Quoted in Friedman, *No Haven for the Oppressed*, 101.

140 **"20,000 ugly adults":** Quoted in Feingold, *Politics of Rescue*, 150.

141 **"following them":** Quoted in Zucker, *In Search of Refuge*, 38.

142 **"leaned toward refusal":** Breitman and Kraut, *Refuge Policy*, 46.

142 **"many years":** Quoted in Zucker, *In Search of Refuge*, 66.

142 **justification for rejection:** Ibid., 114.

143 **"unusual care":** Quoted in ibid., 116.

143 **"own social order":** Ibid., 117.

144 **especially the Foreign Office:** London, *Whitehall*, 278. On anti-Semitism in British society and politics, see Gisela C. Lebzelter, *Political Anti-Semitism in England 1918–1939* (London, 1978); Colin Holmes, *Anti-Semitism in British Society 1816–1939* (London, 1979).

144 **"of unbearable dimensions":** Quoted in Sherman, *Island Refuge*, 17.

144 **to enter Britain:** London, *Whitehall*, 58.

145 **"serious public criticism":** Cadogan to German Ambassador, June 9, 1938, PRO, HO 213/95.

145 **into domestic service:** London, *Whitehall*, 65, 75.

145 **"a lifelong experience":** Quoted in ibid., 133.

147 **"I'll be back":** Interview with KSW.

148 **voyage of the *St. Louis*:** For a good narrative account of this much-publicized incident, see Hans Herlin, *Die Tragödie der "St. Louis" 13. Mai–17. Juni 1939* (Munich, 2000). See also Morse, *While Six Million Died*, 270–288; and Breitman and Kraut, *Refugee Policy*, 70–74.

150 **40 survived the war:** Peter Gay, *My German Question* (New Haven, CT, 1998), 158. Gay and his family, incidentally, were among the German refugees already in Havana who rushed to the harbor to welcome the passengers of the *St. Louis*.

157 **into the country:** I refer specifically to the files of the Central British Fund for Jewish Relief, the Council for German Jewry, the German Jewish Aid Committee, and the Coordinating Committee for Refugees, all housed at the Wiener Library, London.

164 **"in a new country":** Memo to J. A. Calder, Colonial Office, PRO, HO 213/275.

164 **"admitted to the USA":** Foley to Jeffes, January 17, 1939, PRO, HO 213/115.

165 **"commencement of war":** Cooper to Randall, September 18, 1939, PRO, FO 371/24100.

165 **"formed in England":** Quoted in London, *Whitehall*, 131.

CHAPTER 6

167 **"newsboys were shouting":** William Shirer, *Berlin Diary* (New York, 1941), 197.

168 **be handed over:** Zucker, *In Search of Refuge*, 153.

168 **would not be needed:** Interview with KSW, January 14, 2001.

171 **for hard currency:** Herlin, *Die Tragödie*, 32.

171 **no intention of honoring:** Ibid.

173 **anti-Jewish sentiment:** Strauss, "Jewish Emigration," "Jewish Emigration" II: 375–379.

173 **significant financial resources:** Ibid., 369.

173 **"emigrants from Germany":** Warren to Hull, November 25, 1938, Yivo, Joseph Chamberlain Papers, RG 278, Box 3, Folder 67.

173 **"Jews and anarchists":** Strauss, "Jewish Emigration," II: 375.

173 **visas to Jews:** Ibid., 379.

187 **seen as pro-Jewish:** Ibid.

187 **"pastures of America":** *Congressional Report—Senate.* Vol. 86, Part I, 76th Congress, Third Session, 6773–6775.

190 **seizure of power:** Strauss, "Jewish Emigration," II: 374.

191 **arrested and deported:** Ibid., 373–374.

191 **"among the refugees":** Rublee to Warren, November 7, 1938, Yivo, Chamberlain Papers, RG 278, Box 3, Folder 67.

191 **April 1, 1943:** HSAW, Abt. 425, Nr. 432; Schiele, *Juden in Flörsheim,* 455.

192 **August 23, 1942:** Schiele, *Juden in Flörsheim,* 450.

194 **"Welcome to Yugoslavia":** Interview with KSW, January 15, 2002.

196 **"satin and die":** Ibid.

204 **Mussolini and Hitler:** See Misha Glenny, *The Balkans: Nationalism, War and the Great Powers 1804–1999* (New York: 2000), 431–436.

204 **of its own:** Ibid., 435–436.

206 **"Fifth Column":** See Friedman, *No Haven for the Oppressed,* 105–128.

206 **"undesirables":** Department of State Memo, December 18, 1940, LC, Breckinridge Long Papers, Box 202.

206 **"towards such refugees":** Messersmith to Billikopf, November 12, 1940, AJA, Billikopf Papers, Box 19, Folder 10.

206 **entry to America:** Department of State Memo, December 18, 1940, LC, Long Papers, Box 202.

207 **"of another government":** Long memo, February 23, 1940, ibid., Box 195.

207 **for refugee affairs:** Michael Beschloss, *The Conquerors: Roosevelt, Truman and the Destruction of Hitler's Germany* (New York, 2002), 56–57.

209 **royalist Chetniks:** On the Ustaše movement and wartime Croatia, see Gert Fricke, *Kroatien 1941–1944* (Freiburg, 1972); Ladislav Hory and Martin Broszat, *Der kroatische Ustasche-Staat 1941–1945* (Stuttgart, 1964).

209 **"Honor of the Croat Nation":** Quoted in Glenny, *Balkans*, 499.

209 **"first time ever"; "good of society":** Quoted in ibid, 496. See also Hory, 85–92. In November 2001 officials of the United States Holocaust Museum discovered a cache of documents and artifacts from the Jasenovac camp, which are currently on display at the museum. See "Documenting a Death Camp in Nazi Croatia," *New York Times*, November 14, 2001.

209 **"Brother Satan":** Leni Yahil, *The Holocaust. The Fate of European Jewry* (New York, 1990), 431.

209 **20,000 and 30,000 were murdered:** Glenny, *Balkans*, 500.

211 **"correct in every way":** Interview with KSW, January 15, 2002.

211 **in southeastern Europe:** See especially Christopher R. Browning, "Wehrmacht Reprisal Policy and the Mass Murder of Jews in Serbia," *Militärgeschichtliche Mitteilungen* 1/83: 31–47.

211 **"expiratory individuals":** Jürgen Förster, "Wehrmacht, Krieg, Holocaust," in *Die Wehrmacht: Mythos und Realität*, ed. Rolf-Dieter Müller and Hans-Erich Volkmann (Munich, 1999), 959.

211 **in cold blood:** Glenny, Balkans, 502.

211 **Jews they encountered:** On the Volksdeutsche, see Hans-Ulrich Wehler, *Nationalitätenpolitik in Jugoslawien: Die deutsche Minderheit 1918–1978* (Göttingen, 1980), 40–51.

213 **"Jews to the East":** Quoted in Raul Hilberg, *The Destruction of the European Jews* (Chicago, 1967), 455.

214 **"he's lucky":** Interview with KSW, January 15, 2002.

214 **"compounded by bronchial pneumonia":** Death Certificate, Nr. 34039/1943, December 26, 1943. Archive Auschwitz-Birkenau.

214 **T4 (euthanasia) program:** Henry Friedlander, *The Origins of Nazi Genocide. From Euthanasia to the Final Solution* (Chapel Hill, NC, 1995), 100–104.

215 **at the Buna factory:** German Police Decodes, November 18, 1942, item 2, PRO, HW 16/22. See also Richard Breitman, "Auschwitz Partially Decoded," in *The Bombing of Auschwitz. Should the Allies Have*

Attempted It?, ed. Michael J. Neufeld and Michael Berenbaum (New York, 2000), 29.

215 **lived and worked:** Primo Levi, *Survival in Auschwitz* (New York, 1961), 92–130.

215 **three to four months:** Myriam Anissimov, *Primo Levi: Tragedy of an Optimist* (Woodstock, NY, 2000), 108.

215 **"anteroom to the crematorium":** *Auschwitz 1940–1945* (Albuquerque, NM, 1995), 71.

215 **prisoners than guards:** Richard H. Levy, "The Bombing of Auschwitz Revisited: A Critical Analysis," in *The Bombing of Auschwitz*, ed. Neufeld, 120–121. For a skeptical view on the utility of bombing Auschwitz, see also James H. Kitchens III, "The Bombing of Auschwitz Reexamined," in *FDR and the Holocaust*, ed. Verne W. Newton, 183–217.

EPILOGUE

220 **were strictly rationed:** For an account of the difficult conditions prevailing among Jewish displaced persons in the immediate aftermath of World War II, see Angelika Königseder and Juliane Wetzal, *Waiting for Hope: Jewish Displaced Persons in Post-World War II Germany* (Evanston, IL, 1999).

228 **at age sixty-nine:** See Hess obituary, *The Charleston Gazette*, May 3, 1967.

229 **"*Polenlager*":** Becker, *Anmerkungen*, 1029–1031.

229 **the National Socialist regime:** For a good account of the different ways in which the two Germanys dealt with the Nazi legacy, see Jeffrey Herf, *Divided Memory. The Nazi Past in the Two Germanys* (Cambridge, MA, 1997).

230 **supported their claims:** See court records in HSAW, Abt. 518, Nr. 7968.

230 **the *Volksdeutsche* SS:** Hans-Ernst Schilling, September 21, 1949, ibid.

230 **family was making:** Entscheidung in Sache Schohl, November 2, 1950, ibid.

230 **their Croatian allies:** Andreas Joos, September 11, 1954, ibid.

230 **"the appropriate amount":** Liesel Schohl, July 2, 1954, ibid.

231 **ongoing medical attention:** Eidestattliche Versicherung, September 17, 1955, ibid.

231 **"murder of my husband":** Liesel Schohl Erklärung, January 23, 1956, ibid.

231 **liberation of Wiesbaden:** Festsetzungsbescheid, September 7, 1956, ibid.

231 **its final closure:** Interview with KSW, January 14, 2002.

232 **"faith and race":** Quoted in Becker, *Anmerkungen*, 721.

232 **"Heil Hitler":** Ibid., 724.

232 **all its contents:** Jewish Restitution Successor Organization to Entschädigunsbehörde, March 15, 1960, HSAW, Abt. 518, Nr. 1209.

233 **"by older residents":** Quoted in Becker, *Anmerkungen*, 1031.

233 **officially christened:** "Erinnerung an ein verdienter Bürger," *Flörsheimer Zeitung*, December 10, 1984.

233 **"whenever he could":** *Charleston Daily Mail*, May 9, 1985.

233 **"couldn't be there":** Ibid.

Bibliography

U<small>NPUBLISHED</small> S<small>OURCES</small>

American Jewish Archives (AJA), Cincinnati, Ohio
Anti-Semitism
Jacob Billikopf Papers
Felix Warburg Papers
World Jewish Congress

Hessisches Hauptstaatsarchiv Wiesbaden (HSAW), Wiesbaden, Germany
Abt. 418, Nr. 1564
Abt. 425, Nrs. 430, 432, 882, 884
Abt. 483, Nr. 6207
Abt. 501, Nr. 1987
Abt. 518, Nrs. 1209, 7968
Abt. 519

Library of Congress, Manuscripts Division (LC), Washington, D.C.
Wilbur John Carr Papers
William Dodd Papers
Breckinridge Long Papers and Diary

National Archives (NA), Washington, D.C.

150.626 (Jews)

811.111 (Quota)

Pañstwowe Muzeum, Auschwitz-Birkenau

Max Schohl Death Certificate

Public Records Office (PRO), London

FO 371/24100

HO 213/95

HO 213/115

HO 213/275

Schohl Family Papers, Canton, Ohio, and Charleston, West Virginia

Stadtarchiv Flörsheim (SAF), Flörsheim, Germany

Abt. V, Fach 17

Abt. VII, Fach 23

Abt. IX, Fach 34

Wiener Library, London

Archive of the Central British Fund for Jewish Relief, 1933–1960

Council for German Jewry

Yivo Institute for Jewish Research (YIVO), New York

Joseph P. Chamberlain Papers

Exo–29, RG 347.1.29 Germany, State Department Efforts

National Coordinating Committee for Aid to Refugees and Emigrants
Coming from Germany

President's Advisory Committee on Political Refugees

Morris Waldman Papers

PUBLIC DOCUMENTS AND NEWSPAPERS

Charleston Daily Mail

Charleston Gazette

Congressional Report, Senate

Flörsheimer Nachrichten

Flörsheimer Zeitung

Foreign Relations of the United States (FRUS), Washington, D.C.

Frankfurter Allgemeine Zeitung

Höchster Kreisblatt

Kreisblatt für den Landkreis Wiesbaden

Mainspitze, Rüsselsheim
New York Times
Reichsgesetzblatt, 1933–1944
Time Magazine
United States Congressional Record
Washington Post

BOOKS AND ARTICLES

Anissimov, Myriam. *Primo Levi: Tragedy of an Optimist.* Woodstock, NY, 2000.

Auschwitz 1940–1945. Albuquerque, NM, 1995.

Bankier, David. *The Germans and the Final Solution: Public Opinion under Nazism.* Oxford, 1992.

Bauer, Yehuda. *Rethinking the Holocaust.* New Haven, CT, 2001.

Becker, Peter. *Anmerkungen zu Mirjam: Flörsheim Geschichte und Geschichten 1900–1950.* Flörsheim, 2001.

_____. *Mirjam und andere Erzählungen.* Flörsheim, 2000.

Bendarsky, Joseph W. *The "Jewish Threat": Anti-Semitic Politics of the U.S. Army.* New York, 2000.

Benz, Wolfgang. *Flucht aus Deutschland: Zum Exil im 20. Jahrhundert.* Munich, 2001.

_____. "The November Pogrom of 1938: Participation, Applause, Disapproval." In *Exclusionary Violence: Antisemitic Riots in Modern German History*, ed. Christard Hoffmann, Werner Bergman, and Helmut Walser Smith. Ann Arbor, MI, 2002.

Berger, Hans. "Erinnerungen an die Kristallnacht und meine Erlebnisse in KZ Buchenwald." In *Bürger auf Widerruf: Lebenszeugnisse deutscher Juden 1780–1945*, ed. Monika Richarz. Munich, 1989.

Beschloss, Michael. *The Conquerors: Roosevelt, Truman and the Destruction of Hitler's Germany.* New York, 2002.

Biographical Dictionary of the American Congress 1774–1996. Alexandria, VA, 1996.

Blisch, Bernd. "Die 'Separatistenzeit' in Flörsheim am Main—September bis Dezember 1923." *Rad und Sparen: Zeitschrift des Historischen Verein Rhein-Main-Taunus e. V.* 25 (1994): 32–52.

Blumenthal, W. Michael. *The Invisible Wall: Germans and Jews—A Personal Exploration.* Washington, DC, 1998.

Brecher, Frank W. "David Wyman and the Historiography of America's Response to the Holocaust: Counter-Considerations." *Holocaust and Genocide Studies* 5, no. 4 (1990): 423–446.

Breitman, Richard. "Auschwitz Partly Decoded." In *The Bombing of Auschwitz: Should the Allies Have Attempted It?*, ed. Michael J. Neufeld and Michael Berenbaum. New York, 2000.

Breitman, Richard, and Alan M. Kraut. *American Refugee Policy and European Jewry, 1933–1945*. Bloomington, 1987.

Browning, Christopher R. "Wehrmacht Reprisal Policy and the Mass Murder of Jews in Serbia." *Militärgeschichtliche Mitteilungen* I/1983: 31–47.

Buckey, Evan Burr. *Hitler's Austria: Popular Sentiment in the Nazi Era, 1938–1945*. Chapel Hill, NC, 2000.

Ciesulski, Albert. "Das Flörsheimer Notgeld von 1923." *Flörsheimer Geschichtshefte*, No. 2 (September 2000): 13–18.

Craig, Gordon A. *Germany 1866–1945*. New York, 1978.

Curran, Thomas J. *Xenophobia and Immigration, 1820–1930*. Boston, 1975.

Davis, Kenneth S. *FDR: Into the Storm 1937–1940*. New York, 1993.

Dinnerstein, Leonard. *Antisemitism in America*. New York, 1994.

Dippel, John V. H. *Bound Upon A Wheel of Fire: Why So Many German Jews Made the Tragic Decision to Remain in Nazi Germany*. New York, 1996.

Divine, Robert A. *American Immigration Policy, 1924–1952*. New Haven, CT, 1957.

Feingold, Henry L. *Bearing Witness: How America and Its Jews Responded to the Holocaust*. Syracuse, NY, 1993.

_____. "Courage First and Intelligence Second: The American Jewish Secular Elite, Roosevelt, and the Failure to Rescue." In *FDR and the Holocaust*, ed. Verne W. Newton. New York, 1996.

_____. *The Politics of Rescue: The Roosevelt Administration and the Holocaust, 1938–1945*. New Brunswick, NJ, 1970.

_____. "Review of David Wyman's *The Abandonment of the Jews: America and the Holocaust, 1941–1945*." In *FDR and the Holocaust*, ed. Verne W. Newton. New York, 1996.

_____. "Was There a Communal Failure? Some Thoughts on the American Jewish Response to the Holocaust." In *FDR and the Holocaust*, ed. Verne W. Newton. New York, 1996.

Feldman, Gerald D. *The Great Disorder: Politics, Economics, and Society in the Great Inflation 1914–1924*. New York, 1993.

Field, Harold. "Unemployment and the Alien." *South Atlantic Quarterly* 30 (1931): 60–78.

Förster, Jürgen. "Wehrmacht, Krieg, Holocaust." In *Die Wehrmacht: Mythos und Realität*, ed. Rolf-Dieter Müller and Hans-Erich Volkmann. Munich, 1999.

Fricke, Gert. *Kroatien 1941–1944*. Freiburg, 1972.

Friedlander, Henry. *The Origins of Nazi Genocide: From Euthanasia to the Final Solution*. Chapel Hill, NC, 1995.

Friedländer, Saul. *Nazi Germany and the Jews. Volume I: The Years of Persecution, 1933–1939*. New York, 1998.

Friedman, Saul S. *No Haven for the Oppressed: United States Policy Toward Jewish Refugees, 1938–1945*. Detroit, 1973.

Gay, Peter. *My German Question*. New Haven, CT, 1998.

Gay, Ruth. *The Jews of Germany: A Historical Portrait*. New Haven, CT, 1992.

Gilbert, Martin. *Auschwitz and the Allies*. New York, 1981.

Glenny, Misha. *The Balkans: Nationalism, War and the Great Powers 1804–1999*. New York, 2000.

Goebbels, Joseph. *Die Tagebücher von Joseph Goebbels: Sämtliche Fragmente*, pt. I, 1921–1941, vol. 3, ed. Elke Fröhlich. Munich, 1987.

Goldhagen, Daniel Jonah. *Hitler's Willing Executioners: Ordinary Germans and the Holocaust*. New York, 1996.

Gottschalk, Alfred. "The German Pogrom of November 1938 and the Reaction of American Jewry." *Leo Baeck Memorial Lecture* (32).

Graml, Hermann. *Der 9. November 1938: Reichskristallnacht*. Bonn, 1953.

Grunfeld, Frederic. *Prophets Without Honor: A Background to Freud, Kafka, Einstein, and Their World*. New York, 1979.

Hacket, David. *The Buchenwald Report*. Boulder, CO, 1995.

Heppner, Ernst G. *Fluchtort Shanghai: Erinnerungen 1938–1948*. Berlin, 2001.

Herf, Jeffrey. *Divided Memory: The Nazi Past in the Two Germanys*. Cambridge, MA, 1997.

Herlin, Hans. *Die Tragödie der "St. Louis" 13. Mai–17. Juni 1939*. Munich, 2000.

Higham, John. *Strangers in the Land: Patterns of American Nativism, 1860–1925*. New Brunswick, NJ, 1955.

Hilberg, Raul. *The Destruction of the European Jews*. Chicago, 1967.

Hitler, Adolf. *Reden und Proklamationen, 1932–1945: Kommantiert von einem deutschen Zeitgenossen*, pt I, vol. 2, ed. Max Domarus. Munich, 1965.

Holmes, Colin. *Anti-Semitism in British Society 1816–1939*. London, 1979.

Hory, Ladislav, and Martin Broszat. *Der Kroatische Ustasche-Staat 1941–1945*. Stuttgart, 1964.

Die Judische Emigration aus Deutschland 1933–1941: Die Geschichte einer Austreibung. Ausstellung der Deutschen Bibliothek, ed. Buchhandler Vereinigung. Frankfurt, 1985.

Kaplan, Marion A. *Between Dignity and Despair: Jewish Life in Nazi Germany*. New York, 1998.

Kershaw, Ian. *The Hitler Myth: Image and Reality in the Third Reich*. New York, 1989.

Kitchen, Martin. *The German Officer Corps, 1890–1914*. Oxford, 1968.

Königseder, Angelika, and Juliane Wetzal. *Waiting for Hope: Jewish Displaced Persons in Post-World War II Germany*. Evanston, 1999.

Kitchens, James H., III. "The Bombing of Auschwitz Reexamined." In *FDR and the Holocaust*, ed. Verne W. Newton. New York, 1996.

Kohl, Hermann. *Kriegserlebnisse eines Frontsoldaten der 17. bayer. Infanterie-Regiment "Orff."* Stuttgart, 1932.

Kropat, Wolf-Arno. *Kristallnacht in Hessen: Eine Dokumentation*. Wiesbaden, 1988.

———. *"Reichskristallnacht": Der Judenpogrom vom 7. bis 10. November 1938—Ursachen, Täter, Hintergründe*. Wiesbaden, 1988.

Kühl, Stefan. *The Nazi Connection: Eugenics, American Racism, and German National Socialism*. New York, 1994.

Laquer, Walter. *The Terrible Secret: Suppression of the Truth about Hitler's "Final Solution."* New York, 1980.

Large, David Clay. "Out with the Ostjuden: The Scheunenviertel Riots in Berlin, November 1923." In *Exclusionary Violence: Antisemitic Riots in Modern German History*, ed. Christard Hoffmann, Werner Bergmann, and Helmut Walser Smith. Ann Arbor, MI: 2002.

Lazin, Frederick A. "The Response of the American Jewish Committee to the Crisis of German Jewry, 1933–1939." *American Jewish Quarterly* 68 (March 1939): 283–304.

Lebzelter, Gisela C. *Political Anti-Semitism in England 1918–1939*. London, 1978.

Levi, Primo. *Survival in Auschwitz*. New York, 1961.

Lewis, Read, and Martin Schibsby, "Status of the Refugee under American Immigration Laws." *Annals of the American Academy of Political and Social Science* 203 (May 1939): 74–82.

Lewy, Richard H. "The Bombing of Auschwitz Revisited: A Critical Analysis." In *The Bombing of Auschwitz: Should the Allies Have Attempted It?*, ed. Michael J. Neufeld and Michael Berenbaum. New York, 2000.

Lipstadt, Deborah. *Beyond Belief: The American Press and the Holocaust.* New York, 1986.

London, Louise. *Whitehall and the Jews, 1933–1948.* Cambridge, England, 2000.

Martin, George. *Madam Secretary: Frances Perkins.* Boston, 1976.

Mendes-Flohr, Paul. *German Jews: A Dual Identity.* New Haven, CT, 1999.

Morgan, John G. *West Virginia Governors 1863–1980.* Charleston, WV, 1980.

Morse, Arthur D. *While Six Million Died. A Chronicle of American Apathy.* New York, 1967.

Novick, Peter. *The Holocaust in American Life.* Boston, 1999.

Obst, Dieter. "Die 'Reichskristallnacht' im Spiegel westdeutscher Nachkriegsprozessakten und als Gegenstand der Strafverfolgung." *Geschichte in Wissenschaft und Unterricht* 44, No. 4 (1993).

_____. *"Reichskristallnacht": Ursachen und Verlauf des antisemitischen Pogroms vom November 1938.* Frankfurt, 1991.

Pehle, Walter H., ed. *Der Judenpogrom 1938: Von der "Reichskristallnacht" zum Völkermord.* Frankfurt, 1988.

Penkower, Monty. *The Jews Were Expendable.* Urbana, IL, 1983.

Roseman, Mark. *A Past in Hiding: Memory and Survival in Nazi Germany.* New York, 2000.

Ross, Edward A. *The Old World in the New: The Significance of Past Immigration to the American People.* New York, 1914.

Rubenstein, William D. *The Myth of Rescue: Why the Democracies Could Not Have Saved More Jews from the Nazis.* London and New York, 1997.

Sabrow, Martin. "Märtyrer der Republik. Zu den Hintergründen des Mordanschlags vom 24. Juni 1922." In *Die Extremen berühren sich. Walter Rathenau 1867–1922*, ed. Hans Wilderotter. Berlin, 1993.

Sacher, Howard M. *Dreamland: Europeans and Jews in the Aftermath of the Great War.* New York, 2002.

_____. *A History of the Jews in America.* New York, 1992.

Schiele, Werner. *An der Front der Freiheit. Jakob Altmaiers Leben für die Demokratie.* Flörsheim, 1991.

_____. *Auf Roten Spuren: Die Geschichte der Sozialdemokratie in Flörsheim am Main.* Flörsheim, 1988.

_____. *Juden in Flörsheim am Main.* Flörsheim, 1999.

Schmidt, Wolfgang. "Die Juden in der bayerischen Armee." In *Deutsche Jüdische Soldaten*, ed. Militärgeschichtliches Forschungsamt. Hamburg and Bonn, 1996.

Schulzinger, Robert D. *The Making of the Diplomatic Mind: The Training, Outlook, and Style of the United States Foreign Service Officers, 1908–1931*. Middletown, CT, 1975.

Sherman, A. J. *Island Refuge: Britain and Refugees from the Third Reich, 1933–1939*. London, 1973.

Shirer, William. *Berlin Diary*. New York, 1941.

Sievers, Hannelore. *Ein Stück Alt-Flerschem*. Flörsheim, 1981.

Stern, Fritz. *Dreams and Delusions: The Drama of German History*. New York, 1987.

Strauss, Herbert A. "Jewish Emigration from Germany. Nazi Policies and Jewish Responses." Parts I and II. *Leo Baeck Institute Yearbook* 26 (1981).

Strong, Donald S. *Organized Anti-Semitism in America: The Rise of Group Prejudice during the Decade 1930–1940*. Washington, DC, 1941.

Treitschke, Heinrich von. "Unsere Aussichten (1879)." In *Der Berliner Antisemitismusstreit*, ed. Walter Boehlich. Frankfurt, 1965.

Walk, Josef, ed. *Das Sonderrecht für die Juden im NS-Staat*. 2. Auflage. 2 vols. Heidelberg, 1996.

Wasserstein, Bernard. *Britain and the Jews of Europe, 1939–1945*. London, 1979.

Wehler, Hans-Ulrich. *Nationalitätenpolitik in Jugoslawien: Die deutsche Minderheit 1918–1978*. Göttingen, 1980.

Weil, Martin. *A Pretty Good Club: The Founding Fathers of the United States Foreign Service*. New York, 1978.

Westphal, Alfred. "Die Kriegervereine." In *Deutschland als Weltmacht: Vierzig Jahre Deutsches Reich*, ed. Kaiser-Wilhelm-Dank. Berlin, 1912.

Wyman, David S. *The Abandonment of the Jews: America and the Holocaust*. New York, 1984.

_____. *Paper Walls. America and the Refugee Crisis 1938–1941*. Amherst, MA, 1968.

Yahil, Leni. *The Holocaust: The Fate of European Jewry*. New York, 1990.

Zucker, Bat-Ami. *In Search of Refuge: Jews and the United States Consuls in Nazi Germany 1933–1941*. London and Portland, OR, 2001.

Index